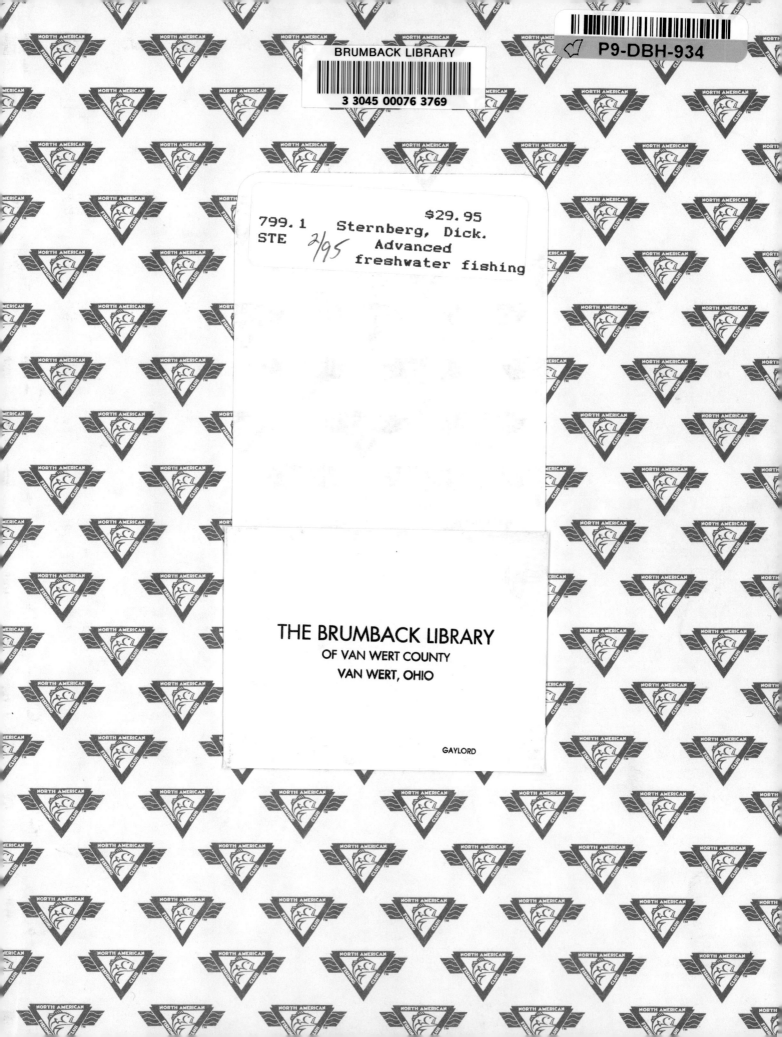

ADVANCED

# Freshwater Fishing Strategies

## Advanced Strategies for Catching North America's Most Popular Gamefish

NON PAGA DORMIRE

DICK STERNBERG blends his years of angling experience and scientific training into a text loaded with important facts about fish and helpful tips for the modern angler. A professional fisheries biologist for 16 years, Dick has fished from the mountain streams of Alaska to the Everglades of Florida. His articles have appeared in numerous regional and national outdoor magazines.

Published in 1994 by
Cy DeCosse Incorporated
5900 Green Oak Drive
Minnetonka, Minnesota 55343

Library of Congress
Cataloging-in-Publication Data

Sternberg, Dick
Advanced freshwater fishing strategies / by Dick Sternberg
p. cm. – (The Hunting & fishing library)
Includes index.
ISBN 0-86573-045-8 (hardcover)
1. Fishing. 2. Freshwater fishes. I. Title.
SH441.S82 1994
799.1'1 - dc20                    94-12933


Printed on American paper by
R. R. Donnelley & Sons Co. (0994)
CREDITS:
*Editorial Director:* Dick Sternberg
*Design and Production:* Cy DeCosse Creative Department, Inc.

# Contents

# Introduction

*Advanced Freshwater Fishing Strategies* is a unique collection of solid fishing information that will help you catch the most popular kinds of gamefish that swim in the fresh waters of North America.

The book contains extensive chapters on bass (largemouth and smallmouth), panfish (crappie, sunfish and perch), walleye, northern pike and muskie, and trout. Another chapter is devoted to catfish and one to white bass and stripers.

By studying this book, you'll learn everything necessary to devise an effective fish-catching strategy for each of these highly sought-after gamefish, including their basic behavioral traits, seasonal movement patterns in different types of waters, and proven live bait and artificial lure techniques.

*Advanced Freshwater Fishing Strategies* takes you well beyond the basics, with in-depth information that will help you find productive fishing spots quickly in a wide variety of waters. Fundamental fishing techniques are shown in detail, but you'll also learn many advanced or unusual techniques that will help you catch fish under tough conditions or in unusual situations.

In the bass chapter, for instance, you'll learn the best methods for catching largemouth when they're holding on different kinds of structure, in various types of aquatic weeds, and around woody cover like flooded brush, trees and stumps. You'll learn when and how to use spinnerbaits, crankbaits, worms, jigs and spoons, along with a diverse collection of largemouth-angling tips — those little things that can make a big difference in your success.

Weather is the nemesis of all fishermen, but this book explains exactly how the weather influences gamefish activity patterns, so you can plan your fishing strategy accordingly. We'll even show you some tricks for salvaging your trip when faced with a severe cold front.

Sprinkled throughout the book you'll find articles detailing techniques used by some of the country's most successful anglers. In the bass chapter, for instance, renowned California trophy largemouth expert, Bill Murphy, divulges the secrets that have made him the all-time champion at catching "teen" bass, those over 13 pounds. Fly-fishing authority Larry Dahlberg demonstrates how to catch smallmouth on a new style of diving fly that bears his name. And in the walleye chapter, Dick (the Grz) Grzywinski, one of the Midwest's top walleye guides, reveals the unique snap-jigging method that has made him a legend.

With hundreds of angling experts from across the United States and Canada as contributors, this book is truly a complete fishing encyclopedia.

# Largemouth Bass

# Where to Find Largemouth Through the Seasons

A prominent bass expert once estimated that "80 percent of the challenge in bass fishing is finding the fish." Locating bass may be difficult because seasonal movement patterns differ in almost every body of water. Temperature, oxygen level, food supply and even the angle of the sun's rays have an effect on bass location in each season.

SPRING. Springtime movements of bass center around spawning. Weeks before spawning begins, bass start moving from deep water toward shallows that warm quickly. Males move in first. During this *pre-spawn* period, look for bass near their spawning grounds, but in slightly deeper water. On a warm day, bass will move into the spawning area, even though spawning is weeks away. They retreat to deeper water when the weather cools. They may repeat this pattern often during the pre-spawn period.

Bass begin to feed when the water temperature edges above 50°F, but catching them is difficult until the water reaches about 55°F. Then they begin a feeding binge that is unequaled at any other time of the year. Anglers catch bass in the shallows throughout the day. Baitfish are scarce, so bass spend most of their time cruising shallow water in search of food. And because the sun is at a low angle, light penetration does not force them into deeper water.

Spawning begins when the water reaches the mid-60s. After depositing their eggs, the females abandon the nests. They feed very little for the next two to three weeks while they recover from spawning. Males guarding their beds will strike lures that come too close.

Water temperatures in the low 70s signal the beginning of the *post-spawn* period and the resumption of good fishing. Females have recovered and males have completed their nest-guarding duties. Both feed heavily in the shallows but spend most of the day in deeper water.

Springtime movements of bass extend from February to April in southern waters. But in the North, they are compressed into just a few weeks, usually from May to early June.

SUMMER. As summer progresses, strong sunlight or warm surface temperatures may force bass out of shallow water. Bass form loose schools along deep structure and cover during midday, but feed in the shallows in morning and evening. Food is easy to find, so feeding periods tend to be short. Some largemouths stay in the shallows all day if the cover is dense enough or the water murky enough to block out sunlight.

Water temperature above 80°F will usually push bass deeper, regardless of water clarity. But in fertile lakes, low oxygen levels in the depths prevent bass from going deeper. They must remain in warm, shallow water, where they become listless and difficult to catch.

FALL AND WINTER. When the water begins to cool in fall, bass in deep water return to the shallows. Early fall is much like the pre-spawn period. In most waters, the summer's predation has reduced their food supply, so bass roam the shallows looking for a meal. And with the sun once again lower in the sky, they can stay shallow all day. But many anglers have quit fishing for the season by the time bass begin their fall feeding binge.

As the surface water continues to cool, it eventually reaches the same temperature as water in the depths. This starts the *fall turnover*. With water at the same temperature and density throughout, wind circulates the lake from top to bottom. Bass may be almost anywhere, so finding them is difficult. In most waters, fall turnover lasts from one to two weeks.

In late fall, the surface water becomes colder than water in the depths. Bass prefer the warmer water, so they move to deep areas of the lake. They remain in these deepwater haunts through winter, whether or not the lake freezes over.

Temperatures below 50°F make bass sluggish and difficult to catch. But a few days of warm, sunny weather may draw them into the shallows. Fishermen aware of this late season movement can enjoy some of the year's best fishing, especially for big bass. However, if water temperatures fall below 40°F, bass are almost impossible to catch.

Ice fishermen sometimes enjoy a short flurry of action just after freeze-up, but very few largemouths are taken during the rest of winter.

# How Weather Affects Largemouth

Weather plays a greater role in the daily activity of largemouth bass than any other factor. To improve your success, you should know how the following weather conditions affect bass fishing.

STABLE WEATHER. When weather conditions are stable or gradually changing, bass go through a routine of feeding and resting that is often predictable from one day to the next. For example, during an extended period of overcast weather, a school of bass may feed on a sharp-breaking point at midday, then drop back into deeper water. The school usually repeats this daily pattern, as long as weather conditions remain stable.

FRONTS. Largemouths feed heavily just before a strong cold front, often providing spectacular fishing for several hours. But once the front arrives, they eat very little until one or two days after the system passes. Catching bass under these conditions is difficult and requires special techniques with lighter lines and smaller lures.

Warm fronts affect bass in different ways, depending on the season and water temperatures. A series of warm days in spring or fall will raise water temperatures in the shallows, causing bass to feed.

In winter, several unusually warm days may draw bass toward the surface to absorb the warmth of the sun. The fish become more accessible to fishermen and more likely to feed or take a lure. But a string of hot days in summer may warm a shallow lake or pond so much that largemouths become sluggish and difficult to catch.

WIND. Like warming trends, wind can either improve or ruin fishing. A steady wind will concentrate minute organisms near shore or along timber and brush lines. Baitfish feed in these areas, attracting bass and other predators. In spring, warm winds blowing from the same direction for several days can pile up warm water on the downwind shore. This warmer water holds more bass than other areas of the lake.

Waves washing into shore loosen soil and debris, creating a band of muddy water. Bass hang along the *mud line*, where they can avoid bright light, but still dart into clear water to grab food.

If the wind becomes too strong, it can impair fishing success in shallow areas. Turbulence caused by heavy waves pushes bass into deeper water, where they are harder to find. In shallow lakes, strong winds often churn the water enough to make the entire lake murky, slowing fishing for several days.

RAIN. Rainy weather usually improves bass fishing. The overcast skies reduce light penetration, so bass are more comfortable in shallow water. In reservoirs, runoff flows into the back ends of coves. The murky water causes bass to move in and feed. The same situation occurs near stream inlets on many natural lakes.

Fishing success may decline during and after heavy rains. Runoff from torrential rains can muddy an entire body of water, causing fish to stop biting. Angling remains slow until the water clears, which may take several days or weeks.

Experienced fishermen can identify certain clouds and other atmospheric conditions that indicate coming changes in the weather. They know how bass react to these changes and plan their angling strategy accordingly. Some of these indicators are described on the following pages.

## How a Cold Front Affects Bass Fishing

CIRRUS CLOUDS usually precede a major cold front. These clouds may be 100 miles ahead of an approaching front. They indicate that largemouths will soon be feeding heavily.

THUNDERHEADS build as a front approaches. Lightning and strong winds often accompany these towering clouds. The feeding frenzy may peak just before these clouds arrive.

## How Wind Affects Bass Fishing

CALM conditions (left) enable bass in clear water to see objects above them. Fishermen and boaters easily spook bass in shallow water. Wave action (right) bends or refracts light rays, making it more difficult for largemouths to see movements on or above the surface.

WAVES breaking against shore dislodge food items. Winds also push plankton toward shore, attracting minnows. Bass move in to feed.

STALLED FRONTS may leave skies overcast for several days. Look for bass feeding in the shallows during this low-light condition.

CLEAR SKY following a cold front filters out few of the sun's rays. Light penetrates deeper into the water, forcing bass to move out of the shallows.

CUMULUS CLOUDS promise better fishing. The white, fluffy clouds signal that the front has passed. Bass will soon resume their normal activity.

## How Rain Affects Bass Fishing

HEAVY RUNOFF into clear lakes creates patches of muddy water. Bass congregate wherever turbid water enters the lake, such as the inlets of streams and drainage ditches, or near storm sewer pipes.

LIGHTNING AND THUNDER drive largemouths into the depths. If the weather looks threatening, head for shore immediately. Your boat may be the highest point on the lake, making you vulnerable to a lightning strike.

# Finding the Pattern

An observer at a professional bass tournament would hear a great deal of talk about finding the best *pattern*. When bass pros use this term, they are not referring to lure design. Instead, a pattern involves an elusive combination of two factors: bass location and the presentation needed to make fish bite. The pattern often changes from day to day and may even change several times a day.

The first step in unraveling a pattern is to locate the right type of fishing spot. Take into account the season, time of day and the weather. For example, on an overcast fall day, bass will most likely stay in the shallows. On a bright day in summer, bass may feed in open shallows in early morning. But as the sun moves higher, they will move deeper or into shaded areas of the shallows.

When scouting for bass, most anglers use some type of fast-moving lure like a crankbait or spinnerbait. Hungry bass will strike almost anything, so this technique is the quickest way to locate an active school.

Concentrate on features within the most likely depth range, but occasionally move to shallower or deeper water. If you catch a bass, carefully note the exact depth and the type of cover and structure. Work the area thoroughly, but continue moving if you fail to catch another fish.

If you find an active school, try to avoid spooking the fish. Keep the boat at a distance and noise to a minimum. Without changing lures, work the school until the bass quit biting.

Presentation becomes more important after you have skimmed the active fish from the school. Switching to a lure with a different action, color or size often triggers a strike immediately. Select a lure based on the situation and continue casting toward the fish. Experiment with various lures and retrieves to find the right combination.

Before you leave a good spot, note its exact location. Some fishermen toss out a marker, then return later to see if the fish have resumed feeding. When a spot no longer produces, try to duplicate the pattern by looking for a similar location nearby. If you found bass on a sharp-breaking point with bulrushes on top, chances are you will find bass on similar points elsewhere. If these areas fail to produce, the pattern has probably changed.

If the weather remains stable, the patterns you find one day will probably be repeated about the same time on the next day. But a change in weather will probably result in a new set of patterns.

In some instances, several patterns exist at the same time. Bass sometimes bite equally well in deep and shallow water, and the type of lure makes little difference. On these rare days, almost anyone can catch fish.

Finding a pattern for deepwater bass can be difficult and time-consuming. These fish often ignore fast-moving lures, so you may have to use a slower presentation. When you hook a fish in deep water, try to land it quickly. Otherwise, its frantic struggling may spook other bass in the school.

At times, there is no definite pattern. You may catch a bass here and there, but seldom more than one in any spot. Keep moving and cover as many areas as possible, including those places where you caught fish earlier in the day.

FAST ACTION rewards fishermen who discover the right pattern. If you locate a school of bass, land your fish as quickly as possible and resume fishing. Use a landing net for only the largest fish. Grab smaller bass by the lower jaw. Untangling a lure from a net takes too much time.

## *Tips for Improving Your Pattern-fishing Skills*

MARK successful spots on a contour map. List any landmarks on shore that can be used as reference points for finding the area quickly.

RIG several rods with different types of lures. This enables you to switch quickly without taking the time to tie on a new lure.

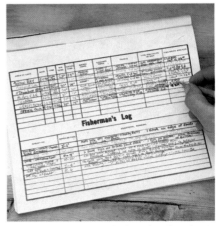

RECORD trip results in a log book. A well-kept log can help you to find successful patterns when conditions are similar in future years.

# Structure-Fishing for Largemouth

Finding structure is the key to finding largemouth bass. Experts estimate that only 10 percent of a typical lake holds bass. And that 10 percent is usually around some type of structure. Fishermen who do not know how to find and fish structure have little chance for consistent success.

Structure simply means a change in the lake bottom. It could be a change in the depth or just a difference in the type of bottom material. Points, sunken islands, rock or gravel reefs, creek channels and shoreline breaks are typical structure in many waters.

Largemouths use structure as underwater highways. It provides easy access for bass moving from deep to shallow water. Structure also supplies bass with something to which they can relate. Given a choice, a bass will select a location near some type of recognizable feature.

The best bass structure has natural cover like weeds, flooded brush or timber, or man-made cover like riprap or brush shelters.

The quickest way to locate structure is to use an accurate contour map and a depth finder. With very little practice, you will learn to identify landmarks on shore for finding the general location of a good area. Then, by crisscrossing the area with your depth finder, you can pinpoint specific structure shown on the map. When you locate fish, note the exact depth. Chances are, bass on structure throughout the lake will be at the same depth.

Fishermen who spend a lot of time fishing one lake usually discover certain pieces of structure that routinely produce bass. In many cases, structure that seems identical produces nothing. Anglers have hired divers to inspect their secret spots, thinking there must be some difference that attracts bass. Often the diver finds nothing that could not be found in dozens of other areas. Bass sometimes choose spots for reasons we do not understand. The only solution for fishermen is to work many pieces of structure. Keep moving, try different depths and presentations until you find the right combination.

TYPICAL STRUCTURE includes: (1) shallow flat, (2) shallow ridge, or saddle, where a creek channel doubles back, (3) outside bend of a creek channel, (4) cliff wall, (5) deep hole, (6) extension of a point, (7) underwater hump, or sunken island, (8) breakline, (9) inside turn on a breakline, (10) rock reef.

## Where to Find Largemouth on Shallow Structure

Locating bass on shallow structure can be challenging even for the best anglers. Most lakes have an abundance of structure in shallow water, providing bass with an endless selection of feeding areas.

All types of structure can be found in either shallow or deep water. The term shallow structure refers to any structure in water 10 feet deep or less.

Begin your search for bass by working the most likely areas based on local reports, the season and your knowledge of the lake. Spend only a few minutes in each spot and keep moving until you find some active fish.

To reduce your scouting time, concentrate on a small section of the lake. Many anglers find it more productive to fish one creek arm thoroughly rather than spending the day roaming the lake.

In clear lakes, you can see shallow structure. Wear polarized glasses to find areas like the sharp break off the side of a weedy point, or a creek channel meandering through a flat. Bass in these areas can feed in shallow cover, then quickly retreat to deeper water. You may need a depth finder to spot structure in murky water.

When fishing on shallow structure, look for something slightly different from the surrounding area. Examples include a small section of reef that drops faster than the rest of the structure, a slight projection along the side of a point, or a shallow depression on top of a flat. These subtle variations frequently hold schools of bass.

### *Where to Fish on Shallow Flats*

CLUMPS of timber or brush attract largemouths on flats. Look for bass in the thickest clumps or in those isolated from other cover.

SMALL CREEKS provide bass with an easy-to-follow migration route leading from deep water into the shallows. They feed on the flats along both sides of the creek.

### *Where to Fish in Shallow Creek Arms*

CREEK CHANNELS (dotted line) winding through shallow arms offer the only deepwater refuge for bass. The channel holds bass just before and after spawning.

FLOWING STREAMS wash bass foods into the back of a creek arm. Streams provide warmer water in spring and cooler water in summer.

SHALLOW FLATS are prime feeding areas for large-mouths. Flats are large expanses of water that have a uniform depth. Look for flats that border creek channels meandering through shallow reservoirs. Bass fishermen also work flats that rise gradually from bottom in mid-lake, or those that extend from shore.

## Where to Fish on Other Shallow Structure

POINTS that taper gradually into deep water attract largemouths after spawning. Bass hang near these points for a few weeks before moving to deeper water.

HUMPS are top bass producers in summer. Those near creek channels draw bass from deep water, especially if there is a ridge connecting the structures.

# How to Catch Largemouth on Shallow Structure

CAST a spinnerbait or some other type of weedless lure onto shallow structure that has trees, brush or heavy weeds. Horse the bass away from cover to keep it from wrapping your line around weeds or limbs.

Fishermen stand a much better chance of catching bass in shallow water than in deep water. Bass in the shallows are usually feeding and more likely to strike a lure.

But bass in the shallows pose two problems for anglers. The fish are often scattered. And they tend to spook easily, especially if the water is clear. To find bass on shallow structure, keep moving and use lures that can be cast and retrieved quickly so you can cover a lot of water. When you catch a fish, remember the exact location. You may want to return later for a few more casts.

When fishing in the shallows, avoid making unnecessary noises. Be especially careful not to drop anything on the bottom of the boat and do not run your outboard. Keep the boat as far away as possible and make long casts. If the water is very clear, watch the angle of the sun to avoid casting your shadow over the fish.

Almost any lure will work for fishing on shallow structure. The lure does not have to bump bottom to catch fish. A hungry bass in 6 feet of water will not

## *Techniques for Fishing on Shallow Structure*

FAN-CAST from atop a shallow flat when the fish cannot be reached by casting from the edge. Quietly slip your boat onto the flat. Use your trolling motor and move back and forth across the flat to cover it thoroughly.

SPOT-CAST to any unusual cover on top of a flat, sunken island or point. A lone tree or bush, or an isolated clump of thick weeds is likely to hold bass. Cast beyond the feature and retrieve the lure along the shaded side.

hesitate to chase a buzz bait ripped across the surface, especially in warm water.

Most anglers prefer spinnerbaits or shallow-running crankbaits so they can cover a large area in a hurry. You may need a weedless lure if the structure has heavy weeds or brush. Carry a rod rigged with a plastic worm so you can work a brush clump or an isolated weedbed slowly and thoroughly.

Casting is the best technique for working most types of shallow structure. Approach quietly and cut the outboard long before you reach the fishing area. Follow the edge of the structure while casting into the shallow water. Cover the shallows first, but if you do not catch fish, try deeper water along the structure's edge.

Drifting sometimes works well for fishing on shallow flats. Start at the upwind side, then let the wind push the boat slowly across the structure. Use your electric trolling motor to adjust the boat's direction. Always cast with the wind. This enables you to cover water the boat has not crossed. You can also cast farther with the wind at your back.

LURES for shallow structure include: (1) Texas-rigged plastic worm, (2) minnow imitation, (3) weedless spoon, (4) spinner, (5) buzz bait, (6) spinnerbait, (7) popper, (8) floating weedless plastic worm.

POSITION your boat over the middle of a creek channel. Cast to the shallows on either side of the channel, then retrieve the lure down the drop-off. Continue casting as you move down the channel.

MOVE SLOWLY along a gradually-sloping shoreline, keeping the boat within casting distance of emergent weeds. Angle some casts toward shore, others toward deeper water.

19

# Where to Find Largemouth on Deep Structure

Before the advent of the depth finder, finding bass on deep structure was largely guesswork. Most fishermen worked shoreline structure because they could find it easily. Much of the deep, mid-lake structure was left unexplored.

The first anglers to buy depth finders enjoyed a fishing bonanza. Some schools of deepwater bass had never seen a lure. Fishing is not that easy today, but the angler who knows how to use a depth finder in conjunction with a lake map can consistently find bass on deep structure.

Prior to fishing any deep structure, explore the area thoroughly with your depth finder. Look for any variations on the structure, because these areas are most likely to hold bass. Make sure you understand the bottom configuration. This will make it easier to follow a contour and to keep your lure at a consistent depth.

When scouting a deep sunken island or flat, criss-cross the area several times. Toss a marker buoy onto the shallowest part of the sunken island or into the middle of the flat. The marker will serve as a reference point. Note the location of any projections or indentations along the edge of the structure, or any deep pockets on top.

To determine the shape of a submerged point, zig-zag across it while edging farther into the lake. When you locate the tip of the point, throw out a marker. Then run the boat along each edge to find any irregularities.

Creek channels bordered by flooded timber are easy to follow. But channels without timber or brush can be difficult to trace. Watch your depth finder as you follow the edge. Drop enough markers to provide a picture of the channel configuration.

To find largemouths near a cliff wall, cruise slowly along the edge while watching the depth finder for signs of trees, brush or rock slides. Any type of projection different from the rest of the cliff will probably hold bass.

## *Where to Find Bass in Creek Channels*

OUTSIDE BENDS (arrows) usually have the deepest water in a creek channel. Steep walls or undercut banks were gouged out by current before the reservoir was formed.

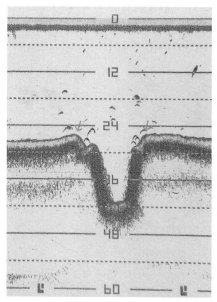

BERMS, or elevated banks (arrows), were formed by current depositing silt along the edges of a creek channel. This graph tape shows bass near berms on both sides of a channel.

ROADS that once crossed creek channels (arrow) may reveal the location of submerged bridge pilings. Bridge decks are usually removed before the reservoir is filled.

20

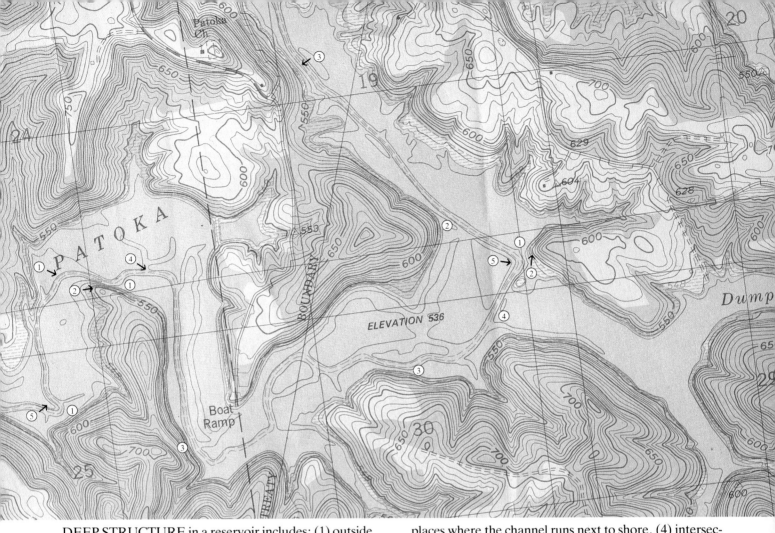

DEEP STRUCTURE in a reservoir includes: (1) outside bends of a creek channel, (2) points along a channel, (3) places where the channel runs next to shore, (4) intersections, (5) submerged point formed by a sharp bend.

POINTS that extend from shore to meet a creek channel (dotted line) provide ideal bass habitat. Largemouths that rest in the deep water of the creek channel must swim only a short distance to feed in heavy timber and brush on top of the point.

INTERSECTIONS of two creek channels (dotted lines) concentrate largemouths, especially if there is ample flooded timber and brush bordering the creeks. If the junction has deep water, bass will generally stay in the area through winter.

## Where to Fish on Deep Points

STEEP DROP-OFFS hold bass in summer, late fall and winter. Largemouths often hang near large boulders or piles of rocks.

SUBMERGED POINTS are difficult to locate without a contour map and depth finder. Look for points projecting from a shoreline break or a sunken island.

## Where to Fish on Other Deep Structure

STEEP LEDGES may provide the only bass cover in deep reservoirs. Scout for areas where wave action has eroded the rock, creating an overhang or causing the bank to cave in.

ROCK REEFS 10 to 15 feet below the surface hold largemouth bass in summer, especially if surrounded by deep water. In clear lakes, bass may inhabit reefs 25 to 30 feet deep.

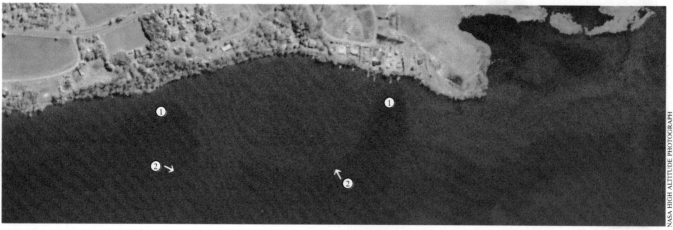

SHORELINE BREAKS provide the best structure in many bowl-shaped lakes. Bass congregate on (1) inside turns and (2) projections along a breakline. But largemouths may be anywhere on a break, especially where there is isolated cover or a distinct difference in the bottom material.

## How to Catch Largemouth on Deep Structure

Bass schooled in deep water are less likely to strike than fish in the shallows. But a lure retrieved slowly will usually tempt a few willing biters.

In warm water, you can generally locate bass along deep structure by using a fast presentation. Even though deepwater bass may not be feeding, chances are one or two fish out of the school will chase a fast-moving crankbait. Maneuver your boat along a drop-off as you cast toward shallow and deep water. When you catch a bass, stick with the crankbait and work the area until the fish quit biting. Then switch to a slower-moving lure and cover the area thoroughly. In cold water, fast-moving lures seldom catch bass. Use slower retrieves or try vertical jigging.

To fish irregular structure, such as a breakline with many sharp turns or the tip of a point, anchor your boat or hover above the spot. If you fish from a moving boat, it is difficult to keep your lure in the strike zone.

When fishing a long breakline with few twists and turns, try speed trolling with deep-running crankbaits or Spoon Plugs. To find the proper depth, make several passes along the breakline while using lures that run at different depths. Note the exact location of any strike and continue to work the area until the fish stop biting. Then switch to a slower presentation, such as slow-hopping a plastic worm.

FOLLOW the contour of a shoreline point or other deep structure by using an electric trolling motor. Flooded timber or emergent weeds on top of a point provide a clue to the location of the drop-off.

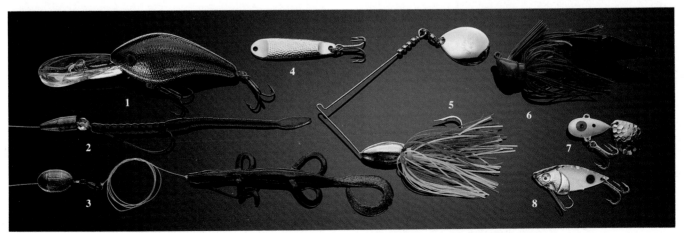

LURES for deep structure include: (1) extra-deep-diving crankbait; (2) brass-and-glass worm rig, with brass sinker and glass bead for extra noise; (3) Carolina-rigged soft-plastic lizard; (4) jigging spoon; (5) heavy single-spin spinnerbait; (6) rubber-legged brushguard jig with pork trailer; (7) tailspin; (8) vibrating blade.

## Techniques for Fishing Along a Sharp Drop-off

CAST a sinking lure such as a plastic worm into the shallows along the outside bend of a creek channel. Bump it along bottom until it reaches the drop-off, then slow your retrieve as the lure drops down the slope.

KEEP the line tight as the lure sinks. Bass holding along the channel edge will grab a plastic worm or jigging lure as it drops. Set the hook immediately and pull the fish away from the cover as soon as possible.

## Other Techniques for Fishing on Deep Structure

VERTICAL JIGGING is ideal for fishing along a steep ledge or any type of structure where bass school tightly. Drop the lure straight below the boat and jig it at different depths until you locate fish.

PARALLEL CASTING works well for covering any sharp drop-off with a straight edge. Position the boat so you can cast parallel to the ledge. Count the lure down to different depths to find bass.

## Techniques for Fishing on a Point

GRADUALLY-SLOPING POINTS should be fished by positioning the boat in deep water and casting toward shore. Retrieve the lure down the slope, keeping it near bottom. Moving too close will spook fish in the shallows.

SHARP-SLOPING POINTS are difficult to fish from deep water. As you retrieve the lure, it loses contact with bottom. Position the boat in the shallows, cast into deep water and retrieve up the break.

## Tips for Fishing on Deep Structure

DIP your fishing rod into the water if you are having trouble getting the lure to bottom. This makes the lure run 4 to 5 feet deeper. Use extra force to set the hook because of water resistance against the rod.

REEL RAPIDLY to make a deep-running crankbait dig into the bottom. The lip will kick up puffs of silt, much like a crayfish scurrying across bottom. This technique gives the plug an erratic action.

25

# Fishing for Largemouth in the Weeds

A largemouth tail-walking above the weeds as it tries to shake an artificial lure is a sight familiar to bass fishermen.

Weeds are the most common type of bass cover and certainly the most important. Bass fry crowd into dense weedbeds to hide from predators. Adult bass hide in weeds to ambush prey. The weeds provide homes for small insects which attract baitfish and other bass foods. Heavy mats of floating weeds prevent the sun's heat from penetrating the surface. Bass move into cool water below the weeds when the rest of the shallows becomes too warm.

Weeds perform yet another important function. Through the process of photosynthesis, they produce oxygen that is vital to the survival of fish.

The aquatic plants used by bass fall into the following categories:

SUBMERGED WEEDS. These weeds grow below the water, although some have flowers that extend above the surface. Water clarity determines how deep these plants will grow. In extremely clear water, they may get enough sunlight to flourish in depths of 30 feet or more. In murky lakes, they seldom grow in water deeper than 5 feet.

A distinct edge forms where the water becomes too deep for submerged weeds to grow. Called a weedline, this edge generally occurs at the same depth throughout a body of water. Weedlines are important bass-holding features.

FLOATING-LEAVED WEEDS. Some weeds, such as lily pads, have leaves that float on the surface. The broad leaves provide more shade than the leaves of most other plants. They offer excellent shallow-water cover for largemouths.

EMERGENT WEEDS. These plants protrude well above the surface. Often they form a band extending around much of a shoreline. Bass frequently spawn among emergent weeds in 2 to 3 feet of water. Emergent weeds in deeper water may hold bass through the summer.

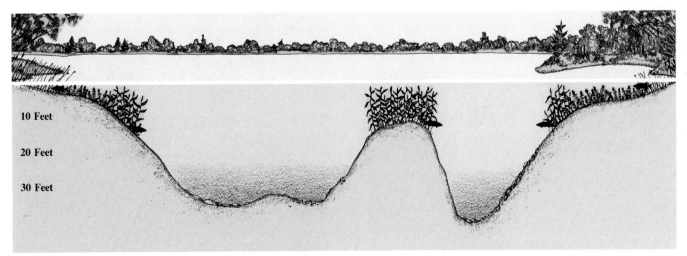

WEEDLINES usually form along drop-offs. This diagram shows submerged weeds that end abruptly at 15 feet. Weedlines also form where there is a distinct change in bottom type. Most bass hang near the edge of the weedline, but some stay in shallow water or near the junction of two different weed types.

## Where and How to Catch Largemouth in Shallow Weeds

Bass fishermen in natural lakes catch more largemouths in shallow weeds than in any other type of cover. Shallow weeds include any type of emergent, floating-leaved or submerged plant in water 10 feet or less. The type of weed matters little to bass, as long as it provides adequate cover.

The best times to find bass in shallow vegetation are spring and early fall. In summer, weeds serve mainly as morning and evening feeding grounds. But some bass stay in the weeds all summer if the cover is dense enough to block out sunlight.

POCKETS in floating-leaved weeds such as lily pads serve as ambush points for feeding largemouths. Avoid large stands of pads in very shallow water with no deeper water nearby.

EDGES of emergent weeds such as bulrushes are top shallow-water locations. The inside edge of a weedbed may hold as many bass as the outside edge. Look for bass in any boat lanes or openings in the weeds.

Shallow weeds near deep water usually hold the most bass. Given a choice, bass will choose a weedbed near a drop-off over one located in the middle of a large, shallow area. Avoid weedbeds so thick that bass would have difficulty moving about.

Bass prefer distinct edges to solid masses of weeds. Look for pockets and projections along weedy edges and open areas within weeds.

Fishing in shallow weeds requires special equipment. Most anglers prefer a powerful rod and a high-speed, bait-casting reel. Once you hook a bass, pull as hard as your equipment allows to head the bass toward the surface. Hold the rod tip high as you reel. Exert strong pressure to keep its head up. If you allow the bass to dive into dense cover, it will probably tangle your line around the stems and break free. Strong pressure also reduces the chance of the bass throwing the hook when it jumps.

Abrasion-resistant monofilament, generally 12- to 17-pound test, works well for most weed-fishing situations. Some fishermen use mono up to 30-pound test when fishing in dense weedbeds. Heavy line does not seem to spook bass in thick cover.

Weedless lures are a must for fishing in most shallow weeds. You may be able to snake a standard lure through scattered weeds, but even moderately dense weeds will foul your hooks and ruin the lure's action. Manufacturers make various types of weed-guards out of wire, plastic, nylon bristle and stiff monofilament. However, if the weedguard is too stiff, it reduces your chances of hooking bass.

Although they lack weedless hooks, Texas-rigged plastic worms and spinnerbaits are among the most weed-resistant lures. Some fishermen bend their hook points slightly toward the hook shank. The point is less likely to pick up weeds, but is exposed enough to hook a bass.

Angling in shallow weeds demands accurate casting. Bass in dense weeds may be reluctant to chase a lure. You must be able to hit small pockets or to cast parallel to a weed edge.

Fly-casting is an extremely effective method of presenting a lure into a small opening in shallow weeds. But horsing a big bass out of heavy cover will test the tackle of any fly fisherman.

Many bass fishermen swear by live bait rigged on a weedless hook. You can dap a frog, salamander or minnow into holes in the weeds; you can let the bait swim through cover with a free line; or you can suspend it from a bobber. Some anglers gently lob the bait a short distance, then skitter it across weed-tops. Long casts will kill most live baits quickly.

SLOP consists of various floating-leaved and sub-merged weeds mixed with *filamentous*, or moss-like algae. The water temperature may be 10 degrees cooler below the slop.

CLUMPS of emergent weeds often break away from dense mats along shore. These clumps float about the lake, providing temporary cover for largemouth bass, usually in early spring.

TALL WEEDS provide bass with shade. Some types of pondweeds may grow to the surface in water as deep as 15 feet.

## Where and How to Catch Largemouth in Deep Weeds

The secret to catching bass in deep weeds is to find a weedline. You can catch some largemouths in a wide expanse of deep weeds, but to improve your odds, concentrate on the edges.

In a clear lake, weeds may grow to depths of 20 or 25 feet. But with a depth finder and a little practice, locating a deep weedline is not as difficult as you might expect. When you find a weedline, throw out one or more markers along the edge, keeping them just inside the weeds.

Use your trolling motor or drift along the weedline while casting a crankbait. Or troll a deep-running crankbait or Spoon Plug® along the edge. Stay just outside the markers while letting out enough line so the lure ticks bottom. Some fishermen use metered monofilament so they can easily find the same depth after catching a bass.

If you catch a bass while trolling or drifting, it is probably an active fish within a school. Mark the spot, then work it thoroughly. You may have to switch to a slower presentation to catch more fish.

If you do not have a depth finder, you must rely on your sense of feel. When your lure tracks through weeds, it catches momentarily, pulls loose, then catches again. Veer toward deeper water until you no longer feel weeds, then slowly angle back toward the weedline.

Most lure types used in shallow weeds will also work in deep weeds. But you may need a larger sinker with your plastic worm, a heavier spinnerbait or jig, or a deeper-diving crankbait.

Bass along a deep weedline sometimes ignore artificial lures. If the fish are not feeding, live bait may be the only solution. Using a slip-sinker rig, cast parallel to the weedline, then inch the bait toward the boat. Or suspend the bait from a slip-bobber. Retrieve it slowly or let the wind push it along the edge of the weeds.

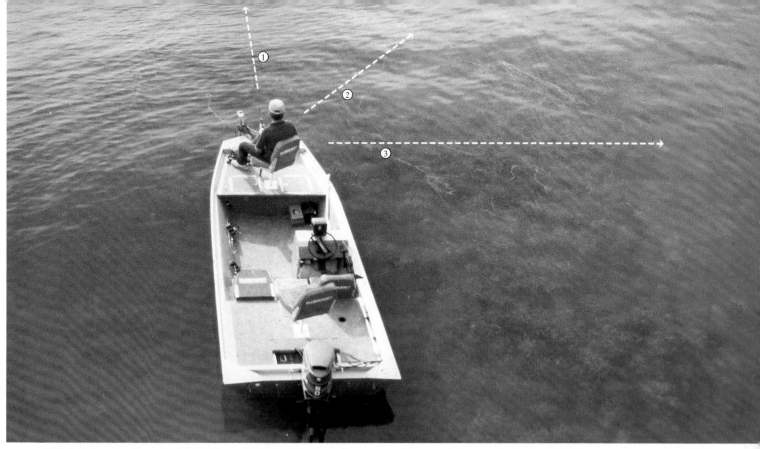

WORK the weedline by (1) casting a deep-running crankbait, plastic worm or jig-and-pig and retrieving it parallel to the weedline. (2) Cast a shallower-running crankbait to the top of the drop-off and retrieve it down the slope just above the weedtops. Or (3) toss a spinnerbait into the shallows and reel it toward the drop-off.

YO-YO a ¾- to 1-ounce brushguard jig with a pork or soft-plastic trailer in dense weedbeds. Make a short cast, shake your rod tip to get the lure down through the weeds, yo-yo it a few times, then reel up and cast again.

SUBSTITUTE a Florida rig for an ordinary worm-sinker rig when fishing in dense weeds. The pigtail on the sinker screws into the worm, preventing the two from separating and eliminating the need to peg the sinker.

# Fishing for Largemouth in Timber & Brush

When a bass feels the sting of a hook, its first reaction is to head for cover. And if that cover happens to be nearby trees or brush, the ensuing battle will test the skill of any angler.

Although it may be difficult to fight and land a bass in woody cover, fishermen who know how to work timber and brush rarely fail to catch bass.

Dams on large rivers have flooded vast expanses of timber and brush over the past few decades. After a reservoir fills, over 100 feet of water may cover the trees. In some impoundments, the entire basin is flooded timber with the exception of farm fields, roads and towns.

A low dam on a river will not cover an entire forest, but it will flood timber and brush in the backwaters. These trees also rot off in time. Waves pounding on stumps in shallow water wash soil away from the bases, exposing the root systems. The spaces between the roots make ideal bass cover. Stumps in shallow areas of reservoirs also have exposed roots under water.

Submerged trees may last indefinitely. Timber that protrudes above water eventually rots off at the waterline, leaving only partially-exposed trunks.

In some cases, the U.S. Army Corps of Engineers or other government agencies cuts the trees as a reservoir is filling. Once filled, the reservoir appears to be void of timber, but it has a forest of tree trunks several feet below the surface. Occasionally, loggers *clearcut* most of the trees before a reservoir is created, leaving only stumps. Although tall timber may be hard to find, the chances of it holding bass are better than if the reservoir was filled with trees.

Some reservoir maps show the location of timber; some do not. If your map lacks such information, obtain a quad map, which shows the location of woodlands before the reservoir was filled. Chances are, the trees will still be there.

Flooded brush decays much faster than timber. You may find brush in deep water in some new reservoirs, but in older ones, brush grows mainly in the shallows. During prolonged periods of low water, brush flourishes along shore. When the water level returns to normal, the brush is submerged, providing excellent bass habitat.

Bass in natural lakes and river backwaters seek cover in flooded brush, especially during spring and early summer when runoff raises water levels. The brush harbors foods such as minnows and insects.

Anglers who spend a lot of time fishing around timber know that certain types of trees are better than others. Generally, the largest trees or those with the most branches attract the most fish. Cedar trees, for example, with their dense network of branches, are consistent bass producers.

In southern lakes and sloughs, water-dwelling trees such as cypress provide homes for largemouths. Erosion along riverbanks often results in trees tumbling into the water. The branches offer cover and break the current.

In steep-walled reservoirs, rock slides carry trees and brush down the slope and into the water. The trees may provide the only cover along a cliff wall. In lakes and ponds that lack good shoreline cover, fishermen sometimes fell trees into the water, then cable the tree to the stump.

# Where and How to Catch Largemouth in Shallow Timber and Brush

When searching for feeding bass in a reservoir, most anglers head for a patch of shallow timber or brush.

Bass use shallow timber and brush the same way they use shallow weeds. It offers a protected spawning area in spring, a morning and evening feeding zone in summer and an all-day feeding area in early fall. Bass abandon this cover in late fall and winter.

The best shallow timber and brush is generally near deep water. Look for bass around isolated patches, along a distinct tree line or brushline, and in deep pockets on brush- or timber-covered flats. Fishermen can sometimes see clues that reveal the location of submerged timber and brush. A small limb extending above the surface may be part of a large tree. *Stickups,* or the tips of small branches, pinpoint the location of submerged brush. A tilted log in open water probably means a tree has floated in and lodged along a drop-off. A clump of trees or brush standing higher than others nearby indicates an underwater hump.

Weedless lures are a must for fishing in brush and stumps. Spinnerbaits and Texas-rigged plastic worms were developed specifically for this purpose. Other popular lures include buzz baits or weedless spoons and brushguard jigs tipped with pork attractors.

With a little practice, you can learn how to work a crankbait through openings in the brush and how to bounce it off stumps without snagging (page 37).

Casting accuracy is important when fishing in shallow timber and brush. A bass holding tight under a log may refuse a lure that passes more than a foot or two away. But when bass begin to feed, they move out of their hiding spots to cruise about in openings between the trees or brush. Anglers often ignore these open areas, thinking that all bass are near cover. Largemouths in clear water generally hold tighter to cover than bass in murky water.

Use heavy, abrasion-resistant line for fishing in timber or brush. The constant friction of line against limbs will soon cause fraying. Check your line frequently. Tug on your knots after catching a bass. A rough spot on the line or a weak knot could result in a lost trophy. Cut off a few feet of line and retie your knots several times a day.

## *Where to Fish in Shallow Timber and Brush*

ISOLATED PATCHES of trees or brush concentrate bass. A small stand of trees away from other cover is more likely to hold bass than a similar stand within a flooded forest or near a large weedbed.

DOWNED TREES offer several types of cover for bass. The fish hang among the branches or under the main trunk. If the entire tree has toppled into the water, look for bass among the roots.

BRUSHY FLATS near deep water often hold feeding bass. If the flat is bordered by a distinct line of brush, fish mainly along the edge. Bass also hold in the thickest clumps of brush on the flat.

TREE LINES and brushlines are similar to weedlines. Look for bass along the edge or several feet inside the cover. Sharp bends, pockets or points along the edge hold more bass than straight portions.

## How to Buzz Trees and Stumps

CAST a spinnerbait several feet beyond a tree or stump. Angle your cast so you can bring the lure within a few inches of the object.

BUZZ the lure across the surface by holding the rod tip high and reeling rapidly. Stop reeling when the lure is next to the tree.

## How to Flip a Lure Next to Stumps

FLIP a jig-and-eel or plastic worm into openings between stumps, trees or brush. Drop the lure into areas with the heaviest shade.

WAIT until the lure hits bottom. Hop the jig through the opening by lifting the rod tip, then lowering the rod to ease the lure back to bottom.

HELICOPTER the spinnerbait down along the tree by dropping your rod tip quickly. Follow the lure with your rod tip, keeping the line tight as the lure sinks.

WATCH your line carefully. Set the hook the instant you see the line twitch or feel a light tap. Bass usually strike as the lure sinks or just after you begin the retrieve.

## *Other Techniques for Fishing in Shallow Timber and Brush*

FLOAT an unweighted plastic lizard or worm over shallow brush. Twitch the lure as you retrieve it slowly. Watch for a slurp that signals a strike.

BUMP a crankbait against the side of a log or bush. The erratic action may tempt a bass. A big-lipped crankbait will bounce off branches, reducing snags.

## Where and How to Catch Largemouth in Deep Timber and Brush

If you ran a graph recorder over a submerged forest, you would probably see a large number of fish scattered among the trees. And a good share of them would be bass.

A graph recorder is valuable for locating bass in deep timber because it enables you to distinguish fish from tree limbs. On a flasher, bass look much like the branches.

Finding bass in deep timber and brush may be difficult, especially in a reservoir that has a lot of trees. The secret is to locate edges or isolated clumps of woody cover.

Prime locations include tree lines along structure such as creek channels. Other good locations include farm fields, orchards, windbreaks or shelterbelts, and powerline clearings. Look for bass in brushlines along road ditches and fencelines. They also congregate in timber and brush on sunken islands, points and deep flats.

In clearcut areas, stumps may provide the only bass cover. If your depth finder shows a jagged bottom, you may be over a submerged stump field.

In summer, look for bass in timber or brush from 15 to 25 feet deep. Fish brushlines or timberlines much as you would a weedline (page 30). Use a deep-running crankbait to find the bass. Then switch to a plastic worm or a brushguard jig. Vary the depth of your retrieve because bass may be suspended halfway up the trees.

During late fall and winter, many bass are caught by vertical jigging in 30 to 40 feet of water. Start jigging at 10 to 15 feet and work your way down. After a few warm days in winter, bass often gather near the surface. Catch them by retrieving a surface lure just above the treetops.

Some anglers prefer 20- to 30-pound test braided dacron line for fishing in deep timber and brush. Dacron has almost no stretch, so it signals a bite better than mono. Dacron also resists nicks and abrasions better than monofilament. Tie on a 6-foot mono leader to reduce visibility.

## How to Fish a Plastic Worm in Deep Timber and Brush

EASE a Texas-rigged plastic worm over the branches. The worm will occasionally catch on limbs or twigs as you retrieve.

DROP the rod tip to give a few inches of slack, then twitch it gently to flip the worm over the branch. Keep the rod tip up after the sinker comes free.

WATCH your line as the worm settles. A strike may feel like a sharp tap or your line may move off to the side. Set the hook immediately.

## How to Vertically Jig in Deep Timber and Brush

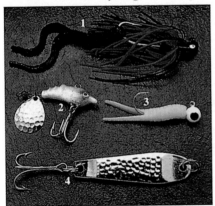

LURES for vertical jigging include: (1) jig tipped with a pork eel, (2) tail-spin, (3) jig tipped with a plastic grub, (4) jigging spoon.

POSITION your boat as close as possible to a large tree. Drop the lure down through the limbs, keeping it close to the trunk.

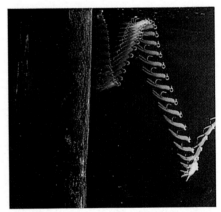

TWITCH the jig, then keep a tight line as it sinks. This lets you detect even the lightest tap. Jig around the tree at different depths.

## Tips for Fishing in Deep Timber and Brush

PEG a cone sinker when using a Texas-rigged plastic worm in brush or timber. Wedge a toothpick into the sinker, then cut off the excess with a nail clipper. Pegging the sinker prevents it from sliding away from the worm when it catches on a branch.

FREE a snagged lure with a plug-knocker. Attach wire pigtails to a heavy weight such as an 8- to 12-ounce sinker. Tie a heavy cord to the weight, then slip the fishing line into the pigtails. Holding on to the cord, slide the weight down the line to knock the plug loose.

# Big 'Dads = Big Bass

by Frank Sargeant

*Bill Murphy, the all-time "teen bass" champion, considers crawdads the deadliest bait*

The object of Bill Murphy's passion came to California some 30 years ago. That's when the first largemouths of the Florida sunspecies were transplanted to the deep impoundments that dot the mountains east of San Diego. The Florida bass took to the strange environment with a vengeance, feeding on hordes of shad and golden shiners, and even on fingerling trout the state had planted in most of the lakes. With the abundant food and the insulating, highly oxygenated depths, the bass grew and fed year round.

By the early 1970s, trophies were being turned out on a regular basis. In a few years more, state records began to topple as monstrous bass showed up in numbers unheard of anywhere else in the country. The little lakes, most less than 5 miles long, became national catchwords: Otay, San Vincente, Casitas, and El Capitan. Less well-known, but also productive, were Marino, Barrett, Hodges, Sutherland, Henshaw, Murray, Jennings, Miramar, Poway, Dixon, Skinner, Wohlford, and Vail.

Murphy was in the vanguard devising techniques for taking the giants now lurking in these lakes — techniques that eventually produced four of the six International Gamefish Association line-class records, including the second-largest bass of all time, a 21-pound 3-ounce behemoth caught by Ray Easley in 1980.

**Bill Murphy**

**Home:** *Santee, California*

**Occupation:** *Dental technician*

In southern California, in the world of big bass, Bill Murphy has earned the nickname ''Lunker Bill.'' Over the last twenty years, from the desert reservoirs around San Diego, he's regularly caught some of the largest bass in the nation.

The red-bearded Irishman extracts these giants with a skill, patience, and attention to detail learned in his job as a dental technician. Sometimes, in fashioning his own tackle, he even employs the same tools he uses in making dental plates for San Diego dentists.

Murphy gained fame by trolling Magnum Rapalas, hand-painted with up to twenty coats to precisely match the rainbow trout forage. He used lead-core line, as much as 200 feet, carrying the lures as deep as 70 feet to hook lunkers untouched by shallower fishing techniques. Another of his methods is fishing homemade giant plastic worms. Some of his worms measure 16 inches long.

But for most of his fishing, Murphy now uses a different method: anchoring and slowly retrieving live crawfish. He feels this technique takes the biggest bass.

At his workbench, Murphy customizes a trolling plug

Murphy's Rapalas, hand-painted to mimic bass forage

Murphy himself has boated 38 bass over 13 pounds, including eight over 15 pounds; his biggest is 16 pounds 15 ounces. This probably makes him the all-time champion of what he calls "teen" fish — the only bass that get him excited.

Bill has lived here twenty years, and the wood of his workbench is burnished black with the continual rubbing of his big forearms as he labors on yet another refinement to yet another custom lure. The early models of his painted Rapalas hang here, now layered with dust. Some wear two dozen coats of translucent paint, laid on over weeks to achieve the living glow of a young trout. The hook points of each have been perfectly triangulated — under the same microscope Murphy uses to perfect the dentures he makes in his lab.

Murphy still trolls with Rapalas in the dead of winter, and says the technique is superb for locating fish. He uses lead-core line, sometimes 200 feet of it, to reach the deep winter haunts of the big bass.

Piled in every corner of the workshop are plastic worms in wild shapes and colors, all designed and poured by Murphy. His worm molds are masterworks, evidence of the skill with tiny tools that has made him a widely sought dental technician. There's the mold for a lead-bodied spinner he calls the Little Murph: he cast it in one of the denture furnaces at his office from old pennies. Lures from this mold look as if they were struck in a coin mint — perfect in every detail.

There are a host of good fishermen around San Diego, a coterie of giant-bass anglers who know each other and keep tabs on each other's catches — but who never, never fish together.

"Only one captain per boat," says Murphy. "Each of us wants to give the orders."

These are incredibly patient men, willing to fish a full day, or even several days, for a single bass. They are comparable to muskie fishermen, to marlin fishermen — and maybe even more so to deer hunters. In fact, Murphy calls one of the techniques he's developed "stand hunting," because he takes a stand and waits there in absolute silence for his giant prey to come to him, the same way he'd await a ten-point whitetail.

"Really big bass survive because they're wary," says Murphy. "They're like trophy bucks, because if they observe the slightest thing that's unusual in their habitat, they won't bite. Remember, these fish have spent maybe eight to twelve years in the same general vicinity, so they know how every rock and twig looks, just what the natural sounds are, and what foods they should find there. It's like a chess game; the challenge is to avoid making a bad move. I don't care if I land them — I release them all now, anyway — but fooling a big one is checkmate."

Murphy says he has been successful because he's willing to set up on a big-fish spot and wait until

*For years, Murphy's giant bass have kept writers and photographers busy at southern California newspapers*

everything returns to normal, so the bass aren't aware of his presence. He looks for rocky points or rubble piles that rise within 15 feet of the surface but drop away sharply, sometimes down to 100 feet of water.

Some of this structure has weed growth, but the usual form of cover is rubble or decaying brush and trees. The biggest bass, Murphy says, have no predators to hide from and require just enough cover to camouflage themselves from their prey. In the really thick cover, only the smaller bass are likely to hang out.

He fishes from a 15-foot aluminum semi-V with a 25-horsepower outboard and a transom-mounted electric motor. The boat's interior is padded from

*Murphy's no-frills bass rig, an aluminum semi-V*

bow to stern with thick carpet. Under the hand-fitted floorboards, poured flotation muffles the noise of waves slapping the hull. Murphy poured it himself to make sure there were no voids to create a drum effect. Carpet is fitted on the inner sides of the boat, to quiet the scraping of rods there when he takes them out of the racks or replaces them. His flasher and graph recorder are mounted on the middle seat.

Also, Murphy has designed and welded up a pair of enormous, multi-clawed steel anchors, each attached to 100 feet of line, which let him rivet the boat over the deep rockpiles and points where he most often finds the giants. "If the anchor goes bouncing through the rocks, you can forget it," he advises. "Noise like that shuts them down every time."

Before he starts fishing, he graphs an area carefully, studying each of the inverted *V* marks that represent fish. With years of experience under his belt, he feels he can tell the approximate size of a fish by the thickness of the mark it makes on the graph paper.

Once he's settled into his "stand," Murphy rarely uses his electric motor, and he keeps the depth finders turned off. "Electronics create noise in the water. I can hear it — and if I can, you know the fish can. They may not spook, but they're less inclined to feed when you're zapping them with sound pulses."

*Murphy deposits his night's catch into his crawdad tank*

*Marking a craw for color-selective bass*

Murphy's favorite bait for the warmer months, spring to fall, is now live crawdads. "In all our lakes 'dads are a natural food, and they're easy for us to catch and keep," says Murphy. In two giant tanks outside his home he stores about a thousand, replenishing them with weekly forays to neighborhood ditches after dark.

When Bill heads for the lake, he takes up to 15 dozen 'dads with him. He keeps a snapping carpet of them in two ice chests, adding an inch of water to keep them happy, segregating them by size so the big ones don't eat the little ones.

Reaching into the box is like reaching into a rattlesnake den. Every crawfish in there rears back, pincers poised like pointed boxing gloves. Some look like miniature — but not very miniature — lobsters. When you get hold of a crawfish — quickly grabbing it by the back of the shell before an adjacent 'dad can nail you — you pull it out and catch it by one of the claws.

Murphy says it's smart to remove one pincer so that the crawfish isn't such a formidable bite for the bass: "A 13-pounder can gobble up the biggest crawfish there is, but if it's got both claws he has to whip its butt first. With one claw, the crawfish just tries to escape when a bass approaches, and that turns on the fish's attack instinct." To remove a claw, you simply crack the shell of it. The crawfish will then activate its escape mechanism, neatly detaching the arm from its body. The craw isn't permanently damaged: if released, it will quickly grow a new pincer.

At times, Murphy uses some unusual tricks to make his 'dads more appealing to the bass. He's found that bass in different lakes prefer different colors, so he paints his 'dads with waterproof

markers, some of which come in two-tone colors like silver and green or silver and blue.

Another secret is to treat his crawdad hooks and the first few inches of his line with a special potion, to conceal his scent. He mixes cod-liver oil, anise, vanilla, saccharin, salt, and even anti-freeze in a mineral oil base, varying the proportions from season to season.

*Home-brewed potion on hook and line masks human scent*

Murphy fishes the crawfish unweighted. In sparse cover, he uses an Eagle Claw 139 Baitholder hook in size 4; in thicker stuff, a Mustad 9174 in size 6 with the bend opened slightly. The line is 6- to 12-pound mono, depending on the clarity of the water. He uses lines in various tints, to match the water color as it changes through the seasons. In summer, when the water has a green color from suspended algae, he uses a line with a greenish tint. In fall and winter, when the algae dies off and the water clears, he prefers line with a grayish tint or clear line. Trophy bass are definitely line-shy, Murphy says.

For angling from late spring through early fall, the hook goes through the "horn" at the front of the crawfish's shell. Inserted here, squarely between the eyes, the hook hits no vital parts. The crawfish can survive for hours, and if it doesn't get eaten, can be returned to the home tank where the hook hole will soon heal shut. Also, a craw hooked this way will dive faster to the productive depth, and can be fished in a single spot more easily: it pulls away from the angler, so he can retrieve it a little and then let it swim out again.

In the cooler months, he hooks the craws through the tail, in the second segment from the tip. The hook must be inserted to the side of the tail vein, not in the vein itself, or the craw will be killed. Tail-hooking conceals the hook better, so it helps deceive cautious bass in the clear water of winter. Lighter line can be used, since a tail-hooked craw is easier to pull through cover without snagging.

A crawdad hooked in the horn usually swims hard straight down, so it's no problem to hit bottom even in 20 to 40 feet of water, the depths Murphy likes to fish early in the summer. In Florida, the ancestors of these fish never visited such deep water haunts — Florida lakes are shallow — but in California lakes the fish thrive in the deepest depths, preferring them to the shoreline all year, except briefly during the spawn.

Murphy fishes the crawdads with an excruciatingly slow retrieve. He gathers short coils of line in his hand, as though retrieving a fly line. "I want to know exactly what's going on down there," he says. "If you run the line directly to the reel, you can't feel it. Sometimes these fish just suck the bait in and hold it a second, and if they feel the slightest line pressure, they spit it. If I retrieve by hand, I know when they take."

*Murphy's hands-on crawdad retrieve*

*How Murphy Rigs Crawfish for Giant Bass*

REMOVE one pincer by crushing it with pliers. The craw has an internal mechanism which then detaches the entire arm. Pulling it off would kill the craw.

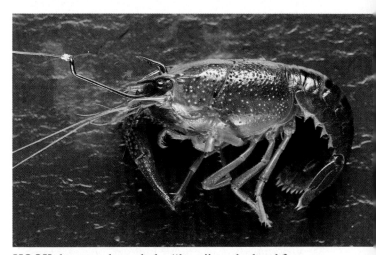

HOOK the craw through the "horn" on the head for warm-weather fishing. Hooked this way, it will dive rapidly to reach bass holed up in the cool depths.

INSERT the hook through the second segment of the tail for cold-weather bass. This conceals it better, an advantage in the clear water of wintertime.

45

Bill fishes the baits on 7-foot spinning rods he's built himself. The rods are jointed, the lower section made from a heavy saltwater spinning blank, the top from a much softer freshwater blank. The combination of sections gives plenty of flex to make long casts with the bait, yet lots of authority to control the fight. The reels are seasoned saltwater spinning models, chosen for their large spools — an advantage in casting light baits because the line peels off with less friction.

Fishing for big bass is normally a slow, painstaking proposition, but Bill has sometimes boated more than 100 in a day while using 'dads. "A few years back, I think it was in October, I caught over 100 bass a day for three days straight," Bill recalls. "They all came from the same spot. It was a rocky hump that topped off at 11 feet. The bass were hitting before the bait ever reached bottom. Nothing really huge, but I had an 11-4, a 9-15, and dozens over 7. They planted rainbows on the third day and that was the end of it. The bass scattered to feed on the trout."

While 'dads now account for most of Murphy's bass, some of his very biggest ones have been caught on plastic worms. In summer and winter, he uses 6- to 7¼-inch worms. A 7¼-incher also works well in spring and fall, but he often uses bigger worms then — much bigger. He can't buy worms big enough, so he molds his own, up to 16 inches long. "Worm" may not be the right term for a lure this size; "snake" would be better. His favorite colors are green, root beer, chocolate, blue

and black. He treats his worms with the potion mentioned earlier.

The retrieve is very slow, much like the one he uses with crawfish. When a fish hits, he gives it slack, reels in his excess line, then lets the fish pull the rod tip down before setting the hook. This way, the line is sure to be tight.

"My partner and I were fishing a tournament on Wohlford Lake some years back," Bill reminisces, "and we hadn't caught a single keeper all day. We had one spot left to try, but a boat was anchored up right where we wanted to fish. They weren't really fishing — it looked like they were all asleep, so we decided to give it a try.

"On the first cast, I moved my worm about 6 inches and she hit. When I set the hook, she tore away, leaped clear out of the water, then headed back toward the boat and swam around the anchor rope. I had to dunk my rod in the lake to get it around the rope, but we finally landed her. She weighed 15 pounds 9 ounces."

That single fish was enough to win the tournament. At that time, it was the largest bass ever caught in a fishing tournament, and it may still be.

The locals were duly impressed. If you look at the official Wohlford Lake brochure, you'll see the spot where Bill caught the fish. It's now designated as Murphy's Rock.

Anyone who can win a tournament with one fish deserves to have a spot named after him.

*An Assortment of Murphy's Favorite Worms*

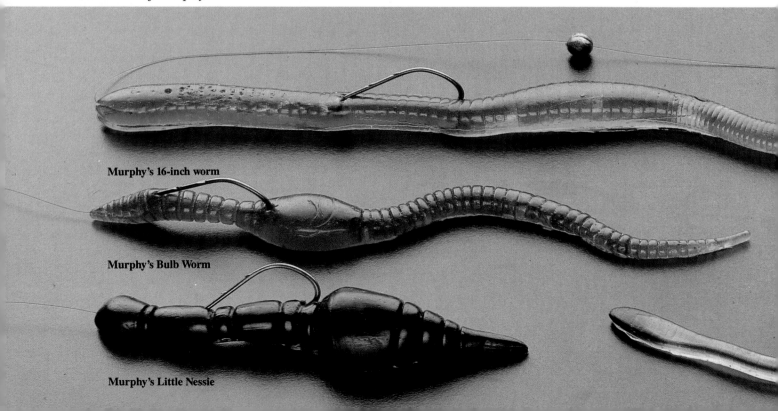

**Murphy's 16-inch worm**

**Murphy's Bulb Worm**

**Murphy's Little Nessie**

*Murphy's Special Plastic-Worm Rig for Trophy Largemouths*

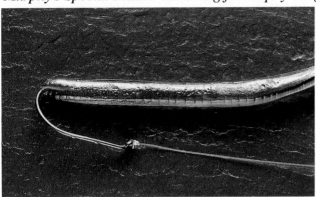

1. PUSH the point of an Eagle Claw 181 Baitholder hook, 1/0 or 2/0, into the head of the worm. Murphy flattens the shank barbs to avoid snagging debris.

2. THREAD the hook through the center of the plastic. Work the hook farther along the length of the worm than you would in rigging Texas-style.

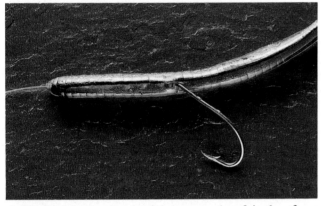

3. BRING the hook out of the worm, 1 to 3 inches from the head; leave the eye embedded. With the hook this far back, bass are less likely to feel it.

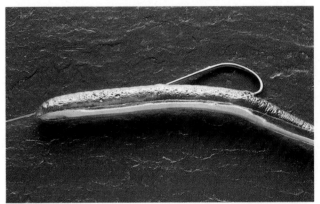

4. INSERT the point into the side of the worm, not deep in the center. The offset hook should point out for best hooking. Add a split-shot about 5 inches up the line.

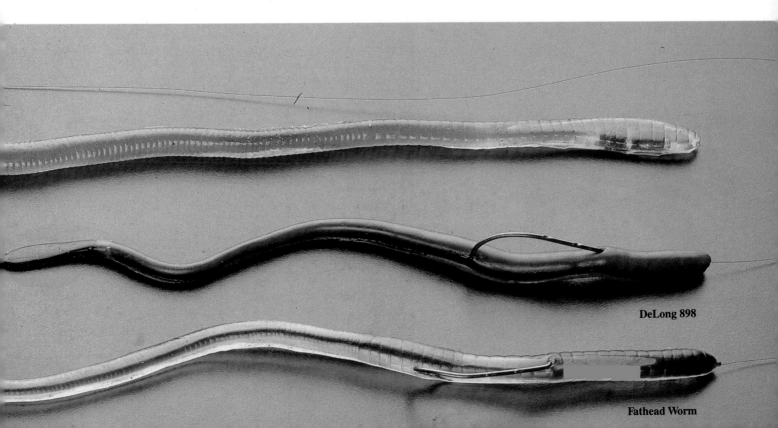

**DeLong 898**

**Fathead Worm**

# Smallmouth Bass

# Where to Find Smallmouth Through the Seasons

Although smallmouth are less migratory than most other freshwater gamefish, you must be familiar with their seasonal movement patterns for consistent fishing success. In many waters, smallmouth stay in the same vicinity all year. The secret to finding them in different seasons may simply be to fish shallower or deeper.

Regardless of the type of water, smallmouth seasonal movements are controlled by the same factors and are surprisingly predictable.

SPRING. Smallmouth remain in a state of near-dormancy until the water temperature approaches 50°F. Then they begin moving toward their spawning area. In streams, the spawning migration may begin at lower temperatures. The exact sites chosen for spawning depend on the type of water. Because smallmouth have a strong homing instinct, they normally spawn in the same area each year.

After recuperating from spawning, the females scatter to deeper water. Males move deeper once they abandon the fry. Both sexes remain in the vicinity of their spawning sites, if there is deep water nearby. Although they are feeding more heavily now than during the spawning period, fishing may be tough because they are not as concentrated.

SUMMER. Smallmouth are even more predictable in summer than during other seasons. Once they take up residence on a particular piece of structure or in a certain pool, they may not move for several months. This stay-at-home tendency can be partially explained by the smallmouth's strong liking for crayfish. Unlike most other types of smallmouth food, crayfish are linked to a specific location. They require rocks for protection and cannot move far from cover. But in waters where baitfish are the primary food, smallmouth must move around to find them.

Deep water is particularly important in summer. With the surface temperature high and the sun directly overhead, smallmouth must retreat to deep water to find a comfortable temperature and light level. How deep they go varies with the type of water. In a clear lake, they may go as deep as 25 feet.

In a murky lake that lacks oxygen in the depths, they may be restricted to water shallower than 12 feet. In a small stream, they may spend the summer in pools only 4 feet deep because there is no deeper water.

EARLY TO MID-FALL. Early fall finds smallmouth in much the same locations as they were in summer, although they spend more of their time in shallow water. The shallows offer more food, and because of the cooler surface temperatures and lower sun angle, smallmouth have no need to go deep.

In most lakes, the surface continues to cool and eventually reaches the same temperature as the water below the thermocline. When this happens the lake turns over, meaning that all of the water circulates and the temperature becomes the same from top to bottom. You may catch one smallmouth at a depth of 5 feet and another at 30 feet. The lack of a consistent pattern results in tough fishing.

In rivers, smallmouth remain in their early-fall locations through mid-fall. They feed more as the water cools, so mid-fall fishing can be the best of the year, particularly for good-sized smallmouth.

LATE FALL AND WINTER. Following the turn-over, the likelihood of finding smallmouth in the shallows diminishes. However, a few days of warm weather may draw baitfish into shallow water and attract smallmouth.

Once smallmouth retreat to deep water, they feed very little. Many fishermen believe that smallmouth simply cannot be caught under these conditions, but if you take the time to do some thorough scouting, you can sometimes locate small but densely packed schools. Although smallmouth are not actively feeding, a slow presentation will tempt a few bites. And the fish you catch are likely to be big.

Stream smallmouth may move to deep pools if their mid-fall locations are too shallow for wintering. They continue to feed and fishing is good until the water temperature drops into the low 40s.

# How Weather Affects Smallmouth

Weather plays a major role in smallmouth fishing. If you had a choice of when to fish, your odds would undoubtedly be best during a period of stable weather. Changes in the weather disrupt the smallmouth's feeding schedule. They may continue to feed, but peak feeding times are not as predictable. Exactly how changes in weather affect smallmouth depends on time of year, type of water, and even type of cover. Following are the weather conditions that have the most influence on smallmouth fishing:

CLOUD COVER. Smallmouth normally bite better when the skies are overcast rather than clear. Although smallmouth are not as light-sensitive as walleyes, low light causes them to move into shallow water and feed more heavily.

But clear weather is nearly always better in early spring, because the sun warms the water and urges smallmouth to begin feeding.

The degree to which cloud cover affects smallmouth fishing depends on the clarity of the water. In lakes that are extremely clear, daytime fishing is usually poor when skies are sunny. In these waters, smallmouth do much of their feeding at night. But in lakes of moderate clarity, they feed sporadically throughout the day even though the skies are clear.

WIND. Windy weather generally spells good smallmouth fishing. The waves scatter the light rays so less light penetrates the surface and smallmouth feeding increases.

In a shallow body of water, a strong wind stirs up the bottom, making the water so murky that smallmouth cannot see well enough to feed. Fishing remains slow until the water starts to clear.

Windy weather may also cause poor fishing when smallmouth are in the weeds. The movement of the vegetation caused by the wave action seems to make them extra-cautious.

RAIN. Rainy weather usually improves smallmouth fishing, especially when the surface is calm. Overcast skies combined with rain droplets dimpling the surface decrease the amount of light that penetrates. And the sound seems to reduce the chance of spooking the fish.

Rain has practically no effect on fishing on a windy day. Because light penetration is already low and the level of background sound is high, smallmouth are not as spooky as in calm weather.

A warm rain in early spring can make a big difference in fishing success. The water temperature may rise several degrees in one day, resulting in an insect hatch which causes semi-dormant smallmouth to start feeding.

A heavy rain usually means poor fishing in streams. Runoff clouds the water so smallmouth cannot see your bait as well. And rising water spreads the fish over a larger area, so finding them is more difficult.

Storms accompanied by lightning and loud thunderclaps cause smallmouth to stop biting. Fishing stays slow for several days if the storm is severe.

COLD FRONTS. Smallmouth often go on a feeding spree before a storm, but if the temperature drops dramatically and the skies clear following the storm, catching them becomes tough.

The negative effects of a cold front are most noticeable in spring and summer, especially if the front follows a period of warm, stable weather. Smallmouth feed heavily during the warm weather, so they can afford to stop for a few days after the cold front passes.

Cold fronts usually do not slow feeding in fall. In fact, it seems as if smallmouth sense the approach of winter and begin feeding more heavily. Anglers willing to brave the elements can enjoy some of the year's best fishing.

The effects of a cold front on smallmouth, as on many other freshwater gamefish, are more severe in clear lakes than in murkier lakes or in rivers.

BAROMETRIC PRESSURE. Most experienced smallmouth fishermen believe that barometric pressure has little effect on fishing success.

# How to Select Smallmouth Waters

Finding a lake or stream with a good smallmouth population can be difficult. Because smallmouth prefer the cleanest and clearest waters available, they generally inhabit a smaller percentage of the waters in a given region than most other gamefish do. And because smallmouth are fairly easy to catch, a healthy population can be fished down quickly once the word gets out.

Natural-resources agencies may not be able to give you much help because smallmouth are difficult to sample. A lake or stream may have lots of smallmouth, but few are found in fish-population surveys because they are very net-shy. They avoid gill nets, trap nets and most other sampling gear, but can be sampled by shocking. Results of shocking surveys are available from some natural-resources agencies.

You can sometimes get good information from tackle shops, marinas and knowledgeable fishermen who have firsthand experience on waters in the area where you will be fishing. You can also find good smallmouth waters by paying attention to fishing-contest results, newspaper reports, regional magazine articles and local outdoor programs on radio and television. If a lake or river is consistently producing smallmouth, chances are you will find out about it through these sources.

The surest way to find a good lake or stream is to hire a competent guide who specializes in smallmouth. He will take you to his prime waters and best spots. And once you get to know him, he may be willing to share his knowledge of other good smallmouth waters.

*How Survey Data Can Help You Find Good Smallmouth Water*

SHOCKING is an effective way for natural-resources agencies to sample smallmouth populations in streams. Current from the electrodes temporarily stuns the fish so they can be weighed and measured.

SURVEY REPORTS list shocking results, including the number of fish per hour of shocking or per acre of water. This report shows that the smallmouth population is highest in sectors 3 to 6.

52

SURFACE ACTIVITY of baitfish can help you recognize structure that holds smallmouth. If the structure holds a lot of baitfish, you can often see them feeding on the surface in early morning or at dusk. In some cases, largemouth or white bass can be seen taking baitfish on the surface while smallmouth feed below.

## How to Recognize Smallmouth Structure

Smallmouth are like most other warmwater gamefish in that structure, which is the topography of the lake or stream bed, dictates where they are found.

A piece of structure that provides food, cover and easy access to the depths may hold smallmouth through the entire year. They simply move deeper or shallower as the seasons change. But if the structure lacks one of these vital elements, smallmouth will move to different pieces of structure to find what they need.

If you find smallmouth spawning in 3 feet of water on a sand-gravel point, you may find them on the same point in summer, but in 12 to 18 feet of water, especially if there are boulders or weeds for cover. In late fall, they will probably stay on the same point but drop into 30 to 50 feet of water.

But if the point lacks summertime cover, smallmouth cannot escape the sunlight, so they will move to structure that offers shade. If the point flattens out at 25 feet, smallmouth may stay there through summer, but will move to a deeper point or offshore reef in late fall.

A good flasher is a must in checking potential smallmouth structure. Smallmouth are almost always found over a hard bottom. By carefully watching for a strong signal, you can quickly locate hard-bottomed areas at the likely depth range.

To understand how a flasher can save fishing time, consider this example. After examining your lake map, you conclude there is a good chance of finding smallmouth along an irregular sandy breakline that runs the length of the north shore. You could try trolling the breakline to find the smallmouth, but that would take several hours. Instead, run the breakline at full speed and watch your flasher for a particularly strong signal which indicates an area of rock or gravel. In only a few minutes, you can pinpoint likely smallmouth spots.

Resort owners or marinas and dock operators may be able to identify specific points, humps or other spots that have been consistently producing smallmouth. If you have a lake map, ask them to mark the spots for you. If you are lucky enough to find a local fishing expert who is willing to share some of his secrets, be careful about the questions you ask. Few serious fishermen are willing to reveal their prime spots, but they will usually tell you what type of structure to look for, and the best depths to fish.

Above-water indicators reveal a great deal about smallmouth structure, if you know what to look for. The examples on the opposite page show how to interpret these clues.

The exact type of structure that smallmouth occupy in different seasons varies greatly, depending on the type of water.

CHANGES in soil composition along the shoreline usually reveal similar changes below water. If you see a line where the soil changes abruptly from sand to rock, visually extend the line into the water. Smallmouth often congregate along the rock margin.

AQUATIC VEGETATION along the shoreline can also provide clues to bottom type. If cattails grow along shore, the bottom probably consists of mud. But bulrushes usually mean a bottom of hard sand or rock, materials better suited to smallmouth.

DEGREE OF SLOPE of the underwater portion of a point can usually be determined by the slope of the above-water portion. A gradually sloping point is normally the best choice in spring; a point with a steeper slope in summer and fall.

JAGGED BLUFFS with many lips and crevices above the water line indicate good smallmouth habitat below water. These irregularities provide shade and attract smallmouth foods. A smooth bluff face lacks these nooks and crannies and holds fewer smallmouth.

## How to Recognize
## Good Smallmouth Cover

Finding productive smallmouth water and determining the type of structure most likely to hold smallmouth are vital to consistent fishing success. But there is still one more piece to the puzzle: you must be able to recognize the specific types of cover that smallmouth prefer.

The primary component of good smallmouth cover is shade, but smallmouth will not use the cover unless a good food supply and deep water are within easy reach. The best cover offers overhead protection as well as shade.

Let's assume that you have located a reef that looks perfect for smallmouth. It is surrounded by deep water and consists mostly of marble- to golfball-sized rock, with a section of scattered boulders along one edge. The entire reef has a good supply of smallmouth foods like crayfish, insect larvae and baitfish, but only the section with the boulders offers adequate shade. This section will hold many more smallmouth than other parts of the reef.

The type of cover that smallmouth use is greatly influenced by other shallow-water predators. If a body of water has a high population of largemouth bass or northern pike, they will occupy weedbeds and woody cover, forcing smallmouth to seek other cover options. But if there are few largemouth or northerns, the weedbeds and woody cover will probably draw smallmouth.

*Good Rocks vs. Bad Rocks*

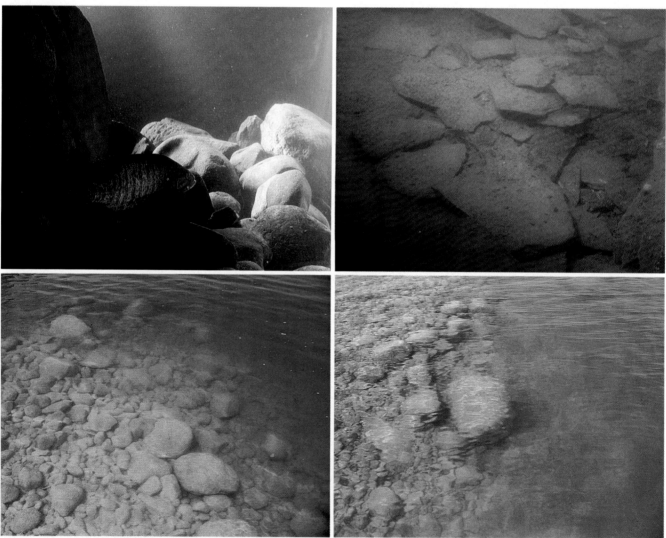

ROCKS tall enough to cast a significant shadow (upper left) make better smallmouth cover than flat rocks (upper right). A reef with large rocks continuing well into deep water (lower left) holds more and bigger smallmouth than a reef that has rocks on the top but sand or silt sloping into deep water (lower right).

### Good Stumps vs. Bad Stumps

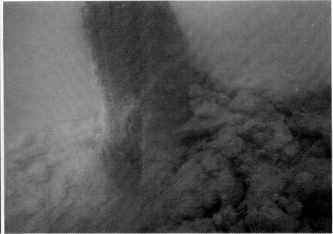

STUMPS with openings between washed-out roots (left) offer overhead cover in addition to shade. This type of stump is much more likely to hold smallmouth than one with embedded roots (right).

### Good Trees vs. Bad Trees

FALLEN TREES that have thick trunks and limbs and slope sharply into the water (left) are best for smallmouth. The thick trunk and limbs offer shade and overhead cover, and the steep slope shows that there is deep water nearby. Spindly trees (right) seldom hold smallmouth, but are attractive to largemouth.

### Good Weeds vs. Bad Weeds

WEEDS that grow on a firm sand-gravel bottom, such as wild celery (left) and bulrushes, are more attractive to smallmouth than weeds that grow on a soft bottom, like lily pads (right) and cattails. Hard-bottom plants located along a breakline attract more smallmouth than those on a shallow flat with no deep water nearby.

# Smallmouth in the Weeds

Smallmouth often conceal themselves along the fringe of a weedbed as they lie in wait for unsuspecting baitfish.

Although smallmouth are not as weed-oriented as largemouth, weeds can be a key in locating them. Weeds make prime smallmouth habitat in oligotrophic lakes, especially if most of the lake basin is rocky. They are also important in rocky mesotrophic lakes. The rocky habitat holds some smallmouth, but you can generally catch more and bigger ones if you can find a sandy-bottomed hump, point or bay with sparse weed growth. The weeds support a different type of food chain: fewer insects and crayfish but more baitfish.

Weeds are not as important in most other types of waters. In lakes where weeds grow virtually every-where in the shallows, smallmouth will seek the typical clean-bottomed habitat, such as rock piles and gravel patches.

Smallmouth may be found in both emergent and submerged vegetation, usually the types that grow on firm bottoms. Seldom will you find them in cattails or other weeds associated with soft bottoms. Low-growing or scattered weeds normally hold more smallmouth than tall or dense varieties. It may be that tall or dense weeds interfere with a small-mouth's ability to catch its prey.

The best smallmouth weeds are within easy reach of deep water. A band of weeds growing along a drop-off is much more likely to hold smallmouth than a large, weedy flat with no deep water nearby.

When a smallmouth takes your bait and winds itself around a stem, you will need fairly stout tackle and heavier-than-normal line to pull it free. Medium power to medium-heavy power spinning or baitcasting gear with 8- to 14-pound abrasion-resistant mono is suitable for most types of weeds.

## Fishing in Bulrushes

These tough, round-stemmed plants grow on sand or gravel bottoms, usually in water from 2 to 5 feet deep. They extend 3 to 6 feet above the surface, so their total height may exceed 10 feet.

Smallmouth are found in and around bulrush beds mainly during the spawning season. But if the bulrushes border deep water, smallmouth may feed in them through the summer and into early fall.

Bulrushes by themselves do not provide much cover, so the best stands have plenty of rocks or logs. They also have numerous open pockets, indentations along the margins, or boat lanes or other types of channels leading through them. Smallmouth hang around the edges of these openings so they can easily ambush baitfish. The openings also make it possible to present a lure without snagging.

When casting into a bulrush bed, try to keep the wind in your face. That way, the bulrushes will be bending toward you, so your lure will tend to slide off the stems instead of snagging.

In addition to the lures shown on this page, other choices for fishing in bulrushes include surface plugs like chuggers and propbaits, Texas-rigged plastic worms, fly-fishing lures like jigging flies and divers, and split-shot rigs with weedless hooks.

TWITCH a floating minnow plug over the surface rather than using a steady retrieve. By twitching it, you can snake it through the bulrushes without snagging. If you reel too fast, the hooks will catch on the tough stems. The same type of presentation works with a propbait.

WORK deep bulrush beds with a ¹⁄₁₆- to ¹⁄₈-ounce brush-guard jig tipped with pork rind or some type of live bait. When smallmouth are not active, a light jig fluttering to bottom is more effective than a minnow plug or propbait twitched on the surface.

RETRIEVE a small spinnerbait through the bulrushes by reeling steadily, pausing to let it helicopter when you reach an open pocket, a boulder or a log. A spinnerbait seldom snags in bulrushes, so you can work it through the thickest part of the bed.

TEXAS-RIG a grubtail (inset) to make it completely weedless. Peg the sinker with a piece of toothpick so it will not slide up the line when the lure rides over the leaves. If the sinker slides up, you will lose feel.

## Fishing in Cabbage

Given a choice, smallmouth prefer the broad-leaved varieties of cabbage to the narrow-leaved types. Normally, smallmouth are found in cabbage beds in 6 to 14 feet of water.

Smallmouth are most likely to use cabbage beds from late spring through early fall. Later, when the cabbage turns brown, they retreat to deeper water.

The cabbage beds best suited to smallmouth are those where the individual plants are spaced several feet apart. Smallmouth are rarely found in dense beds where the plants grow close enough together to form a canopy.

Cabbage has crisp leaves that shatter easily. A fast-moving lure will usually rip through the leaves without fouling, and a slow-moving lure can be freed with a sharp tug.

Surface techniques are usually not as effective as mid-water or bottom techniques for fishing in cabbage. Besides the lures and rigs shown on this page, you can also catch smallmouth in cabbage on spinnerbaits and crankbaits.

RIP a light jig with an open hook through a cabbage bed. The jig may catch on the leaves, but you can free it with a sharp tug. An open hook snags more often than a brushguard hook, but increases your hooking percentage.

TIE a special slip-sinker rig (inset) for working live bait through cabbage. With a brushguard hook and a cone sinker, the rig will rarely snag. In sparse cabbage, you may be able to use an open hook.

## Fishing in Sandgrass

Sandgrass or muskgrass, technically called *Chara,* is a brittle, narrow-leaved plant that grows in water as deep as 35 feet. It often forms a blanket several inches thick covering a large area.

You can find some smallmouth in sandgrass in summer, but the best time is late fall. Sandgrass grows in deeper water than practically any other aquatic plant, and often is the only deep-water cover.

Large sandgrass flats may hold some smallmouth, but these areas are difficult to fish because the smallmouth are scattered. A deep hump or point carpeted with sandgrass would be a better choice.

Fishing in sandgrass is tricky. If you use a jig or live-bait rig, the hook catches on the tiny branchlets. When you pull, one branchlet snaps and the hook stops abruptly as it catches on another. This creates a tugging sensation hard to distinguish from a bite.

Almost any deep-running lure or live-bait rig will work in sandgrass. But you must be alert for excess drag, because small pieces of sandgrass will often cling to your hook.

RETRIEVE a deep-running crankbait over sparse sandgrass. Make sure the lip occasionally digs bottom. The lure usually rips through cleanly, and the bottom disturbance may trigger a strike.

## Fishing in Other Weeds

Although smallmouth prefer the previously shown weeds, they will use many other weeds when their favorite types are not available.

Savvy smallmouth anglers do not hesitate to try any weeds that offer food and cover. Even weeds not normally associated with smallmouth, such as lily pads, can be productive at times. Shown below are some of the other weeds in which smallmouth may be found.

MILFOIL. The feather-veined leaves grow in whorls around the stem. These plants resemble coontail, but coontail leaves are forked.

WILD CELERY. The long leaves have a light-colored center stripe. Small flowers grow at the tops of long, spiraling stems.

CANADA WATERWEED. The leaves are shorter and wider than those of milfoil or coontail, and an individual strand is much narrower.

# Smallmouth in Woody Cover

Woody cover makes ideal smallmouth habitat because it harbors smallmouth foods like insects and minnows in addition to providing shade and protection from larger predators. In rivers, woody cover also creates pockets of slack water where smallmouth can get out of the current.

The best woody cover is in areas where smallmouth can fulfill all of their needs without moving too far. Consequently, a fallen tree on a rubble or boulder bottom would attract more smallmouth than a similar tree on a mucky bottom. Crayfish and aquatic insect larvae living on the rubble or boulder bottom make it more appealing.

If the fallen tree is adjacent to deep water, it would be even more appealing. Then, smallmouth could easily move to deeper water should the light become too bright or the water temperature too warm.

Smallmouth make use of many kinds of woody cover. Besides fallen trees, possible smallmouth hangouts include standing timber, submerged logs, standing or toppled stumps, flooded shoreline brush, beaver lodges and piles of beaver cuttings.

TREES, LOGS AND STUMPS. Experts know that certain trees, logs and stumps hold more smallmouth than others that look practically the same. Part of the difference lies in the bottom composition and the depth of the surrounding water, but there are also differences in the cover itself.

Smallmouth prefer cover that offers overhead protection as well as shade, so a toppled tree with a thick trunk and limbs is more attractive than one with a thinner trunk and limbs, assuming that the habitat is similar.

Standing timber offers some shade, but little overhead cover. It often draws largemouth, but is not as attractive to smallmouth. The lack of overhead cover also explains why a log lying flat on the bottom attracts fewer smallmouth than one that is somehow propped up from the bottom.

FLOODED BRUSH. In spring, when river or reservoir levels rise high enough to cover shoreline vegetation, smallmouth move into flooded brush. They stay in the brush as long as the water continues to rise or remains stable. But as soon as it begins to fall, they move deeper.

Fishermen sink brush piles into deep water, but the water where you find naturally flooded brush is usually shallow. Brush will survive seasonal flooding, but once it is flooded permanently it soon rots away. This explains why new reservoirs have an abundance of brushy cover, but old reservoirs have very little, if any.

Seasonally flooded brush is usually too dense for smallmouth to hide between the branches. Instead of attempting to work your bait or lure through the brush, concentrate on any pockets or fish the edges.

BEAVER LODGES. The idea of fishing around beaver lodges never occurs to most smallmouth fishermen. The areas where beavers build their lodges usually look too shallow and marshy for smallmouth. What many anglers do not realize is that beavers excavate deep entrance holes and runs leading into their lodges. The combination of deep water and overhead logs and brush makes excellent smallmouth habitat.

Another reason that smallmouth like beaver lodges: the mud used to cement the logs and brush attracts many types of burrowing aquatic insects, so smallmouth enjoy a built-in food supply.

Smallmouth also hang around beaver feed beds, especially in small streams. These piles of fresh cuttings are usually close to the lodge.

When fishing in woody cover, remember the old adage "no guts, no glory." To catch the biggest smallmouth, you must work the thickest, shadiest part of the cover. This usually means casting into small openings in the branches instead of casting around the edges. There is no way to avoid getting snagged and losing some lures; that's the price you must pay for success.

If you do get snagged, simply break your line and tie on another lure. If you jerk the branches back and forth or move your boat into the cover to retrieve your lure, you will surely spook the smallmouth.

The techniques for fishing in woody cover are similar to those used in weeds. Most fishermen cast with snag-resistant artificials like spinnerbaits, brushguard jigs and Texas-rigged soft plastics. When rigging Texas style, peg your cone sinker to keep it from sliding away from your worm or grub. Pegging gives you better feel and reduces snagging.

You can fish live bait in woody cover by freelining, or by casting a split-shot or cone-sinker rig. Use a brushguard hook or a fine-wire hook that will bend enough to pull free if you get snagged.

If there are pockets in the cover, you can flycast with bass bugs or jigging flies, jig vertically with a jigging spoon, twitch a surface plug or minnow plug through the openings, or dangle live bait from a bobber. Other techniques for fishing in woody cover are shown on the opposite page.

Fishing in woody cover demands heavy tackle, like a medium-heavy or heavy power baitcasting outfit with 12- to 20-pound abrasion-resistant mono. With heavy tackle, you are better able to free a snagged lure. And you can horse a smallmouth out of the cover before it has a chance to wrap your line around a branch.

*How to Find Submerged Woody Cover*

LOOK for a tree line along the shore of a reservoir, then visually extend the line into the water. Smallmouth often hold along the edge of the submerged trees.

CHECK the location of timber and brush in your favorite smallmouth water at normal water stage (top) or during a drawdown. Then, you will have a better idea of what is beneath the surface when the water is higher (bottom).

WATCH for collapsed banks in reservoirs, pits or big rivers. If the remaining bank is covered with timber or brush, there is a good chance of finding submerged timber and brush where the bank slid into the water.

# Smallmouth in Rocks & Boulders

Smallmouth spend more of their time around rocks and boulders than any other freshwater gamefish. Fishing in this snaggy cover can be extremely frustrating, but there are many techniques to help you keep the problem of snagging to a minimum.

The best way to avoid snags is to keep your bait or lure riding just above bottom. Smallmouth hiding among the rocks are accustomed to darting upward to grab food, so there is no need to drag bottom.

If you attempt to drag your bait or lure along a bottom strewn with rocks, you will always get some snags, even if you use sinkers and hooks that manufacturers claim to be snagless.

Keeping your bait or lure just above the bottom sounds easy, but requires a great deal of concentration. Many fishermen are not comfortable unless they can feel the bottom, so they continually drop their rod tip back to test the depth. Before long, the sinker or lure will wedge into the rocks.

To avoid snags, you must resist the urge to continually feel the bottom. Instead, touch bottom once, then reel up a foot or two and try to maintain that depth. When casting, try to find the retrieve speed that will keep the lure or bait just off bottom. If you are trolling or drifting, watch your depth finder closely. When the depth changes, adjust your line accordingly. Should you lose your concentration and fail to reel in line when the water gets shallower, you will probably get snagged. Should you fail to let out more line when it gets deeper, your bait or lure will pass too high above the fish.

When casting, use the lightest sinker that will take your bait to the bottom. This way, you can retrieve slowly, yet keep the sinker gliding above the rocks. If you are using artificials, select one intended for the depth at which you are fishing. If you are casting into 5 feet of water, for instance, you will get fewer snags with a 1/16-ounce jig than with a 1/4-ounce jig.

When trolling in deep water, use a relatively heavy sinker so you can keep your line nearly vertical. This allows you to hold the sinker just off bottom, and the steep line angle reduces the chances of the sinker wedging in the rocks. The same principle applies to artificials. And keeping your line as short as possible makes it easier to feel your lure tick bottom.

Although nothing is completely snag-free, you can substantially reduce the number of snags by using the right tackle. If you rig your bait on a floating jig head and use a bottom-walking sinker, for instance, you will get only about half as many snags as you would with a standard hook and sinker. And a long-lipped crankbait will deflect off the rocks better than a short-lipped model.

If snagging continues to be a problem, you can always use some type of snag remover or plug knocker. One of the simplest gadgets for freeing a snag is a large clip-on sinker attached to a string (shown on opposite page).

When you combine the right tackle with the right technique, snagging will become the exception rather than the rule. And your smallmouth fishing will become more enjoyable and more successful.

TACKLE for fishing in rocky cover includes: (1) snag-resistant sinkers; (2) a dropper rigged with split-shot that slide off the line if they get snagged; (3) floating jig heads and other floats that lift your bait off the bottom; (4) a worm blower, for inflating a crawler to make it ride higher; (5) a slip-bobber rig, which can be adjusted to keep your bait dangling just above the rocks; and (6) abrasion-resistant mono.

*Tips for Fishing in Rocks and Boulders*

MAKE your own snag-resistant sinker using a piece of coat hanger. Pound one end flat, drill a small hole and insert a snap-swivel.

USE a long rod, 8 to 8½ feet. Then, if you get snagged, you can reach out and change the angle of pull without moving your boat.

UNSNAG your lure by clipping a removable sinker attached to a string onto your line. Lower the sinker fast; the impact will free your lure.

# River Fishing for Smallmouth

Some anglers maintain that river smallmouth fight more than their counterparts in lakes; others say that it just seems that way because of the flowing water. Either way, you are in for some excitement when you hook a river smallmouth.

In many parts of the country, river smallmouth offer an almost untapped fishing opportunity. If an area has a lot of natural lakes or reservoirs, these waters draw the vast majority of fishing pressure.

Smallmouth inhabit a wide variety of flowing waters, ranging in size from small creeks only 10 feet wide to the largest rivers. The best smallmouth populations are in medium-sized rivers with recognizable pool and riffle areas. Big, slow-moving rivers with silty channels rarely have good populations of smallmouth bass.

The best time to fish rivers is during periods of low water. Smallmouth will be concentrated in deep holes and easy to find. When the water is high, they could be almost anywhere. Smallmouth bite better when the water is rising or stable than when it is falling. But if a torrential rain causes the water to rise quickly and become muddy, fishing is poor.

Smallmouth in rivers tend to be in shallower water than those in lakes. Most smallmouth rivers have enough current so there is continuous mixing, so smallmouth cannot find cooler water by going deep. Except in late fall and winter, when they move into deep holes, river smallmouth are seldom found at depths exceeding 10 feet.

River smallmouth avoid strong current, but they will tolerate a moderate current. In rivers that have both smallmouth and walleyes, smallmouth are found in water that moves slightly faster. In many cases they inhabit the same pool, but smallmouth spend more time in the upper portion of the pool, while walleyes are in deeper, slacker water farther downstream. Smallmouth and spotted bass divide up the habitat in much the same way.

With the exception of heavy rains, weather seems to have less effect on smallmouth in rivers than in lakes. They continue to bite despite cold fronts, severe thunderstorms or extremely hot weather.

The ideal rig for most river fishing is a 14- to 16-foot jon boat with a 10- to 15-horsepower outboard. A jon boat draws only a few inches of water, so it will float over shallow riffles. Yet the flat-bottomed design gives it good stability.

If the river has deep holes, a flasher comes in handy. But in most river-fishing situations, you can visually identify the prime smallmouth spots.

Many rivers can be fished without a boat and a lot of expensive equipment. All you need is a rod and reel, a few lures and a pair of hipboots or waders. In summer, you can get by with shorts and tennis shoes.

## How to Recognize a Good Smallmouth River

HIGH-GRADIENT rivers are not suited to smallmouth because the current is too fast. Smallmouth are seldom found in a river whose *gradient,* or slope, exceeds 25 feet per mile.

LOW-GRADIENT rivers, with a slope less than 2 feet per mile, hold few smallmouth. The slow current allows the water to get too warm, and results in a silty, flat bottom.

MODERATE-GRADIENT rivers, with a slope of 7 to 20 feet per mile, support the most smallmouth. They normally have cool temperatures and plenty of riffles and pools.

SIDE-CAST a weighted nymph under overhanging branches in a pool. Smallmouth lie beneath the branches waiting for insects to drop into the water, and will usually strike when the fly hits the surface or soon after it sinks.

## Fishing Techniques for River Smallmouth

The secret to catching river smallmouth is learning to read the water. Eddies caused by boulders, logjams, pilings and other above-water objects that break the current are easy to recognize. And with a little experience, you can also recognize eddies caused by underwater obstructions.

Every river has a few key spots that always hold smallmouth. Once you discover such a spot, you can catch the fish that are there, and more will move in to take their place. Some always hold big smallmouth, others only little ones.

After fishing a stretch of river once or twice, a river-fishing expert can identify practically all of these prime spots. By concentrating his efforts on these spots and bypassing less productive ones, he can catch as many smallmouth in an hour as the average angler could in a day.

Once you learn to identify these prime locations, the rest is easy. Smallmouth in rivers are generally not as fussy as those in lakes. They are conditioned to grab food as it drifts by, so they do not take much time to make up their mind.

*Tips for Catching River Smallmouth*

DRAG a heavy chain to slow your drift speed. Attach about 4 feet of logging chain to a rope, then lower it to bottom (left). You can regulate the angle at which the boat drifts by attaching the chain rope at different positions along another rope running from the bow to the stern (right). To drift with the bow pointing upstream, attach the chain rope toward the bow; to drift with the bow downstream, attach it toward the stern. Most experts believe that the chain does not spook the smallmouth. In fact, some think that the sound attracts them.

The lead-head jig is probably the most consistent producer of river smallmouth. One of the major advantages of a jig is that it sinks quickly, so it will reach bottom before the current sweeps it away from the spot you are trying to fish.

A ⅛-ounce jig works well in pools or eddies as deep as 7 feet. In deeper or swifter water, you may need a ¼- to ⅜-ounce jig. You can reach bottom more easily if you angle your casts upstream and retrieve downstream. But if the current is slow enough, it pays to cast downstream and retrieve upstream. Your jig will have better action and you will get fewer snags. However you retrieve the jig, always keep it bouncing bottom.

Standard spinners also work well for river smallmouth. Because they are conditioned to respond so quickly at the sight of food, the flash of a spinner blade immediately draws their attention. But standard spinners are limited mainly to shallow water. Unless the water is very shallow, angle your casts upstream. If you attempt to cast downstream, the water resistance causes the blade to turn too fast and forces the lure to the surface.

Small spinnerbaits are better than standard spinners for casting into snaggy cover like logjams, fallen trees or brush piles.

Crankbaits and minnow plugs allow you to cover a lot of water quickly. You can cast to pools, eddies and riffles while drifting or wading. Or you can troll a long stretch of uniform cover, like a riprap bank.

Select a crankbait or minnow plug suited to the type of water you are fishing. A short-lipped floating minnow plug is an excellent choice for cranking through the riffle at the upper end of a pool, but a deep-diving crankbait is more effective for fishing the pool itself.

The best way to work a pool is to cast into the fast water at the upper end, then crank the plug downstream so it moves faster than the current. Smallmouth are accustomed to lying at the upper end and grabbing food as it drifts into the pool.

Fly fishing is an excellent technique for river smallmouth because you can cast to precise spots, like a small pocket below a boulder. Subsurface flies such as streamers, crayfish and leech flies, and nymphs are the top choices. In summer, when smallmouth feed heavily on floating insects, bass bugs and dry flies also work well.

River fishermen also use a variety of live-bait rigs. A slip-sinker rig works best for large baits, like frogs and crayfish, because you can let the fish run and give it ample time to swallow the bait. A split-shot rig is better suited to smaller baits, like leeches and nightcrawlers. Use just enough weight to keep the bait drifting naturally along the bottom. When you feel a bite, simply drop your rod tip back, then set the hook. A slip-bobber rig is a good choice for fishing an eddy. Set the bobber to the right depth, then let the current sweep it around. A slip-bobber rig is ideal for hellgrammites and crayfish, because it keeps them from crawling under the rocks.

REDUCE your chance of snagging by hooking your bait on a floating jig head and adding just enough split-shot to make the bait sink. The hook will ride above the rocks and the shot will barely tick the bottom as the rig drifts downstream with the current.

LOOK for smallmouth around heated discharges from power plants or municipal treatment plants during the winter months. The discharge water may be 70°F or higher, so smallmouth will be active enough to strike fast-moving lures such as crankbaits and minnow plugs.

# Trophy Smallmouth

Anyone who spends much time fishing for trophy smallmouth has heard stories about the big one that got away. All respectable-sized smallmouth have a knack for throwing your hook, pulling your knot loose or breaking your line, but trophy smallmouth magnify the problem many times. So when you land a big one, there is a great feeling of accomplishment.

In most parts of the country, any smallmouth over 4 pounds is considered a trophy. But in mid-South reservoirs, a smallmouth must be 6 or 7 pounds to attain trophy status.

Waters that consistently produce big smallmouth have several things in common. Most have a significant area deeper than 50 feet. The deep structure has flat shelves for feeding and resting. If the structure plunges rapidly into deep water, it is of little value to smallmouth.

Good trophy waters seldom have heavy fishing pressure. Heavily fished waters produce few trophies because anglers catch the smallmouth before they have a chance to reach trophy size.

Most waters that produce a lot of trophy smallmouth do not have large smallmouth populations. Where smallmouth are numerous, there is a lot of competition for food and living space, so they do not grow as large. If you are interested in trophy fishing,

be prepared to put in some long days with only a strike or two for your efforts.

Waters where baitfish are the main food source are more likely to produce big smallmouth than those where the major food is crayfish or insects. And waters dominated by small baitfish are more likely to grow trophy smallmouth than those where most of the baitfish are large.

In mid-South reservoirs, for instance, threadfin shad make up a large part of the smallmouth's diet. Because threadfins seldom exceed 6 inches in length, smallmouth in these waters often grow to trophy size. Farther north, however, most reservoirs are dominated by gizzard shad which grow to 18 inches in length. The total food crop in any body of water is limited, and with so much of it consisting of oversized shad, smallmouth have less food that is usable and rarely grow to trophy size.

Your chances of catching a trophy smallmouth are generally better in reservoirs or natural lakes than in rivers. Most small- to medium-sized rivers lack the abundant baitfish crops needed for fast growth. Some big rivers, however, produce a fair number of trophy-caliber smallmouth.

It pays to do some research in advance to maximize your chances of locating good trophy water and being there at the time when the big ones are biting. State and provincial conservation agencies can give you some helpful hints, as can local bait shops and tackle stores. Outdoor magazines and newspapers that serve the area you are interested in can also help. Another source of information is the results of past fishing contests held in the area.

Most trophy hunters agree that big smallmouth bite best in spring, from 2 weeks before spawning until

*Types of Waters Likely to Produce Trophy Smallmouth*

MID-SOUTH RESERVOIRS have an ample food supply and a long growing season. Overfishing is seldom a problem because of their vast acreages and complex basins.

REMOTE NORTHERN LAKES have an abundance of rocky habitat ideal for smallmouth. Your chances for a trophy are best in lakes that cannot be fished with motorboats.

FERTILE NATURAL LAKES have poor spawning habitat for smallmouth, but abundant food. The few smallmouth that exist grow rapidly, but are overlooked by anglers.

BIG BAITS and lures work well for trophy smallmouth during the spawning period, in late fall and at night. In spring, when smallmouth are guarding their nests, larger baits and lures pose more of a threat. By late fall, the size of the smallmouth's natural food has increased, so they are accustomed to eating larger food items than they would earlier in the year. At night, big baits and lures are more likely to draw a smallmouth's attention than small ones. Larger-than-normal baits and lures are not recommended at other times.

spawning ends; on warm summer nights; and in fall, when the water temperature drops to about 60°F. Fall fishing remains good until the water cools to about 45°. Another good time to catch big smallmouth in streams is in late summer, when water levels are low and the fish are confined to deep pools.

Exactly where you find smallmouth during these periods depends on the type of water you are fishing. Refer to the seasonal-location section for specific situations.

As smallmouth get older, their personality and behavior patterns undergo dramatic changes. They lose their aggressive nature and become much more selective about what they eat. They hang tighter to cover and do more of their feeding at night. And they spend more of their time in deep water.

To catch big smallmouth with any degree of consistency, you must be aware of these changes and tailor your fishing techniques accordingly.

Although trophy-sized smallmouth are very skittish, the following steps will reduce the chances of spooking them:

· When they are in water less than 15 feet deep, do not run your outboard over them. Instead, hold your boat within casting distance with an electric motor or drop anchor.

· Avoid dropping anything in the boat.

· Keep a low profile and do not allow your shadow to fall on the spot you are fishing.

· Do not use big hooks or swivels, a heavy leader, or any type of highly visible terminal tackle.

· Use light, clear monofilament. Many trophy fishermen prefer 4-pound mono and few use mono heavier than 8 pound, unless they are fishing in heavy cover.

Big smallmouth almost always stay deeper than smaller ones. If you are catching 1- to 2-pound smallmouth in 10 feet of water, you will probably have to fish 15 to 20 feet deep to catch a trophy. But big smallmouth may feed in shallow water on a cloudy, windy day or at night.

In a given body of water, only a small fraction of the smallmouth spots produce trophy smallmouth. Typically, these spots have ample cover, easy access to deep water and a good food supply nearby. A spot that lacks any of these components will hold only small to average-sized smallmouth.

When you catch a big smallmouth, note the location carefully because the spot may hold more. Even if it does not, there is a good chance it will at a later date. Once a trophy smallmouth is removed, another usually moves in to take its place.

*Where to Find Trophy Smallmouth*

CAST directly into thick cover to catch the biggest smallmouth. The big fish force the smaller ones out of the best cover. If you fish only the edges, you will seldom catch a trophy.

LOOK for the steepest portion of a gradually sloping breakline. The biggest smallmouth prefer the sharpest break because they can reach deep water more easily.

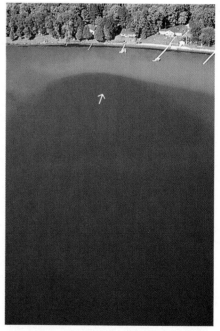

CHECK any inside turns along a breakline. Plankton collects in the inside turns, drawing baitfish and other foods. The big smallmouth take over these preferred feeding zones.

If you know of some of these spots, work one for a few minutes, then move on to the next. If nothing happens, check them again in a few hours. Continue to check them throughout the day; the big smallmouth have to feed sometime. Concentrate only on these spots and resist the urge to try others that hold smaller fish which are easier to catch.

Although larger-than-normal baits and lures work well for trophy smallmouth at certain times, they are no more effective than smaller ones most of the year. And big baits and lures definitely reduce your chances of catching average-sized smallmouth. Bright or flashy lures catch big smallmouth at spawning time or in murky water, but dark or natural colors usually will work better.

Your choice of rod and reel depends on your fishing technique and the type of cover. You may need a stiff baitcasting rod and 14-pound mono for fishing in dense brush or vertically jigging with a vibrating blade. But a light- to medium-power spinning rod works better in most other situations. Big smallmouth can be extremely line-shy, and with a lighter outfit, you can use lighter line.

Inexperienced anglers often make the mistake of using heavy gear regardless of the situation, thinking it is needed to land hefty smallmouth. But if you learn to play the fish properly, you can land any smallmouth on light gear.

RELEASE any big smallmouth you do not intend to mount. Even prime trophy waters contain a surprisingly low number of large fish, so if you keep the big ones for food, you jeopardize your future fishing.

## Tips for Trophy Smallmouth

EXAMINE your line often for frays. Most anglers believe that smallmouth cannot damage the line, but the tiny needle-sharp teeth (top) can easily cause fraying (bottom).

SELECT the best-looking spots in the area you intend to fish, then make a few casts in each one. Chances are, a trophy fish will bite right away or not at all. Try the spots again later.

APPROACH a likely spot from deep water. Drift or use your electric motor to get within casting range. If you approach from shallow water, you will probably spook any big smallmouth.

# Buggin' Bronzebacks

by Nat Franklin Jr.

*Stream smallmouth can't resist the bass bugs
created by Larry Dahlberg*

Picture a young boy during a drowsy 1950s summer, in a village in the pulpwood country of northwestern Wisconsin. On this particular afternoon he dawdles on his way from Bible school, his mind inflamed as usual with fishing. He halts atop the dam of a public pond called Memory Lake — a romantic label at varience with the silt-clogged reality — and from this vantage spots numerous porker carp wallowing in the shallows below.

For a moment, he mulls the probable consequences of what he has in mind. Then, in a flash, he's up to his waist in Memory Lake, thrashing the sour water so the carp come bumping into him in a frenzy of mistaken identity. One by one he drags them buckling from the pond, their scales as big and shiny as half dollars. When the water flattens out, twenty fat carp lie gasping on the grassy bank. Out of breath himself, the boy delivers the whole mess to

---

**Larry Dahlberg**

**Home:** *Brainerd, Minnesota*

**Occupation:** *Independent TV producer and outdoor writer*

---

*Larry Dahlberg is well known among fly fishermen as the creator of the Dahlberg Diver, the most important new fly design in several decades for bass and other warm-water fish. Though the fly was not introduced to anglers until 1983, when an article about it appeared in* Fly Fisherman *magazine, he first tied and fished it in the mid-1960s, while still a teenager. Dahlberg also introduced the revolutionary material called Flashabou, which resembles narrow metallic tinsel but is far more flexible, for use in fly wings, jig tails, and other lure dressings.*

*He started fishing at age four with his father, tossing Dardevles on 50-pound-test line into a small pond in*

*Grantsburg, Wisconsin. His father was a stickler for casting accuracy, setting a box under a swing set as a target and having him practice long hours. Dahlberg's first fly rod was an ice-fishing pole 4½ feet long that his father rigged for him with a weight-forward line — a tough rig to cast under the swings with, but he persevered and in time became expert.*

*Dahlberg may have set a record for youthfulness in the guiding profession: he began work as a smallmouth bass guide on the St. Croix River near his home when he was only eleven. A fly-fishing club on the river needed someone who knew the river and could row a boat. "I'd only fished for smallmouths incidentally," he says, "catching a few while out for muskies. And I'd fly-fished only for sunfish with my 4½-footer." But he had the knack, and wound up guiding 23 summers; in time, he also started managing the club facilities for the wealthy owners.*

a family of grateful Hungarian immigrants who live nearby.

Such benevolence cuts no ice when he arrives back home. His mother surveys his carp-slimed Bible-school clothes and orders him to the backyard, there to give them a prompt and decent burial. The clothes won't be alone out there. It isn't the first time all this has happened.

Larry Dahlberg, the hero of this drama, is not and never has been a purist of any sort. He's famous today as an expert fly fisherman — a reputation which could easily give some people the wrong idea. But the angler who noodled for carp and buried his trousers is not about to limit himself to fly tackle, nor to trout or any other single species of fish. Most of the time, in fact, he fishes with spinning or baitcasting gear. And the range of fish he pursues — with flies and otherwise — includes everything from bass and trout to muskies and tarpon.

But it's true, certainly, that fly fishing is his favorite method. And the fish he'd far rather catch than any other is the smallmouth bass. "It's the first in my heart," he says, "maybe because I guided fly fishermen for smallmouths for so long."

As he speaks, he stands thigh-deep in the St. Croix River, the stream on the Wisconsin-Minnesota border where he did all that guiding. It's now late summer, and the water is low and clear. To avoid spooking

fish, he's waded quietly into position about 60 feet from a stony, brush-covered point extending into the stream. The point is undercut, and the intervening water is fast and broken, with a bottom of rocks the size and color of bread loaves. Smallmouths might be almost anywhere. The prime spot, surely, is the undercut itself — but the irregular bottom away from the bank could also hold resting or feeding fish.

After casting very close to the point, Dahlberg begins retrieving with a series of short strips. His fly is a Dahlberg Diver, chartreuse. With each quick

*Dahlberg Diver*

strip of line, it darts slightly under the surface; then, immediately, it floats back up in the brief pause before the next strip begins. Dahlberg holds

*Dahlberg fishes his Diver past an undercut point on Wisconsin's St. Croix River*

his rod tip high, at nearly a 45-degree angle from the water, giving it a little flip every time he strips, to make the fly dart more vigorously. When the fly has moved out 6 or 7 feet from the point, he retrieves with longer, faster skips that pull it a foot or so under the water and keep it at about that level, darting forward.

On his second cast to the same spot, a smallmouth hits beside the undercut and he plays it for a couple of minutes in the swift current — a 2-pounder. He explains how he settled on his tactics. The diver was an ideal choice for this spot, he says, since it could make some disturbance at the surface on the first part of the retrieve, attracting any fish tucked up under the point; then, as it worked farther out, he could plunge it deeper for fish holding on the rocky bottom of the run.

Divers are the only flies that you can fish on the surface and well beneath it on the same cast. They're unsurpassed for any fishing situation where such a double-feature retrieve is called for. You can work a diver through shallow water or over weeds or deadfalls, then pull it down under when deeper or more open water is reached. Dahlberg got the inspiration for his diver when fishing with spinning and baitcasting plugs that float at rest but dive when retrieved. "I wanted to make a fly with an up-and-down diving action, something like a Suick [a muskie jerkbait]."

Not surprisingly, the Dahlberg Diver bears some resemblance to a plug. The head is large and rounded, made of trimmed deer hair, with a collar of untrimmed hair at its upper back edge; the whole thing is shaped like a badminton shuttlecock. When the fly is pulled sharply, water flows over the head and hits the collar, pushing it underwater. Dahlberg's innovation, originally intended for bass, has now been used to catch everything from trophy rainbows to tarpon to innumerable weird-named fish on faraway continents.

Dahlberg ties his diver in a number of different ways. One variation has a wing of marabou and saddle hackles, with a few strands of Flashabou for extra attraction. This works well for smallmouths, but he considers a rabbit-strip diver even better. It has a long, narrow tail made from a strip of rabbit fur still attached to the tanned hide. For smallmouths he generally ties the diver in white, yellow, chartreuse, or a natural rabbit gray. When he fishes it fast, he prefers the brighter attractor colors; slow, the natural gray.

The best diver sizes for smallmouths, Dahlberg says, are 1 and 1/0. To help keep the diver from soaking up water (this is true of his other hair bugs as well), he applies a paste floatant sparingly to the head before fishing.

For nearly all his smallmouth fishing, with the diver or any other fly, Dahlberg uses a 7-weight, 8-foot 9-inch Sage RP graphite rod. He prefers a standard weight-forward line to a bug taper; he feels that the standard type forms a smoother casting loop and reaches longer distances when necessary. His leaders are 9½-footers with 8- to 12-pound tippets. All the lines he uses for smallmouths are floaters.

When he wants to get deep in current, he simply attaches a split-shot a foot up the leader from the fly, then another shot 8 inches farther up. He points out that a floating line can be picked up off the water for a new cast far more easily than a sink-tip line, a type he avoids altogether. The split-shot are easy enough to cast, he says. The trick is to keep your line speed fast, so the shot-loaded leader won't sag in the air and foul on the fly line.

Later, a different stretch of the St. Croix: the water is flat here, a long pool that extends out of sight both upstream and down but has a visible current around deadfalls along both banks. Dahlberg faces shore from a casting position on the bow deck of his 13-foot Boston Whaler. Though short, the boat is broad and stable. The casting deck is a slab of marine plywood he installed himself, affixing it atop the gunwales for maximum casting height and visibility.

*Dahlberg battles a smallmouth from his casting deck*

Mounted on this forward deck is a powerful 24-volt electric motor. The outboard is a 40-horse whose speed enables him to fish stretches of the river that lie far from any bridge, and to do so in a single day's fishing rather than making a two- or three-day expedition. The shallow-draft hull floats in only 2 or 3 inches of water, so he can slip down through the thinnest riffles by tilting the outboard up and maneuvering with a 12-foot graphite push pole of the type used for saltwater flats fishing.

Back under the deadfalls, big smallmouths lie in ambush. But getting them out is no cinch. Where the trunks and limbs rest directly on the water, Dahlberg shoots out a cast parallel to them but several feet upstream. For this, he typically uses a hair popper, letting it drift motionless on the surface until it moves within a foot or two of the obstruction. Then he brings it in at medium speed, with short strips so the bug makes a series of light popping sounds. He calls this his "buzzbait retrieve." His cast goes just far enough back along the obstruction — and then his retrieve is just fast enough — that he can pull the bug into open water before it drifts onto the snag and hangs up. These tactics work best in water 4 feet deep or less, Dahlberg says.

Where leaning trees and brush have not quite collapsed onto the water but still hang just above it, he casts back under as far as possible. The trick here — and Dahlberg is a master — is to side-cast low,

sometimes within inches of the water, keeping the line moving rapidly so the tip and fly don't sag to the surface and spoil the presentation. The keys to line speed are the double haul and extremely narrow casting loops — only a foot wide at most. "In fly fishing for smallmouths," Dahlberg says, "a narrow loop is *always* best." He's able to flick a bug all the way back to the bank, even where a tree hangs down near the water some 50 feet out in the stream.

Once he's got a bug adrift under the cover, he may work it back out with the steady popping retrieve already described. Or he may substitute a retrieve that simulates a swimming frog — allowing the popper to rest briefly, then popping it two or three times in quick succession, following this with another rest, and so on. With either type of retrieve, he advises sliding the bug about 3 feet across the surface just before lifting it off for another cast. "If they're looking at it, they may show themselves when you do this and you'll know where they are. Then you cast right back to the same place on your next shot."

Yet another productive retrieve with the popper is simply to let it sit motionless while it floats past logs. This works especially well, Dahlberg says, when the smallmouths are spooky in low, clear water. The one thing to avoid is exactly the sort of retrieve that most bass fly-rodders generally use: giving the bug one big pop and letting it sit awhile,

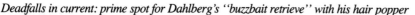

*Deadfalls in current: prime spot for Dahlberg's "buzzbait retrieve" with his hair popper*

*Dahlberg Slider*

then uncorking another big pop — the same tedious procedure over and over. "That's the least productive retrieve there is, in all my experience," he says.

One more important point that Dahlberg emphasizes in fishing poppers for smallmouths: always fish upstream or across stream. If you try to retrieve a popper against the current, it will dig into the water and make an enormous fish-spooking boil — not to mention that the popper will be almost impossible to pick off the water for another cast.

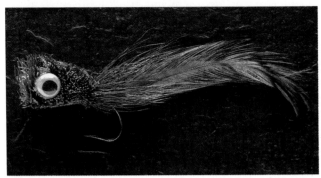

*Hair popper tied by Dahlberg*

Dahlberg's deer-hair poppers have a flattened face, doll eyes, and saddle hackles separated to suggest the legs of a frog. He prefers hair poppers to cork or plastic types. Hair bugs cast better, because of their lighter weight, and the softness of the body seems to fool a striking bass into holding on a moment longer, giving the angler some extra reaction time for making the hook-set. Since the popper is fished relatively slow, he likes natural colors — green and light gray-brown — the latter the shade of undyed deer hair. The best sizes for smallmouth bass are 1 and 1/0.

Another great surface bug — one that few bass fly rodders are likely to have fished — is the Dahlberg Slider. This design also has a head of clipped deer hair, but it's bullet-shaped. Unlike the diver, the slider is designed to stay on the surface. And unlike a popper, it can be fished in any direction relative to the current. Even if you retrieve it straight upstream, it skims across the water with no tendency to dig in.

"Slider-type bugs were developed in the early days of fly fishing in the U.S.," Dahlberg says. "I just went from an old type called a Wilder-Dilg that had a cork head, and tied my own fly with a hair head." He uses sliders in sizes 1 and 2. White and yellow are his color choices, so he can see the fly easily on the surface.

His favorite place to fish the slider is what he calls a "current push" — a slick run of rocky water 1 to 4 feet deep, just above a riffle that acts like a dam. He casts across stream or slightly downstream, then

allows the fly to skate on the surface and swing until it's straight below him. All the while the fly is skating, he holds his rod up at a 45-degree angle, to avoid getting too much belly in the line. A small amount of belly will make the fly skate at just the right speed; a large belly will drag it too fast and may also make hook-sets difficult.

He follows the swing with his rod tip. Though a steady drift will take fish, an erratic one often is better, accomplished by bouncing the rod tip while holding it upward. If he sees the fly is going to swing short of some spot he wants to reach — a large boulder, for instance — he'll feed as much line as needed on the drift. A smallmouth may surface out of nowhere at any moment during the drift, bulging up beneath the river's gloss to slam the slider.

When the fly has swung straight below him, Dahlberg retrieves just enough line to enable a pickup for another cast. He makes four casts in one spot, then moves on downstream to the next. "It's an easy technique for beginners," he says. "And you can do it while wading, but it helps to get up high in a boat. Why do smallmouths hit this dumb-looking bug skidding along like nothing they've ever seen before? I don't know."

SKATE a slider over a "current push." After casting across stream, raise the rod as shown; a moderate belly forms in the line, skating the fly.

For smallmouths in faster water, Dahlberg's usual choice is his Flashdancer, a streamer with a deer-hair head and a wing consisting entirely of strands of Flashabou. This material squirms in the current, emitting flashes of light in every conceivable direction. It comes in a variety of metallic colors — blue, red, pearl, you name it — but gold and silver are

*Flashdancer, an attractor pattern*

by far his favorites. The Flashdancer may resemble a baitfish, but Dahlberg sees it mainly as a nonrealistic attractor pattern. He calls it his "Mepps imitation." For smallmouths he prefers sizes 1/0 to 2.

The trick to fishing an attractor, he says, is to keep it moving fast enough that the bass don't have time to study it closely. If they do, they'll see it's a fake, something to avoid. "Smallmouths are programmed through natural selection to hit anything that looks like it doesn't belong, to get rid of it. You especially want to fish an attractor fast if the water is clear. You want them to glimpse it, just get a look. Give them the impression that if they don't hit it right now, it'll get away."

Dahlberg usually casts the Flashdancer across stream, then retrieves it in short jerks as it swings with the current. The jerks are produced partly with his line hand, partly by shaking the rod tip. He doesn't mend line, just holds the tip high to keep much of his line off the water; the minor drag caused by the remaining belly does not discourage strikes from smallmouths.

Flashabou, the main ingredient of the Flashdancer, is now sold by virtually every dealer in fly-tying materials and is used in countless other flies and lures. Its history goes back to Dahlberg's early days on the St. Croix. He was fourteen or fifteen at the time, guiding a woman who wasn't highly skilled at fly fishing. "She had to fly-fish, because her husband would bring her along to the club and that's all they did there. She had to put in a dollar bet for the biggest fish every day, a dollar for the first, a dollar for the most. She paid off gamely for years."

Then Dahlberg got the idea of tying streamers with some flexible gold Christmas-tree tinsel he'd seen; he gave all the new flies to his female client. "The tinsel was 1/32 inch wide, much wider than Flashabou is now, but it worked. She'd keep track of her bass by bending over matches in a matchbook. Before lunch, she'd have all the matches bent, and notches in the cover besides. I kept the fly just to her for a couple of years. We let all the others stew, all trying to figure out how she was doing so well."

Much later, Dahlberg trademarked the name Flashabou for a material similar to the tree tinsel. Flashabou was first sold in the late 1970s; it's now made in twenty colors and is used in flies of all types, from the tiniest trout midges to the biggest tarpon streamers.

This material was followed by another of Dahlberg's innovations, a colored synthetic fiber called

*Dahlberg casts across a riffle, setting up a drift with his Flashdancer streamer*

Hairabou. His idea was to make a hair especially for big flies, a material much longer than any animal hair that was readily available. The stuff also had to be wavy, so it would give the fly a bulky look with relatively few fibers: a fly tied with too much thick, wind-resistant hair would make casting difficult. A friend of Dahlberg's who was a chemist in the wig business came to his aid. Today, Hairabou has become a favorite material in extra-long flies for lunker bass, and also for pike, muskies, and saltwater fish.

Toward the end of a day on the river, as Dahlberg works along a shoreline in his Whaler, casting poppers and divers to logs crisscrossed like Oriental calligraphy, he hooks, boats, and releases dozens of smallmouths weighing up to 4½ pounds. The particular appeal of fly fishing — obvious to some anglers, obscure to others — seems absolutely clear to Dahlberg: "Fly fishing is comparatively non-mechanical. When you fight a smallmouth with fly tackle, you're not using a reel, just your hands on the line. There's no drag device between you and the fighting fish.

"When you were a little kid and you hooked a fish, you had this feeling of … who's got who? You weren't at all sure you were going to catch him. He might get off any moment. It made your heart beat faster. Fishing with a fly rod is like that, even now. You can't just roll 'em over on their side and reel 'em in. Fly fishing really is more exciting."

*Dahlberg admires a 4-pound St. Croix smallmouth, which he'll quickly set free*

# Largemouth & Smallmouth Tips

## Better "Pegging" Technique

Plastic-worm anglers peg bullet sinkers with toothpicks to keep the worm and sinker from separating on the cast and retrieve. But the toothpicks jam in the holes, making the sinkers difficult to remove and later reuse without first punching out the toothpick. Here's a method that let's you re-rig quickly:

SLIP a rubber sinker stop onto your line before adding the bullet sinker, hook and worm. To re-rig, simply slide the stop up the line a few inches, snip off the hook, change sinkers, tie on a new hook and slide the stop back into place.

## Mono Loop Fends off Weeds

Texas-rigged worms are weedless, but with the hook buried in the worm, you'll miss fish. A worm hooked on a plain jig head has an exposed hook, so you'll hook more fish but snag more weeds. Here's how to rig a worm so it's nearly weedless but still allows a good hook set:

1. TIE a piece of 30-pound stiff mono behind the eye of a 1/0 straight-shank worm hook. Run the line through the eye.

2. SLIDE the worm on the hook, and poke the mono into the worm at the hook bend so the mono forms a loop over the hook point. The loop is stiff enough to fend off weeds and brush but supple enough to give on a strike. Fish the worm with a bullet sinker. Set the hook as soon as a bass hits.

## Plastic Surgery Improves Worms

If bass ignore a normal plastic worm, try a high-buoyancy worm made with air bubbles in the plastic, such as a Sportsman's Super Floater, and enhance its action with a razor blade or X-Acto knife.

Slice the worm lengthwise, from the midpoint to the tail. Then slice each half lengthwise again to form four tentacles. Thread the worm on a jig. With the jig head on the bottom, the tentacles wiggle enticingly.

## Keep Curly-Tails From Twisting

If you're bothered by severe line twist after casting with a curly-tail plastic worm, you're not alone. Even if the worm is hooked straight, without a kink in the body, it may twist on the retrieve. Here's how to rig a curly-tail worm to keep it from spinning and twisting your line:

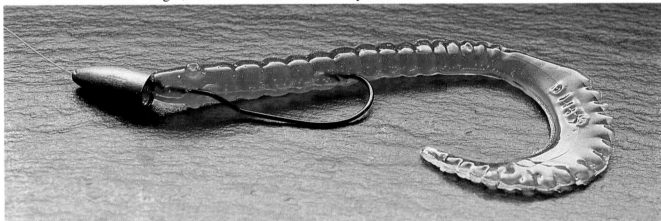

HOOK the worm so the curly-tail rides *down* when the hook point rides up. Make sure the body isn't kinked. If the tail is turned up, the worm is much more likely to spin as it moves through the water.

*Bass Tips from Tony Bean*
# Trimming the Pork for Tailored Action

One of Bean's favorite smallmouth lures is what he calls a "fly and rind" — actually a ⅛- or ¼-ounce hair jig dressed with a pork chunk. The chunk is an Uncle Josh 101 or 11; both styles have the size and shape he likes. At times, Bean trims part or all of the fat from the chunk, to change the sink rate and action of his offering. When the water is cold or the smallmouths are sluggish for any other reason, he wants a slower drop and less action. When the water is warm and the fish more active, he prefers a fast-sinking lure with increased action.

## Easy-to-Open Pork Rind

As you use pork rind, the brine corrodes the cover of the jar and forms a salty deposit on the threads. As a result, the jar can be impossible to open by hand. Try this trick to keep the cover from sticking.

Spread a thin coat of petroleum jelly on the threads of the cover and jar when you first use the pork rind; repeat occasionally during the season. The petroleum jelly will prevent corrosion and lubricate the cover, so it comes off easily.

TONY BEAN has caught more than 200 smallmouth bass weighing 5 pounds and up. He lives in Nashville and guides anglers for smallmouths on Percy Priest Reservoir and other southern waters. He's written a book, *Tony Bean's Smallmouth Guide*.

## Offset Hook for Sure Sets

To increase his hooking percentage with jigs, Bean bends the hook so the point aims slightly to the side. This way, he says, the point takes a better bite in the side of the fish's jaw. He believes it should be bent to the left (looking at the lure head-on) for a right-handed angler, and the opposite way for a left-hander.

SLICE fat off a pork chunk to alter the sink rate and action. An untrimmed chunk (left) sinks slower and has less action than a trimmed one (right).

TURN the hook point of a jig outward with needlenose pliers, shifting it only a short distance from the original position.

## Bobby Brewster
## Soft Jigging Spoon for Deep Bass

A highly effective slow-dropping lure for large-mouths is a $\frac{1}{16}$-ounce jig with a Gitzit or other tube-style soft-plastic dressing. One drawback of the lure is that for deep fishing — 15 feet down, or more — it takes too much time to sink. Bobby Brewster, a guide and competition angler from Elephant Butte, New Mexico, says that he and other pros who fish deep southwestern reservoirs have a solution. They combine a larger tube-style dressing with a heavy jigging spoon. The spoon has a rapid sink rate, ideal for fishing the depths, and the dressing gives the whole lure a soft texture so the bass won't spit it out before you have a chance to set the hook.

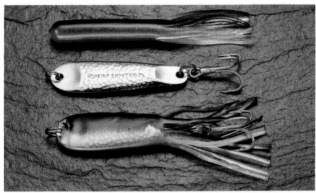

SLIP a tube-style dressing over a $\frac{3}{4}$-ounce Hopkins jigging spoon, just far enough that the eye and split-ring of the spoon protrude. The treble will be partially hidden in the legs of the dressing.

## Mike Teigen
## Weedless Bullet-Sinker Jig

One big problem with ordinary weedless jigs is that stems, leaves, and other bits of debris catch too easily on the hook eye where it protrudes from the head. Mike Teigen, a guide and competition angler from Osage, Minnesota, fishes for large-mouths in wild rice, bulrushes, and reeds, and makes his own special weedless jigs to solve the problem. For a jig head he uses a bullet sinker that has a live-rubber skirt, such as the Culprit Captivator or the Gopher Worm Dancer. Behind this he positions a keeper worm hook, with a piece of plastic worm covering the keeper and hook point. Part of the keeper is clipped off, so it won't fill the hook gap and interfere with hooking. The piece of worm is what makes the lure so weedless; hard worms such as Creme and Culprit hold up best. Though he could attach a whole plastic worm this same way for snag protection, Tiegen prefers a pork-chunk trailer. When fishing slow in the weeds, he says the chunk will catch more bass.

## Conrad Peterson
## Double Trailers for Sure Hooking

At times, a buzzbait cranked across the surface at high speed will trigger bass like nothing else. The problem, though, is that they often miss the speeding lure, striking somewhere behind it. This happened to Conrad Peterson, a tackle-company owner from Aitkin, Minnesota, on a trip to Texas. The buzzer would draw bass out of flooded trees, but he couldn't connect. He decided to attach a trailer hook, but didn't stop at just one. His strung-out buzzbait — with one trailer riding point-down, and another point-up — did the trick. The rear hook extended past the skirt on the bait, getting even the shortest strikers. And Peterson noticed that many of his bass were hooked in the upper jaw, on the downturned hook. These fish apparently struck from below: he would probably have missed them if all the hooks had been turned up in the usual way.

ADD a pair of trailer hooks to increase your hooking percentage with a high-speed buzzbait or spinnerbait retrieve. The point on the front trailer rides down; on the rear trailer, up.

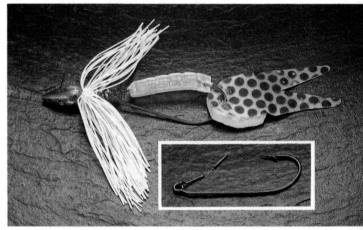

RIG a weedless bass jig by threading 20-pound mono through a skirted bullet sinker, then tying it to a 5/0 Mister Twister keeper hook. Push a section of toothpick into the sinker hole from the bottom, to peg the sinker in place against the hook eye. Attach a pork chunk to the hook. Clip part of the keeper off the hook (inset), leaving only the last two barbs. Thread a 1-inch piece of hard plastic worm onto the keeper and then onto the hook point.

## Good Vibrations

Fishing gets tough with a sudden change in weather — the dreaded cold front. Still, cold-front bass aren't impossible to catch. Bass are sure to notice big baits that make strong vibrations in the water. Here are a couple of examples.

A big, single-bladed spinnerbait with a size 6 or 8 Colorado blade (above) produces a strong, slow vibration that can tempt lethargic bass. Put a jumbo pork frog on the hook to slow the sink rate. Cast the lure into heavy cover and retrieve slowly.

Crankbaits run deep enough to reach bass that have been pushed into deeper water by a cold front, and the strong vibrations can trigger strikes, even from inactive bass. Cast out a big, sinking, deep-diving crankbait. Reel fast to get it deep, then slow down so it swims along the bottom.

## Looking for Active Fish

Under cold-front conditions, most anglers slow down their presentation to entice fish that aren't interested in feeding. Some fishermen, however, do just the opposite: they work fast, hoping to find and catch the few fish that are relatively active.

Fish water you know well and move quickly from one proven spot to another, fishing each no more than 10 minutes. Pepper the areas with lures you can work fast, such as spinnerbaits and crankbaits. By covering a lot of water, you should be able to find a few active, catchable bass.

## Stick to Bread-and-Butter Spots

During a cold front, fish the spots that normally produce bass; exploring new water is a bad bet when fish aren't feeding. Usually bass will be in the areas you found them before the front passed. But they may hold tighter to cover or in slightly deeper water.

## Finding Weedline Bass

As a cold front passes, bass holding at various depths along a weedline move to the base of the weeds. Inside turns in the weedline are usually best.

## Slow and Subtle

Although big, noisy lures can catch cold-front bass, a slow presentation with a small lure usually works better. Here's one proven method for cold-front bass: Rig up with clear, light mono and a ⅟₁₆-ounce to ⅛-ounce tube jig. If the water is deep or cloudy enough that you can put the boat over fish without spooking them, try vertical jigging, which lets you work a lure right in front of fish until one decides to strike.

If the water is clear or shallow, and scaring fish is a possibility, cast and jig instead. Either way, work the jig as slowly as you can.

## "Doodlin' " Brass and Glass

Doodlin' — twitching a Texas-rigged plastic worm along the bottom — catches bass in a lot of situations, but it can be one of the best approaches to try after a cold front has passed. Doodlin' can be even more effective if you add a brass bullet weight and a glass bead to the worm. As you're trolling, drifting or retrieving, twitch the rod tip rapidly, keeping the worm on the bottom. The brass and glass will click together, making far more noise than an ordinary lead sinker. Here's how to rig the brass and glass:

SLIDE a brass bullet weight and a good-sized glass bead onto 6-pound-test monofilament. Tie on a worm hook and rig a plastic worm Texas style. Brass is not as dense as lead, so you'll need a larger-than-normal sinker to get down. (Get brass weights and glass beads from Cemco, Box 1015, Starkville, MS 39759.)

## Jigging a Worm in Place

Working a Texas-rigged plastic worm slowly through heavy cover is an effective cold-front technique. But even the slowest retrieve may be too fast when bass are off the bite. Here's a way to entice them.

When the worm hangs up on submerged branches or weeds, resist your first reaction to rip it free. Instead, after you feel the sinker hit the obstruction, drop the rod tip a bit so the worm sinks a few inches. Then pull the line tight again to raise the worm. If a bass is around, the action of a worm jigged repeatedly in front of its nose may be too much to resist.

## Target Shallow Weeds

With the change in weather, many bass will head to the thickest weeds available. Some of this cover may be deep, some as shallow as 3 or 4 feet. Make best use of your time by trying the shallow weeds first.

In the shallows you can easily see where the cover is thickest and provides the most security, so you can flip or pitch a jig-and-pig or plastic worm practically on a fish's nose. Getting close in deeper water is far more difficult, because you can't see the nooks and crannies of the cover and aren't so sure where fish are likely to be holding.

Walleye

# Where to find Walleye Through the Seasons

SPRING. In early spring, walleyes often travel great distances to reach their spawning areas. In large lakes and reservoirs and in big river systems, migrations of over 50 miles are not uncommon.

Walleyes have a strong homing instinct. An individual fish will usually return to spawn in the same area each year. Once you discover a heavily used spawning area, chances are you will find walleyes there in subsequent years. The locations where walleyes spawn are described on page 35.

Once walleyes recover from spawning, they move gradually toward their summer haunts, scattering as the water temperature warms. During this period, food becomes the major driving force in their lives. They spend most of their time in shallow water, where baitfish and other foods are most plentiful. Because the previous year's baitfish crop has been drastically reduced by predation and the current year's crop is not yet available, walleyes may have to roam the shallows all day to find enough food. They can comfortably remain in the shallows because surface temperatures are still cool, and the angle of the sun is low enough to make light levels tolerable.

SUMMER. By midsummer, baitfish hatched in spring have grown large enough to interest walleyes. Because food is much easier to find, it has less influence on walleye location. The fish can spend more of their time in deeper water where temperatures are cooler and light levels more to their liking.

Most walleye waters stratify into temperature layers in summer. The *thermocline,* the layer where the water temperature changes rapidly, separates the warm upper layer, or *epilimnion,* from the cold lower layer, or *hypolimnion.*

In the far North, the epilimnion remains cool enough for walleyes. But further south, the upper portion of the thermocline is most likely to have the moderate temperatures that walleyes prefer.

Some walleye waters do not stratify into temperature layers, so the fish are less likely to stay at a specific depth. Rivers, reservoirs with a large quantity of inflowing water, and shallow, windswept lakes seldom form temperature layers.

Oxygen supply affects summertime walleye location in some shallow to medium-depth lakes and reservoirs. If these waters stratify, the hypolimnion loses oxygen in summer. Because the cold water in the depths is heavier than the warm water in the shallows, the wind does not circulate the deep water and replenish its oxygen supply. Plankton, fish and other organisms use up what oxygen there is, making water below the thermocline off limits to walleyes, except for occasional feeding forays.

FALL. Walleyes spend more time in the shallows when the surface water starts to cool. As the season progresses, more and more young-of-the-year baitfish fall victim to predation. Because food is again harder to find, walleyes must spend more time searching the shallows. They can stay in shallow water because the sun is again lower in the sky and the light level is less intense.

When the surface temperature cools enough to match the temperature in the depths, wind circulates the water from top to bottom. This mixing process is called the *fall turnover.* With temperature and oxygen levels equal throughout, walleyes can be found almost anywhere.

By late fall, the surface temperature is colder than that in the depths, so walleyes move deeper to find water closer to their preferred temperature range. They often hold near sharp drop-offs, where they can quickly move into shallower water to feed.

In waters that do not freeze in winter, walleyes generally remain where they were in late fall. They become less active as the winter wears on, but a period of warm, sunny weather may draw them into shallower water in search of food. In late winter, they become more active again.

# How Weather Affects Walleye

Weather can be a walleye fisherman's greatest ally or his greatest foe. Exactly how weather affects walleyes, however, is a topic on which few anglers concur. Although there has been little scientific research on the influence of weather on walleye behavior, most expert anglers believe the following:

• The best walleye fishing results from conditions that cause rapidly decreasing light levels. For instance, a sudden increase in wind velocity creates a *walleye chop* which scatters the light waves and often triggers a feeding spree. Similarly, dark clouds from an approaching thunderstorm usually start a period of frenzied feeding.

• Wind direction can have a dramatic effect on where walleyes in a given body of water will be most likely to bite. In a clear lake, for example, walleyes may feed along windward shores while fishing on the lee side of the lake is poor. Silt churned up by the wave action reduces the light level enough to allow shallow-water feeding.

Wind can also cause currents in narrows or around reefs and points, concentrating food and attracting walleyes. Wind-induced currents can wash food off a reef and draw walleyes to the downwind side.

• Cloudy or rainy weather usually spells good walleye fishing. But where the water is extremely turbid, heavy cloud cover or the disturbance caused by raindrops striking the surface may keep the light level too low for walleyes to feed.

• Walleye fishing is generally good during periods of stable weather because the fish maintain fairly predictable feeding patterns.

• The poorest fishing follows the passage of a severe cold front or an intense thunderstorm, especially if there are frequent lightning strikes.

After a severe cold front, the sky often becomes exceptionally clear. Because there is no haze to filter out the sun's rays, 10 to 20 percent more light penetrates than normally would. This condition causes walleyes to stop feeding and move deeper or seek cover beneath the weeds.

• For some unknown reason, cold fronts and thunderstorms seem to have less effect on walleyes in rivers than in lakes.

• Calm, sunny weather in a clear body of water makes walleyes stop biting earlier than usual in the morning and start later than usual in the afternoon. But in low-clarity water, it makes them begin feeding earlier in the morning and continue later into the afternoon.

In clear waters that do not stratify, walleyes may feed in midday in calm, sunny weather. Because there is no thermocline, they can simply move as deep as necessary to avoid sunlight.

• There is no evidence that barometric pressure plays a major role in walleye fishing. Some walleye experts believe that the fish bite best when the barometer is rapidly falling. But the increase in feeding activity is more likely the result of the decreasing light intensity associated with an approaching storm.

*Poor Conditions for Walleye Fishing*

LIGHTNING accompanied by loud thunderclaps makes walleyes bury in the weeds or move deeper. If lightning and thunder continue for several hours, the fish may not feed regularly for the next two or three days.

COOL, BLUSTERY weather following a cold front makes walleyes very sluggish. They generally move deeper and refuse food. Like a thunderstorm, a cold front can slow fishing for two or three days.

IDEAL WALLEYE WEATHER for waters that are relatively clear usually consists of a moderate chop and overcast skies. On a typical overcast day, only one-fourth as much light reaches the surface as would on a sunny day.

Choppy water scatters the rays so that much less light penetrates. Because of the low light level, walleyes may feed throughout the day. In highly turbid water, ideal walleye weather is calm and sunny.

## Good Conditions for Walleye Fishing

DARK CLOUDS from an approaching storm cause the light level to decrease rapidly, making walleyes bite faster than at any other time. But be sure to get off the water before the storm arrives.

ROILY WATER along a windswept shore is a good spot for walleyes to feed in a clear lake. The waves stir up silt, decreasing the light level. They also dislodge bottom organisms which attract baitfish.

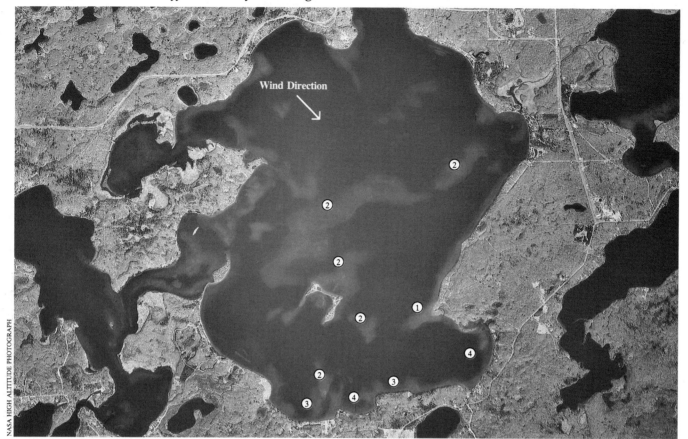

WIND DIRECTION determines where walleyes are most likely to be feeding. With a northwest wind, for example, walleyes in the lake shown above would feed most heavily in the following areas: (1) a gradually sloping point and (2) shallow reefs, all exposed to the wind. Walleyes in these areas are triggered to feed by reduced clarity from wave action, wind-induced currents and food washed loose from the bottom. Walleyes also feed in (3) inside turns on the breakline that gather windblown plankton which in turn attract baitfish, and (4) bays on the south end that trap warm surface water blown in by the wind, resulting in temperatures a few degrees higher than on the other end of the lake. The warm water draws baitfish, especially in spring.

*How to Select a Lake on the Basis of Wind Direction*

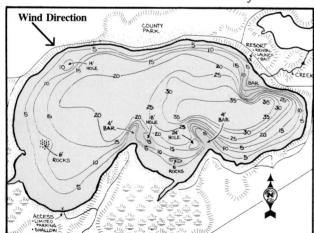

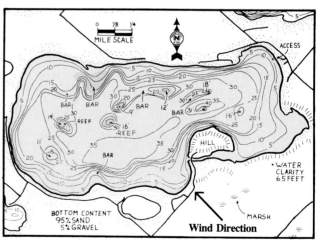

CHECK the weather forecast before deciding where you are going to fish. With a northwest wind, for example, the lake on the left would be a better choice than the one on the right, all other factors being equal. The best walleye structure (shaded) is on the southeast side, so a northwest wind creates enough wave action to make the walleyes bite. With the same wind, the lake on the right would be a poor choice because the best structure is on the northwest side where it is sheltered from the wind. But this lake would be a better choice with a southeast wind.

TEST NETTING gives natural-resources agencies a measure of the fish population in a body of water. Gill nets (above) catch fish by snaring them around the gills when they try to swim through the mesh. Most gill nets are designed to catch small to medium-sized fish because they are the ones most important to the future of the fishery. The gill nets used for sampling do not have mesh large enough to catch big walleyes.

# How to Select Good Walleye Waters

North America has over 100 million acres of walleye water, so you should have no problem finding a place to fish. But many waters, especially those near population centers, are heavily fished, so the walleyes run on the small side.

If you are content with a mess of eating-size walleyes, you can easily get information on these well-known waters by inquiring at almost any bait shop or tackle store. For bigger walleyes, you will have a better chance in a more remote area. But gathering information on lesser-known waters is considerably more difficult.

Knowledgeable anglers are understandably tight-lipped when it comes to revealing their favorite walleye waters. If you cannot find a good fisherman willing to share his secrets, you can gather information from the following sources:

FISHING-CONTEST RESULTS. Certain waters annually produce surprising numbers of contest winners. If a lake or river never shows up in contest results, chances are it holds few big walleyes. Contest results may also provide information on the best baits and lures and the best times to fish.

LAKE SURVEYS. Many natural-resources agencies conduct lake surveys to provide information for fish management. If current information is available and you know how to analyze it, you can uncover some secret walleye waters of your own. Survey reports usually contain the following:

## Test Netting Summary

a. Gillnets: __6__ sets          250 ft. Experimental Nylon Net

| Species | Total Number | Number per Set | Numbers per Set Statewide Median | Numbers per Set Local Median | Total Pounds | Pounds per Set | Pounds per Set Statewide Median | Pounds per Set Local Median |
|---|---|---|---|---|---|---|---|---|
| White Sucker | 17 | 2.83 | 1.90 | 1.24 | 43.5 | 7.25 | 2.53 | 2.84 |
| Carp | 2 | 0.33 | 1.20 | 2.44 | 21.4 | 3.57 | 1.80 | 2.53 |
| Black Bullhead | 10 | 1.67 | 1.50 | 4.82 | 5.5 | 0.92 | 0.90 | 1.02 |
| Yellow Bullhead | 72 | 12.00 | 1.18 | 3.52 | 43.1 | 7.18 | 0.70 | 2.72 |
| Northern Pike | 95 | 15.83 | 2.67 | 6.87 | 138.3 | 23.05 | 5.62 | 14.68 |
| Yellow Perch | 36 | 6.00 | 8.00 | 48.50 | 5.7 | 0.95 | 1.51 | 6.39 |
| Walleye | 113 | 18.83 | 3.60 | 4.55 | 57. | | | |
| Largemouth Bass | 11 | 1.83 | 0.50 | 1.69 | | | | |
| Pumpkinseed | 53 | 8.83 | 1.17 | 7.25 | | | | |
| Bluegill | 36 | 6.00 | 1.61 | 14.80 | | | | |
| Black Crappie | 8 | 1.33 | 2.00 | 10.82 | | | | |
| Hybrid Sunfish | 6 | 1.00 | 0.67 | 2.40 | | | | |

b. Trapnets: __11__ -Total Pots     __0__ Double Pot Sets

SURVEY REPORTS are usually available to the public from state natural-resources agencies. The netting results on the above survey show an excellent population of walleyes and a low population of perch, the primary baitfish. The walleye catch, 18 per gillnet set, is about four times higher than the local median. The perch catch, 6 per set, is only one-eighth as high as the average. Because of the baitfish shortage, fishing should be good.

*Fish-population data.* Survey crews generally sample walleye populations using nets or electrofishing gear. These sampling devices cannot determine how many walleyes there are in a lake or river, but they provide an index of relative abundance. In other words, they give you an idea of the density of the walleye population compared to that in other waters sampled in similar fashion.

Population data from prior years can serve as an indicator of current walleye abundance. For instance, a strong year-class of age-two walleyes in test netting conducted one to two years ago means that the present fishing is probably good. Once the young fish reach two years old, they have escaped the most serious threats. At a typical growth rate, they will reach catchable size at three to four years of age.

Another important thing you can learn from studying fish-population data is the abundance of baitfish. A lake with an extremely high perch crop, for example, will usually have poor fishing despite a healthy walleye population.

*Average depth.* This is an important consideration when choosing a lake for fishing in early spring. A shallow lake warms more quickly than a deep one, so the walleyes begin to bite sooner. In fall, a shallow lake cools more quickly, so the turnover is earlier and walleyes may be harder to find than in a deeper lake that is still stratified.

Maximum depth is not a good indicator of how quickly a lake will warm. If a lake has one deep hole, but the rest of the basin is shallow, it may warm earlier than a lake where the maximum depth is not as great.

*Clarity.* Biologists measure water clarity by lowering an 8-inch black-and-white disc, called a *Secchi disc,* into the water until it is no longer visible.

The Secchi disc measurement gives you an indication of the time of day when fishing will be best. If the reading is a foot or less, chances are walleyes will feed intermittently from midmorning through midafternoon. If the reading is 10 feet or more, walleyes may feed only at night. Your best choice is a lake where the reading is between 3 and 8 feet. Here walleyes feed heavily around dusk and dawn with occasional feeding periods during the day.

*Thermocline.* Whether or not a lake has a thermocline, and the depth at which the thermocline is located, can play an important role in your walleye-fishing strategy.

Most shallow, windswept lakes do not form a thermocline. Walleyes may be as shallow as 5 feet or as deep as 30 feet, depending on light conditions and location of the forage.

Deeper lakes generally form a thermocline in summer. The walleye's preferred temperature zone is usually near the upper limit of the thermocline, so walleyes spend most of their time around that depth. As a result, summertime walleyes are usually easier to find in a deep lake than in a shallow one.

*Oxygen.* Survey reports often list dissolved oxygen levels at intervals from the surface to the bottom. Walleyes need a level of at least 4 parts per million to be comfortable. The oxygen readings will not tell you where to fish, but they will tell you where *not* to fish.

*Boat traffic.* Most survey reports mention the amount of boat traffic and other types of recreation

*How to Select a Lake on the Basis of Structure*

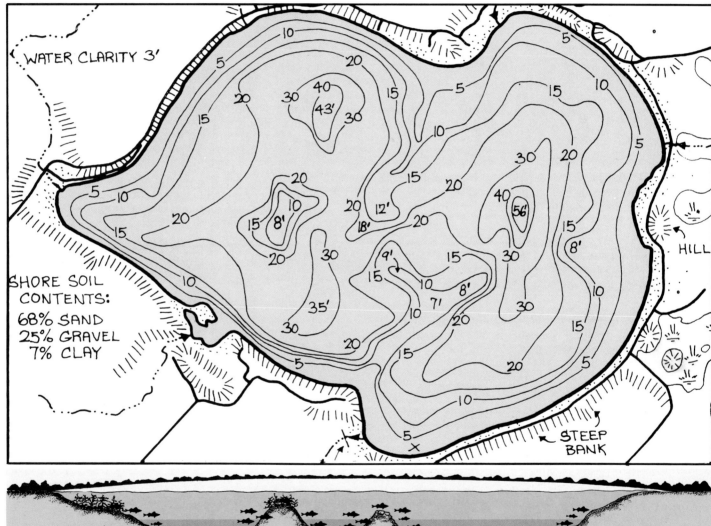

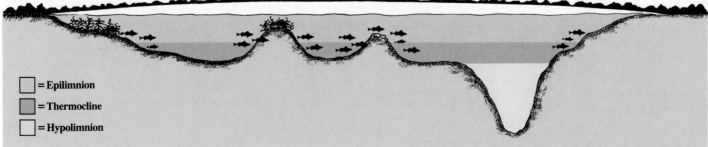

= Epilimnion

= Thermocline

= Hypolimnion

PRIME walleye lakes generally have a moderate amount of structure such as points, irregular breaklines, and offshore reefs and sunken islands (top). The offshore structure should top off in the thermocline or above it (bottom) and should be linked to other walleye structure rather than isolated by deep water.

that could interfere with fishing. In lakes or rivers where walleyes spend a good deal of their time at depths of 15 feet or less, heavy traffic from water-skiers and pleasure boaters will cause walleyes to stop biting and move to deeper water. So even though there is a good population of walleyes, you may have difficulty catching them, especially on weekends. On these waters, walleyes usually bite best early in the morning, before the traffic starts.

STOCKING RECORDS. Records kept by natural-resources agencies can give an indication of the size of the existing walleye population. If the lake was stocked heavily several years earlier, it may hold good numbers of walleyes. However, these records can be misleading because the survival of young fish, especially fry, is very uncertain.

CONTOUR MAPS. Hydrographic maps are available for most important fishing waters. They tell you a great deal about the walleye-fishing potential of these waters, if you know what to look for. The examples on these pages show you how to evaluate that potential based on the shape of the lake basin. All of the examples show typical walleye location in summer, after the thermocline has formed.

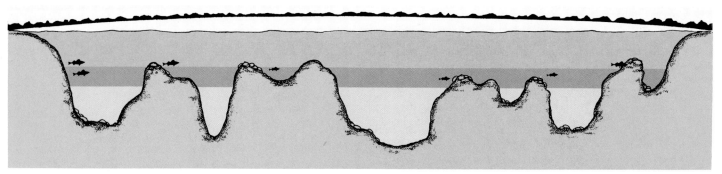

TOO MUCH STRUCTURE can make walleye fishing difficult, even if the lake has a good population. Often, you can find a walleye or two on a seemingly good spot, but seldom a big school. Walleyes are not as likely to be concentrated as in the lake at the left because they have many more good spots to choose from.

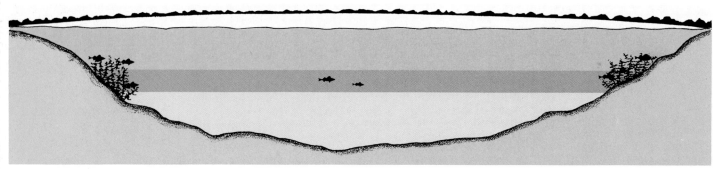

LACK OF STRUCTURE can also make walleye fishing tough. A lake may be teeming with walleyes, but they can be hard to find if there is no structure to concentrate them. In this bowl-shaped lake, some of the walleyes suspend in the thermocline; others scatter along the shoreline, in the weeds or along the weedline.

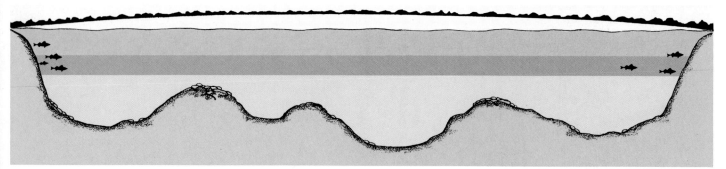

DEEP STRUCTURE has little value to walleyes during the summer. The humps and reefs in this lake top off at 30 to 40 feet, but the thermocline ends at 25 feet. Below the thermocline, the water is too cold and may lack oxygen, so walleyes will most likely be scattered along the shore-line or suspended in the thermocline.

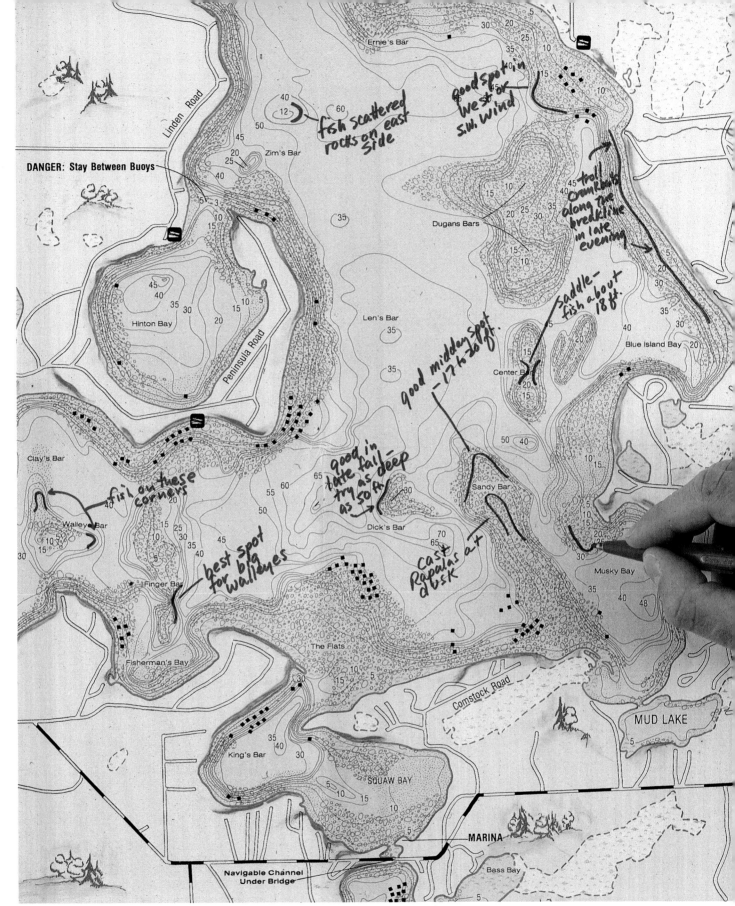

CONTOUR MAPS marked with the best walleye spots can be extremely valuable when fishing a strange lake. Instead of spending hours searching for a good spot, you can spend your time fishing. If you know someone who fishes the lake frequently, inquire about the possibility of sending you a marked map. If you cannot obtain a map in advance, buy one at a local tackle shop and ask the proprietor to mark some good walleye spots.

# Walleye in the Weeds

In years past, few walleye anglers ever considered fishing in the weeds. They were told at an early age that walleyes always preferred a hard, clean bottom, so that is where they fished. But largemouth bass fishermen knew differently because they often pulled walleyes from the weeds using spinnerbaits, crankbaits and plastic worms.

Even today, the average walleye angler seldom fishes in the weeds. Many do not realize that walleyes spend a significant amount of time in the weeds; others think that walleyes in the weeds cannot be caught.

Walleyes move into weeds to find food, shade or cooler temperatures. Many types of baitfish use the weeds for cover, so a walleye cruising through the tangle can easily grab a meal. On a bright day, walleyes can often find adequate shade and cool temperatures in a weedbed, instead of retreating to deep water. The temperature in the weeds may be five degrees cooler than elsewhere in the shallows.

If walleyes are raised in rearing ponds during their first summer of life, they become accustomed to living in weeds. It is possible that these walleyes, after being stocked into a lake, have a greater tendency to live in the weeds than walleyes reared naturally in the lake. If a lake also has natural reproduction, there may be separate populations of weed-dwelling and reef-dwelling walleyes.

Weeds produce oxygen, but it is unlikely that walleyes would move into weeds for that reason. Only in rare cases would oxygen levels in shallow water reach levels low enough to affect walleyes, even in waters where there are no weeds.

Eutrophic lakes are most likely to have populations of weed walleyes. Because the depths lose oxygen during the summer, walleyes may have no choice but to remain in the epilimnion where weeds offer the only shade. But you may find weed walleyes in mesotrophic and even in oligotrophic lakes. And walleyes in big rivers frequently feed in weedy backwaters, or in weedbeds in slack pools or along current margins. Occasionally, you will find reservoir walleyes in weeds, but fluctuating water levels prevent most types of weeds from taking root.

Not all weeds attract walleyes. The best weedbeds are in or near deep water. Seldom will you find the fish on a shallow, weedy flat with no deep water nearby. Broadleaf weeds generally hold more walleyes than narrowleaf varieties; submergent weeds more than emergent or floating-leaved types.

You can find walleyes in weeds almost any time of year. But weed fishing is usually best in summer and fall, the times when young-of-the-year baitfish are seeking cover from predators.

*Types of Weeds that Hold Walleyes*

LARGELEAF PONDWEED, sometimes called broadleaf cabbage, grows in water as deep as 14 feet. The leaves are up to 7 inches long and 1½ inches wide. The flowering heads may extend above the surface.

RICHARDSON'S PONDWEED, often called curlyleaf cabbage, grows in water as deep as 10 feet. The wavy leaves are up to 5 inches long and ¾ inch wide. The flowering heads always extend above the surface.

COONTAIL grows in water as deep as 30 feet. The plants are not rooted, but grow in large masses on the bottom. Tiny leaves grow in whorls around the stem and are usually forked. There is no flowering head.

WATER MILFOIL grows in water as deep as 30 feet. The plants are usually rooted. Tiny leaves grow in whorls around the stem and are shaped like the veins of a feather. The top of the plant may have small flowers.

CHARA, also called sandgrass, or muskgrass because of its skunk-like odor, blankets the bottom in water as deep as 35 feet. Coarse branchlets grow in whorls around the stem and are usually coated with calcium deposits.

HARDSTEM BULRUSH grows in water as deep as 5 feet and may extend up to 6 feet above the surface. Dark green in color, the tough-stemmed plants grow only on a firm bottom, usually sand or gravel.

99

# Techniques for Weed Walleyes

Fishing along the edge of the weeds is easy. Simply cast or troll a slip-sinker rig or a jig along the weedline, keeping it as close to the weeds as possible. But when walleyes are actually in the weeds or suspended above them, fishing is much more difficult.

What seems like a bite often turns out to be a weed. If you hook a strand of sandgrass, for instance, tiny branchlets break off as your hook slides along the stem, creating a jerking sensation. On the other hand, what feels like a weed may be a walleye.

If you attempt to fish with live bait, the bait will often come off the hook when you pull free of a weed. And regardless of what technique you use, you will continually have to remove bits of weed from your hook.

Different types of weeds demand different fishing techniques. You can retrieve a lure through some types of weeds without fouling, but other types will catch on the hooks. To fish effectively in weeds, you should be aware of these differences (see below).

## How Weeds Differ

BROADLEAF weeds, including most varieties of cabbage, are crispy enough that a sharp tug will rip the leaf and free your hook.

LONG, STRINGY weeds, such as coontail, are almost impossible to free from your hook. Use a weedless hook or fish only the edges.

BRITTLE NARROWLEAF weeds like sandgrass cling to your hook. But a sharp tug will bend the branchlets enough so you can pull free.

## How to Fish Jigs in Weeds

RIP your jig through tall broadleaf weeds by making a sharp sweep with your rod tip when you feel resistance. Any type of jig weighing from $\frac{1}{16}$ to $\frac{1}{8}$ ounce will work, but many anglers prefer pyramid jigs because weeds slide over the head instead of catching on the eye. If the weeds are dense, keep the jig riding above them rather than trying to rip through them.

WORK the edges of a bed of long, stringy weeds. These weeds grow in clumps and walleyes often hold in the open water nearby. A jig fished in the weeds would foul continuously.

## How to Fish Spinners in the Weeds

BAIT a mono-leader type spinner with a minnow, leech or nightcrawler. Troll at a slow speed, keeping the rig just above the weedtops. If you feel the rig touching weeds, lift your rod tip. A floating spinner (page 109) will keep the bait riding higher.

RETRIEVE a spinnerbait through dense weeds, letting it helicopter to bottom when it comes to a deeper pocket. Use a standard spinnerbait with a minnow or plastic curlytail in place of the skirt, or a safety-pin spinner arm attached to a hair or feather jig.

## How to Fish a Slip-bobber in Weeds

CAST a slip-bobber rig into a pocket in tall broadleaf weeds. Adjust the bobber stop so the bait dangles just above bottom. Slip-bobbers also work well for fishing above a blanket of sandgrass or alongside beds of coontail, milfoil or other long, stringy weeds.

## How to Fish Other Lures in the Weeds

PLUGS. Cast a shallow-running crankbait or minnow plug over a weedy flat or point, keeping the plug just above the weedtops. Trolling may spook the walleyes. A deep-running crankbait or minnow plug works well for trolling along a deep weedline. Clip the leading hooks (inset) to reduce fouling.

FLOATING RIG. Tie a sliding cone-sinker rig, then attach a float ahead of your bait, or hook your bait to a floating jig head. Troll or retrieve over sandgrass or other low-growing weeds. The tapered sinker slips through the weeds and the float or jig head rides above them.

SMALL JIGS are effective in the rocks, if you do not let them drag bottom. Keep the jig swimming just above the rocks; let it touch occasionally to check the depth. If you use a heavy jig, it will quickly wedge in the rocks. You may lose a few small jigs, but they are less expensive than most other lures.

# Walleye on a Rocky Bottom

A bottom of jagged and broken rocks is one of the best places to find walleyes. But it is one of the most difficult places to fish, especially when using live-bait rigs.

With an ordinary slip-sinker rig, the rocks seem to reach out and grab the sinker. You can reduce the frustration and catch a lot more walleyes by using the following techniques:

• Suspend your bait from a slip-bobber. Position your bobber stop so the bait hangs just above the rocks.

• When trolling, lower your rig to the bottom, then reel in a foot or two so the sinker does not drag on the rocks. Occasionally drop your rod tip back until the sinker touches the rocks, to make sure the depth has not changed.

• Float your bait off bottom with a floating jig head or some other type of floating rig, or use an in-flated nightcrawler. For extra flotation, hook the crawler through the middle and inject both ends

with air. A floating rig will keep your hook out of the rocks but will not prevent your sinker from snagging.

• Use a snag-resistant sinker or some type of break-away sinker (shown at right). Or, use a Wolf River rig tied with a dropper lighter than the standing line. When you get snagged, you lose only the sinker instead of the entire rig.

• Use tough, abrasion-resistant monofilament instead of soft, limp mono. Soft line nicks too easily when fished over rocks.

Some types of artificial lures also work well over rocky bottoms. Small jigs, floating crankbaits and weight-forward spinners are among the best choices. Select a crankbait that will run just above the rocks. If the lure should hit a rock, the lip will usually keep it from snagging. With a weight-forward spinner, reel just fast enough to keep it off bottom. By tipping it with a nightcrawler, you can increase its buoyancy and fish it more slowly.

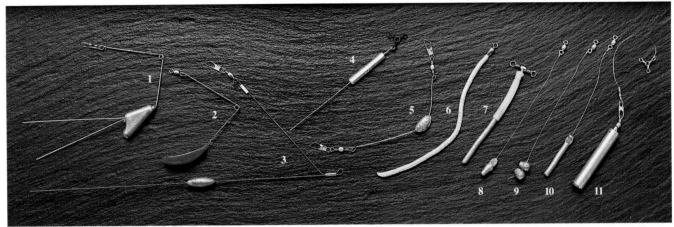

SNAG-RESISTANT SINKERS include: (1) Bottom Cruiser, (2) Bait-Walker™, (3) Bottom Walker, (4) Needle Weight™, (5) Bait-Guide, (6) Flex-O-Sinker, (7) Lead Cinch®, (8) dropper with drift sinker, (9) dropper with split-shot, (10) dropper with hollow pencil lead, (11) pencil sinker on 3-way swivel rig.

## *How Line Angle Affects Snagging*

KEEP your line as close to vertical as possible when fishing on a rocky bottom. When trolling with a light sinker, you must let out a lot of line to reach bottom. Because your line is at a low angle, your sinker can easily wedge between the rocks (left). With a heavier sinker, you can use a much shorter line. The line is at a greater angle to the bottom, so the sinker usually climbs over the rocks instead of wedging between them (right).

## *How to Make and Use Breakaway Sinker Rigs*

CUT a slit in the eye of a walking sinker (inset), then close the gap with a pair of pliers. If the sinker snags, a strong pull will open the eye and free the line. You will lose the sinker but keep the rest of your rig.

SUBSTITUTE a mono dropper for a slip-sinker. Tie a barrel swivel on one end of the dropper and pinch split-shot on the other. If the split-shot snag, give a strong tug to slide them off the dropper, then pinch on new ones.

103

# Walleye in Timber & Brush

In many rivers and reservoirs, timber and brush provide the only shallow-water cover. Weeds are scarce or non-existent, so walleyes rely on timber and brush to provide a supply of food and a shady resting spot.

You can find some walleyes around almost any kind of submerged timber, including flooded trees, stumps, logs on the bottom, and trees toppled into the water from an eroded bank. But your chances of finding good numbers of walleyes will be better if you know what type of timber to look for.

The best timber is near deep water. A timbered flat along the edge of a creek channel, for instance, will hold more walleyes than a timbered flat with no deep water nearby. A tree toppled into deep water off a steep riverbank will attract more walleyes than a tree toppled onto a shallow sandbar.

Timber may hold walleyes anytime from the pre-spawn period until late fall. But brush holds walleyes mainly in spring, when high water floods willows and bushes along the bank.

Walleyes move into the brush when the water level begins to rise. As long as the water continues to rise or stabilizes, they remain in the brush. But when the water begins to drop even the slightest bit, they move to deeper water. This movement may be an instinctive reaction, to avoid being trapped in an isolated pool.

Anglers who specialize in fishing timber and brush prefer cone-sinker rigs with weedless hooks, brush-guard jigs, or jigs with fine-wire hooks. Other good lures and rigs include spinnerbaits, jigging spoons, slip-bobber rigs, and crankbaits and minnow plugs with clipped trebles.

If you are afraid to drop your bait or lure into the thickest tangle of sticks and logs, you will catch only the most aggressive walleyes, which are also the smallest ones. The bigger walleyes usually hang out where the cover is densest, so you will have to risk losing a few rigs to catch them.

## Types of Timber and Brush that Hold Walleyes

TOPPLED TREES with the small branches intact are better than old trees with only large limbs remaining. Walleyes can find baitfish and insects among the small branches.

STANDING TIMBER near deep water can hold walleyes, if the trees are close enough together to provide ample shade. Avoid fishing a flat where the trees are widely scattered.

FLOODED BRUSH often holds walleyes in high water. The brush itself may be too dense to fish effectively, but you can cast into pockets or work the edges.

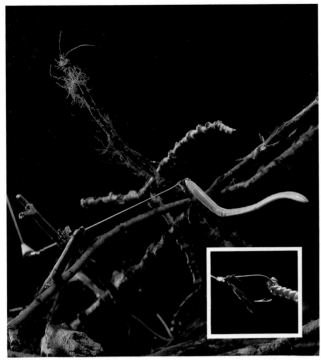

RIG a nightcrawler or minnow on a size 4 weedless hook (inset) attached to a sliding cone-sinker rig. Then crawl the bait slowly through dense timber or brush. The weedguard will prevent the hook from snagging, and the cone sinker will easily slide through obstructions.

RETRIEVE a brushguard jig tipped with a pork trailer through toppled trees or standing timber. The jig will seldom hang up, and the trailer will stay on the hook indefinitely. A brushguard prevents snagging in the dense cover but may cause you to miss a few strikes.

CAST a 1/16- to 1/8-ounce jig with a fine-wire hook into a pocket in flooded brush. Tip the jig with a minnow and retrieve slowly, raising your rod tip to avoid snags. A fine-wire hook will improve your hooking percentage, and if it does snag, it will usually bend enough to pull free.

# Suspended Walleye

For generations, the basic rule of walleye fishing was: keep your bait on the bottom. But modern-day walleye anglers know that this is not always good advice. Walleyes may suspend off bottom for any of the following reasons:

TEMPERATURE. In a clear lake, walleyes retreat to deeper water after feeding to avoid sunlight. But in low- to moderate-clarity water, they often move laterally rather than vertically, especially if the water is stratified into temperature layers. By moving laterally, they can avoid drastic temperature changes.

Walleyes that feed on reefs, for instance, often suspend in nearby open water when feeding is completed. They usually move less than 100 yards. Many fishermen make the mistake of assuming that the walleyes have moved deeper, so they waste a great deal of time searching barren water.

OXYGEN. If the deep water lacks sufficient oxygen in summer, and there is a shortage of shallow-water structure, walleyes may have no choice but to suspend.

TOXIC GASES. Walleyes often suspend on calm, sunny days in summer. Many anglers have witnessed this behavior and wondered about the cause.

In many instances, the fish are suspending to avoid high levels of toxic gases near bottom. Calm, sunny weather allows maximum sunlight penetration. Sunlight promotes decomposition of organic bottom sediments, which produces levels of carbon dioxide, hydrogen sulfide and methane gas that could be toxic to walleyes.

To escape, walleyes suspend above the layer of toxic gases. If the bottom is rich in organic materials, they may move up as much as 10 feet.

In windy weather, water circulation prevents toxic gases from accumulating, so walleyes need not suspend to avoid the gases.

FOOD. The walleye's favorite foods are not necessarily linked to the bottom. Open-water baitfish like shad and ciscoes, for example, can be found at almost any depth. On calm mornings or evenings, you may see baitfish schools dimpling the surface. Walleyes will ignore their oxygen and temperature preferences for an easy meal, so they pursue the baitfish in open water or hang just below the surface schools. Walleyes may suspend to feed on immature insects, particularly emerging mayfly nymphs.

*How a Graph Recorder Can Help You Find Suspended Walleyes*

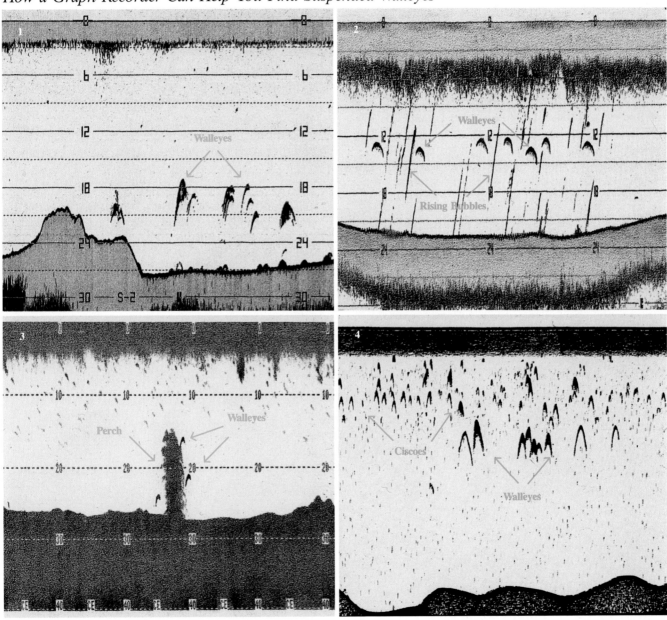

GRAPH RECORDERS can provide clues to how walleyes suspend. On tape 1, the walleyes have moved laterally into open water in order to stay in the same temperature zone where they fed earlier in the day. Tape 2 shows bubbles rising to the surface and walleyes suspended about 8 feet off bottom. The bubbles are a sign of high concentrations of toxic gases above the bottom sediment. Tape 3 shows plumes of small yellow perch, a favorite walleye food, reaching from the bottom almost to the surface. You can see walleyes suspended at various depths alongside the perch. Tape 4 shows walleyes scattered below a layer of ciscoes.

# How to Catch Suspended Walleye

Finding and catching suspended walleyes can be a difficult assignment. Walleyes suspended off structure are there to rest, not to feed. Walleyes suspended in pursuit of baitfish are willing to bite, but they may not notice your bait among the clouds of natural food.

To catch suspended walleyes, you must present the right bait or lure at precisely the right depth. Finding this depth requires either a graph or flasher or a lot of experimentation.

One of the simplest ways to catch suspended walleyes is to use a slip-bobber rig. Set your bobber stop at the appropriate depth, bait up with a leech, nightcrawler or minnow, and wait for a bite. This technique works especially well for walleyes that are not actively feeding.

If the walleyes are within a few feet of bottom, you can float your bait up to them rather than lowering it down. Most anglers use a slip-sinker rig with some type of floating jig head or a float that attaches to the leader.

The major drawback to these floating rigs is the difficulty of controlling the depth. In most cases, the bait will not float nearly as high as you would expect. To get an idea of how high it will float, try trolling alongside the boat in shallow, clear water. You can make the bait float higher by increasing the amount of flotation, lengthening the leader or reducing the boat speed.

You can also catch walleyes that are within a few feet of bottom by jigging vertically with a vibrating blade or tailspin. While drifting with the wind, jig with long sweeps of the rod; keep the line taut as the lure sinks to bottom.

To catch walleyes suspended more than a few feet off bottom, cast or troll with crankbaits or minnow plugs designed to run at the appropriate depth (see below). Determine the exact depth at which a plug runs by starting to troll in deep water, then gradually moving shallower until the plug bumps bottom.

You can catch walleyes suspended at any depth by casting or trolling with vibrating plugs, jigs, vibrating blades, and weight-forward spinners. To locate walleyes with these lures, use the countdown technique. Many fishermen prefer to tip their jigs and spinners with live bait.

## *How to Select Plugs Based on Running Depth*

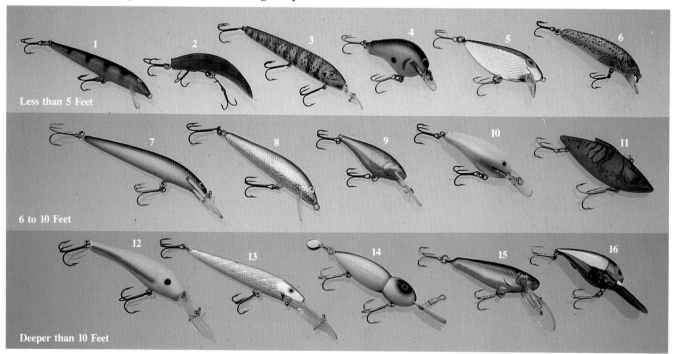

**Less than 5 Feet**

**6 to 10 Feet**

**Deeper than 10 Feet**

POPULAR PLUGS for suspended walleyes include models that run less than 5 feet deep such as (1) Floating Rapala®, (2) Flatfish, (3) Baitfish, (4) Kill'r "B"1, (5) ThinFin® Silver Shad®, (6) Mini Long A®. Models that run from 6 to 10 feet include (7) Diving Bang-O-Lure, (8) A.C. Shiner 375, (9) Shad Rap™, (10) Fat Rap®, (11) Rat-L-Trap, which can be counted down to any depth. Models that run deeper than 10 feet include (12) Shadling®, (13) Spoonbill™ Minnow/Floater, (14) Hellbender, (15) Small Fry Shad, (16) Wiggle Wart®.

## How to Use a Floating Rig

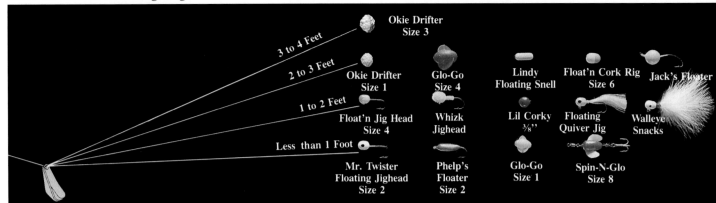

FLOTATION of various floating rigs was determined in tests by The Hunting and Fishing Library research staff. Each rig was tied to a 10-foot leader of 8-pound monofilament, baited with a medium-sized leech, then trolled at a slow speed (1.5 feet per second). The long leader was used to accentuate differences in flotation. With a shorter leader, the heights would be reduced in proportion to leader length. The same rigs baited with minnows and nightcrawlers yielded similar results. The height that each rig floated above bottom is shown in the above chart.

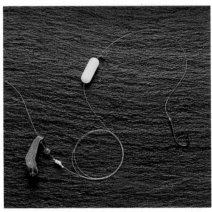

TIE a floating rig with an adjustable leader by using a bead and slip-bobber knot as a stop for the sinker. To adjust the leader length, simply slide the knot along the line.

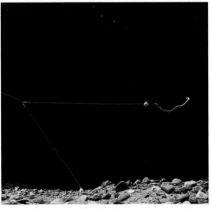

FLOAT your bait higher by using a sliding-dropper rig. Instead of a slip sinker, use a length of mono with a barrel swivel tied to one end and a bell sinker to the other.

AVOID trolling or drifting too fast when using a floating rig. Too much speed will offset the flotation, dragging your bait to the bottom where suspended fish will not see it.

## Tips on Fishing for Suspended Walleyes

THREAD half of a nightcrawler onto the hook of a weight-forward spinner. To prevent short strikes, the worm should trail no more than an inch behind the hook.

INJECT air into the front half of a nightcrawler to make it float. If you inject air into the tail or over-inflate the worm, it will look unnatural. Use a worm blower or hypodermic needle.

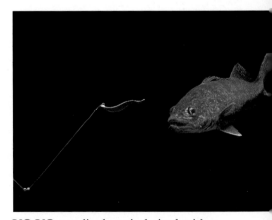

YO-YO a split-shot rig baited with a leech or nightcrawler through a school of suspended walleyes. Use as little weight as possible so the bait does not sink too fast.

109

# Cold-Front Walleye

The toughest time to catch walleyes is after a severe cold front. Normally, crisp temperatures and ultra-clear skies follow passage of the front. Walleyes respond by tightly hugging the bottom or burying themselves in dense weedbeds. They feed sporadically if at all. Depending on the severity of the cold front, it may take up to three days for the fish to resume normal activity.

Post-cold front conditions present problems for even the best fishermen, but the following tactics may improve your success:

• Do your fishing very early or very late in the day, or at night. Your odds of finding active walleyes are best during low-light periods. In early spring, however, they may bite better during the warmest part of the day. Feeding periods following a cold front are likely to be short.

• Fish 5 to 10 feet deeper than you normally would at a given time of day. Increased light penetration from the clear skies drives the walleyes into deeper, darker water.

COLD-FRONT conditions cause walleyes to lie on bottom in a state of near-dormancy. Normally walleyes are extremely shy of divers, but after a cold front, a diver can often swim up to a walleye and touch it. The increased light penetration causes a reaction called *dazzlement*, or partial blindness due to bright light.

- Try fishing in the weeds. Some walleyes will seek cover in shallow vegetation rather than move to deep structure. Weed walleyes resume normal activity before the walleyes in deeper water.

- Use live bait. A small bait will usually work better than a large one. Walleyes in a lethargic state are not likely to chase a fast-moving artificial.

- Fish slowly. Walleyes may even ignore live bait if it is moving too fast. Anchoring is often more effective than trolling or drifting.

- Attach a stinger hook if the fish are striking short. A half-interested walleye will often take a nip at the tail of a minnow or crawler, then let go

- before you can set the hook. With a stinger, you will hook a good percentage of these fish.

- Use light, clear line. Post-cold front walleyes are particularly line-shy. Some fishermen use monofilament as light as 4-pound test.

- If you are fishing on a relatively clear lake with no success, try a lake with darker water or a river.

- In large, shallow lakes with silty bottoms, the strong winds accompanying a cold front stir up the bottom. For several days after the front, the water may be so turbid that you have to fish shallower than normal if the walleyes are to see your bait. In most cases, midday fishing is best.

*Tips for Fishing Under Cold-front Conditions*

DANGLE a minnow or leech from a lighted slip-bobber starting at dusk. A stationary bait may tempt inactive walleyes to bite, and you can easily see the bobber.

TIE a slip-sinker rig using a leader no more than 18 inches long. A lethargic walleye will not swim upward to grab your bait; a short leader keeps your bait near bottom.

USE a lighter-than-normal jig, and tip it with live bait. A lighter jig takes more time to sink, so it forces you to retrieve very slowly and gives the fish extra time to strike.

# River-Fishing for Walleye

A glance through a list of state-record walleyes reveals that a large number were caught in rivers. There is no doubt that rivers offer some excellent walleye-fishing opportunities. One reason that rivers support good walleye populations is that they generally are not fished as heavily as nearby lakes.

Versatile walleye anglers spend their time fishing in rivers when cold fronts have slowed the action in their favorite lakes. Cold fronts do not seem to have as much effect on river walleyes. Rivers are also a good bet in late summer, when lake fishing may be poor due to high water temperatures and hefty crops of forage fish. When lake walleyes are scattered because of the fall turnover, river walleyes continue to feed in the same places where you found them in summer.

In the North, portions of many big rivers stay open through the winter months. Walleyes congregate in the tailwaters of dams and around warmwater discharges all winter long, offering the only open-water fishing opportunity.

Inexperienced anglers have more trouble learning to fish in rivers than in lakes. Many do poorly on their first trip to a river, so they do not come back. The secret to catching river walleyes is knowing how current and fluctuating water levels affect their behavior, and adjusting your tactics accordingly.

CURRENT. Walleyes will tolerate a slight current, but seldom will you find them in fast water, unless there is some type of cover to serve as a current break. When searching for walleyes in rivers, you can immediately eliminate a good share of the water because the current is too swift. Just how much current walleyes will tolerate depends on the season.

You can find river walleyes in slack pools, in eddies, or downstream from some type of current break like an island, a bridge pier or a large boulder. But many anglers make the mistake of fishing only the downstream side of obstructions. For instance, walleyes usually hold just upstream of a wingdam, a rocky

structure intended to deflect current toward the middle of the river to keep the channel from silting in. Current deflecting off the face of a wingdam or other current break creates a slack pocket on the upstream side, providing an ideal spot for a walleye to grab drifting food.

Current edges are to a river what structure is to a lake. Walleyes will hold along the margin between slack and moving water. This way, they can rest in the still water and occasionally dart into the current to get a meal.

FLUCTUATING WATER LEVELS. Most good river fishermen prefer low, stable water for walleye fishing. Under these conditions, the water is at its clearest, and the walleyes are concentrated in well-known spots.

A rapidly changing water level caused by a heavy rain or release of water through a dam can turn a productive walleye hole into dead water. The increase in flow changes the current patterns and drives the walleyes to different areas.

But if you know where to find walleyes when the water is rising, fishing can actually be better than when the water is stable. Rising water often triggers a feeding spree because of the worms, insects and other foods that are washed into the river.

Rising water also causes walleyes to move shallower. They often feed near the base of flooded willows or brush, sometimes in water only a foot deep. If current in the main channel becomes too swift, the fish move into backwater lakes, oxbows, sloughs or cuts where there is practically no current. Or, they may swim into the mouths of feeder creeks that are normally dry.

If the increase in flow causes the river to become extremely muddy, walleyes cannot see well enough to find your bait. In many cases, the muddy water comes from a tributary stream. You may be able to find clearer water by moving upstream of the tributary or far enough downstream so the mud has a chance to settle out.

Walleyes continue to feed as long as the water level is rising or stable. But when it begins to fall, they immediately sense the change and move to deeper water to avoid getting trapped in a dead-water pool. Once they move deeper, feeding slows and fishing becomes much tougher.

River walleyes are predictable in that they generally move to the same areas at a given water stage. By keeping a log book, you can look back to see where you found fish at a similar stage in previous years. Most sizable rivers have water-level gauges that will give you an exact reading.

113

# Where to Find Walleyes at Different Water Stages

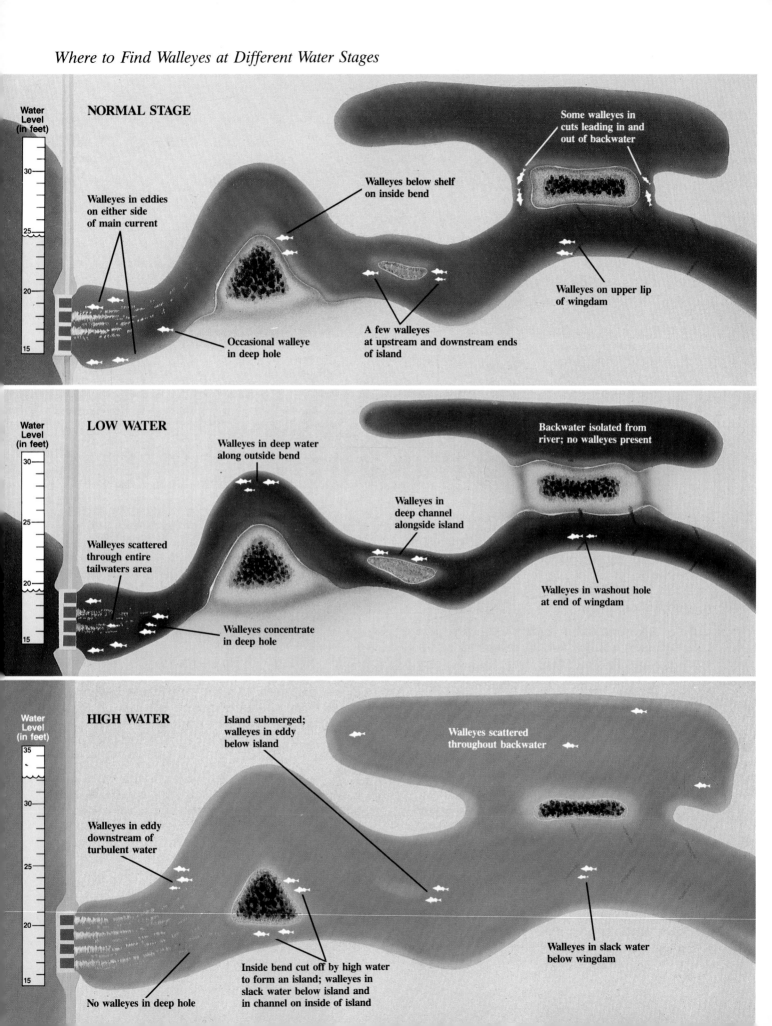

**NORMAL STAGE**

Water Level (in feet)

Some walleyes in cuts leading in and out of backwater

Walleyes below shelf on inside bend

Walleyes in eddies on either side of main current

Walleyes on upper lip of wingdam

Occasional walleye in deep hole

A few walleyes at upstream and downstream ends of island

**LOW WATER**

Water Level (in feet)

Walleyes in deep water along outside bend

Backwater isolated from river; no walleyes present

Walleyes in deep channel alongside island

Walleyes scattered through entire tailwaters area

Walleyes concentrate in deep hole

Walleyes in washout hole at end of wingdam

**HIGH WATER**

Water Level (in feet)

Island submerged; walleyes in eddy below island

Walleyes scattered throughout backwater

Walleyes in eddy downstream of turbulent water

Walleyes in slack water below wingdam

No walleyes in deep hole

Inside bend cut off by high water to form an island; walleyes in slack water below island and in channel on inside of island

With a few modifications, many of the popular techniques for catching walleyes in lakes will also work in rivers.

JIG FISHING. More river walleyes are taken on jigs than on any other lure, but the best sizes and styles may differ from those used to catch walleyes in lakes. In still water, you can easily reach bottom in 15 feet of water with a ⅛-ounce jig, but you will need a ¼-ounce jig to reach the same depth in moderate current. Most anglers prefer round-head or bullet-head jigs for fishing in current because these types have less water resistance than others.

Jigs are normally fished by casting from an anchored position just upstream of a pool or eddy, by casting to pools and eddies while slipping downstream, by vertically jigging while drifting with the current, or by jig trolling.

When jig trolling, motor downstream slightly faster than the current while hopping the jig along bottom. Although most types of lures work best trolled upstream, jigs are more effective trolled downstream. Because you can keep your line closer to vertical, you can hop the jig farther off bottom and detect strikes much easier. When casting a jig from an anchored boat, an upstream retrieve is best. Retrieved downstream, the jig would drag along bottom and quickly snag (page 117).

A jig tipped with a minnow usually works well in spring, when the water temperature is below 45°F. But at warmer temperatures, an untipped jig often works better, especially if the water is on the murky side. Under these conditions, walleyes strike at any kind of movement, and tipping with live bait only reduces your hooking percentage. Fluorescent colors seem to be a bigger attraction than live bait.

FISHING WITH VIBRATING BLADES. Vibrating blades are well-suited to river fishing because they sink rapidly in the current and emit vibrations which attract walleyes even if the water is muddy. They work best when jigged vertically while drifting with the current. But they can also be fished by anchoring upstream of a pool or eddy, casting downstream, then jigging against the current as you would with a lead-head jig.

PLUG FISHING. Trolling with crankbaits, minnow plugs and vibrating plugs accounts for a tremendous number of river walleyes. If the current is not too swift, you can often catch fish by trolling along the edges of the main channel. Other productive trolling areas include long riprap banks, edges of long sandbars and islands, and rocky shoreline.

When trolling with plugs, always move against the current. Much has been written about the logic of trolling with the current because fish are accustomed to seeing their food drifting at them. But experienced river fishermen know that a plug trolled with the current will seldom catch a walleye. Trolling against the current gives the plug good action and enables you to move much more slowly.

Because the current is lightest near the bottom, river walleyes seldom suspend. As a result, keeping your plug near the bottom is especially critical in river fishing. Many anglers use lead-core line or heavy sinkers to keep their plugs ticking bottom.

Another productive plug-fishing technique is casting to a riprap or rocky shoreline while the boat drifts with the current. River walleyes often lie tight to the bank, especially if the water is rising. Casting a plug or spinner within a few inches of shore and retrieving rapidly is one of the best techniques for catching these bank-hugging fish.

FISHING WITH LIVE BAIT. If the bottom is relatively clean, you can lower a slip-sinker rig to bottom and drift with the current. Let out just enough line to reach bottom. If you allow your line to drag on bottom, it will be more difficult to detect a bite and you will get snagged more often. If the bottom is strewn with logs, brush and rocks, you will probably do better with a floating rig or some other rig intended for a rocky bottom (pages 102-103).

You can also fish a live-bait rig by casting to pools or eddies from an anchored position or while slipping downstream. Many anglers prefer a plain split-shot rig for this type of fishing.

Almost all rivers have murky water at least part of the time. In discolored water, a fluorescent spinner ahead of your bait can make a big difference.

## How to Fish Important River Features

SMALL EDDIES created by obstructions like points, islands, submerged sandbars and bridge piers are usually fished by anchoring alongside the eddy. Position your boat so you can cast a jig or live-bait rig into the upstream portion of the eddy, then walk it downstream.

WINGDAMS at normal stage should be worked by anchoring as shown, then casting a jig or plug to the upper lip. Walleyes hold just above the wingdam. At low water, work the washout hole at the end of the wingdam. At high water, fish downstream of the wingdam.

LARGE EDDIES hold the most walleyes near the slack-water zone, especially in cold-water periods. Upstream is reverse current; downstream, the current resumes its normal flow. Anchor in the slack water, then work the area with a jig.

## The Upstream Retrieve: Why It Works

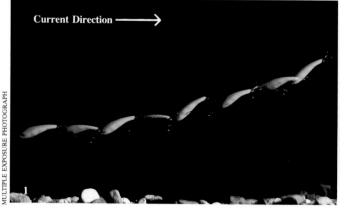

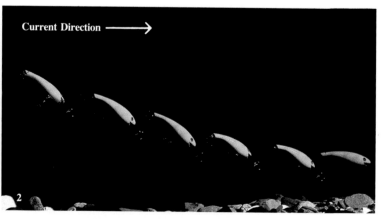

RETRIEVE your lure upstream for more action and fewer snags. When a crankbait is retrieved or trolled upstream (1), it has an intense wobble. When moving downstream (2), it wobbles very little. A jig retrieved upstream (3) sinks slowly, giving the fish time to strike, and the dressing has good action. The jig will ride over

POOLS can be fished by anchoring well upstream, then casting a jig or live-bait rig and retrieving over the upstream lip. Active walleyes lie at the head of the pool to grab drifting food. Let out more anchor line to reach the less active walleyes in the middle of the pool.

FALLEN TREES and logjams must be worked by anchoring below them, if you cannot reach the eddy from upstream. Because you must retrieve downstream, use a brushguard jig or a jig with a light-wire hook so that you can easily free it from the branches.

WARMWATER DISCHARGES from power plants and waste-disposal plants attract walleyes during cold-water periods. Using a jig, crankbait or live-bait rig, fish at different distances from the discharge until you find the temperature zone that holds the most walleyes.

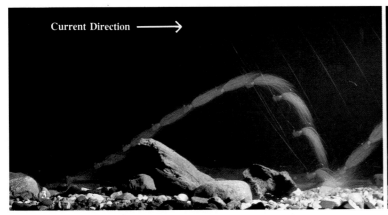

Current Direction →

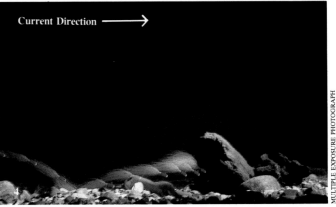

Current Direction →

MULTIPLE EXPOSURE PHOTOGRAPH

most obstructions; if it snags, simply let out some line, then jerk sharply to exert a downstream pull which frees it. With a downstream retrieve (4), the jig sinks more

rapidly and has less action. It snags more often, and is impossible to unsnag because there is no way to pull from the opposite direction.

117

# Fishing for Trophy Walleye

A walleye over 10 pounds ranks among the greatest prizes in freshwater fishing. Catching a walleye that size is a difficult and often frustrating task, even for an accomplished angler.

Few bodies of water contain large numbers of big walleyes. In a moderately fished lake, for instance, the combination of natural mortality and angling catch reduces the number of fish of a given age by about 50 percent each year. Thus, if a population contained 1000 age-one walleyes, 500 would remain at age two, 250 at age three, and only 2 at age ten.

Adding to the challenge is the fact that big walleyes are much warier than small ones. Their exceedingly cautious nature explains why they live so long. If a big walleye sees or hears anything unusual, it stops feeding and heads for deeper water. Trophy hunters know that the poorest time to catch a big walleye is on a weekend when the lake is overrun with water skiers and pleasure boaters.

If you fish long enough, you may catch a trophy walleye using the same strategy you would employ for average-sized walleyes. But you can greatly boost your odds by selecting waters likely to produce big fish, carefully choosing your fishing times, and using techniques suited to trophy walleyes.

SELECTING THE WATER. One of the best-kept secrets in fishing is the location of a spot that produces trophy walleyes. It is highly unlikely that a fisherman who specializes in big walleyes will tell you where he catches his fish.

Many types of water are capable of producing big walleyes. You may find your trophy in a deep oligotrophic lake or in a shallow eutrophic lake infested with rough fish. In general, rivers are poorer choices than natural lakes or reservoirs because the fish grow more slowly. But large rivers impounded by dams produce some of the finest trophy-walleye fishing to be found anywhere.

In recent years, much has been written about trophy-walleye fishing in the Southeast. Reservoirs in this area produce some giant walleyes because of the fast growth rate. But walleyes in the North are more abundant and have a much longer life span. Even though the top-end weights are not quite as high, northern waters produce many more walleyes of 10 pounds or more.

If you want to catch a big walleye, but do not know where to go, base your choice on the following:

*Water area* — All other factors being equal, a large body of water is more likely to support big walleyes than a small one. A 500-acre natural lake may hold a few 10-pound walleyes, but on a per-acre basis, a 5000-acre lake would hold a lot more.

*Size of walleye population* — Waters that produce lots of small walleyes generally yield few trophies. Competition for food and living space makes it

CHECK fishing-contest results for information on where to catch trophy walleyes. Sometimes the results reveal dates when they were caught as well as lures or baits. In the contest results shown in the above magazine, note that the largest entries (circled) from each region of the country were about equal in size.

more difficult for the fish to grow to a large size. Strange as it may sound, your chances of boating a big walleye are often better in a body of water not known for good walleye fishing.

Waters where walleyes are plentiful usually attract large numbers of anglers. Heavy fishing pressure reduces the average size of the walleyes and cuts your odds of boating a trophy.

*Usable forage* — A body of water may be full of forage fish, but if they are not of a size acceptable to walleyes, they do not contribute to the trophy potential. In fact, a large population of unusable forage is detrimental. The productivity of any body of water is limited, so the larger the population of oversized forage, the smaller the crop of usable forage.

For example, many lakes in the North contain large populations of ciscoes. But in most cases, the cisco crop consists mainly of fish over 10 inches in length, too big for the vast majority of walleyes. These lakes produce few trophies. A few northern lakes, however, have populations of *dwarf ciscoes,* a strain that never grows longer than 7 inches. These lakes have much greater potential for big walleyes.

## WHEN TO CATCH TROPHY WALLEYES.

Anglers catch by far the most trophy walleyes during the following three periods: just before spawning; in early summer, when the big females have completely recuperated from spawning; and in late fall, when the fish are feeding heavily in preparation for winter.

During the pre-spawn period, large numbers of big females crowd into a relatively small area. Although they are not feeding heavily, you may be able to catch a fish or two because of the sheer numbers present. Good fishing lasts until spawning begins.

About two weeks after spawning, the big females start to bite again, but they are still scattered and can be very difficult to find. You may catch an occasional large walleye, but seldom more than one. Your chances of finding a concentration of big walleyes are much better after they have settled into their typical summer locations. The best fishing begins about five to six weeks after spawning and generally lasts two to three weeks.

Late-fall fishing is extremely unpredictable, but if you can find the walleyes, a high percentage of them will be big. The preponderance of large walleyes in late fall can be explained by the fact that most of them are females. To nourish their developing eggs, females must consume more food than males, up to six times more according to some feeding studies.

In waters that stratify, the depths are warmer than the shallows once the fall turnover is completed. Big walleyes may swim into shallow water for short feeding sprees, but at other times may be found as deep as 50 feet. Although difficult to find, they form tight schools, so you may be able to catch several from the same area.

## TECHNIQUES FOR TROPHY WALLEYES.

Catching a walleye over 10 pounds is a once-in-a-

*Tips on Night Fishing for Trophy Walleyes*

SCOUT likely walleye structure during midday, when fishing is slow. Anchor a large white jug on the edge of a shallow reef or shoal likely to hold walleyes at night. Remember the position of the jug so that you can find the exact spot after dark.

LOCATE the jug with a spotlight, but avoid shining the beam into the water because it may spook the fish. When you spot the jug, shut off your outboard. Let the breeze push you into position or move in with an electric motor. Anchor upwind of the spot you want to fish.

lifetime accomplishment for most anglers. But some fishermen catch several that size each year. If you spend a lot of time fishing waters known for trophy walleyes, but seldom land a big one, you are probably making one or more of the following mistakes:

- You may be fishing at the wrong depth. In most waters, big walleyes feed in the shallows during low-light periods, especially in spring and fall. But at most other times, they prefer relatively deep water, deeper than the areas where you typically find smaller walleyes.

  Often, big walleyes use the same structure as the smaller ones, but hang 10 to 15 feet deeper. This behavior can be attributed to a walleye's increasing sensitivity to light as it grows older. In addition, bigger walleyes prefer cooler water, and they can usually find it by moving deeper.

  In deep northern lakes, however, the shallow water stays cool enough for big walleyes through the summer. If the walleyes can find boulders or other shallow-water cover to provide shade, they may spend the summer at depths of 10 feet or less. In these lakes, most anglers fish too deep.

- You may be using baits and lures too small to interest trophy walleyes. If you have ever cleaned a big walleye, you were probably surprised to find one or more 6- to 8-inch baitfish in its stomach. Yet few walleye anglers would consider tying on a bait this large. Instead, they use smaller baits and, not surprisingly, catch smaller walleyes.

Big baits draw far fewer strikes than small ones, and most anglers are not willing to fish all day for one or two opportunities. But if you are intent on catching a trophy, that is the price you must pay.

- You may be fishing at the wrong time of day. If the water is very clear, or if there is a great deal of boat traffic, big walleyes will feed almost exclusively at night.

- Your presentation may be too sloppy. Many fishermen assume that they need big hooks and heavy leaders to catch trophy walleyes, but the reverse is actually true. Big walleyes are extremely cautious. They are much more likely to take a bait attached to a size-6 hook and a 6-pound-test leader than one attached to a 1/0 hook and 15-pound leader. In clear water, some trophy specialists use a 4-pound leader.

A small hook allows a walleye to swallow the bait without feeling anything unusual. And a small hook will not break or pull out. Most big walleyes are hooked under snag-free conditions, so if you take your time and do not attempt to horse the fish, light line will do the job.

Another common mistake is making too much noise. Unless the fish are in water deeper than 20 feet, you should not troll over them with your outboard motor. Avoid dropping anything in the boat and do not attempt to anchor on top of the fish. Set your anchor at a distance and let the wind drift your boat into position.

## Other Tips for Trophy Walleyes

SELECT a jig with a hook larger than normal (top) when tipping with big minnows. A smaller one (bottom) will hook fewer fish because too little of the hook is exposed.

CHECK your line frequently, especially when fishing for trophy walleyes. You may get only a few bites each day, so you do not want to lose a fish because of a frayed line.

USE minnow plugs up to 8 inches long. Big lures work better than small lures; a big walleye can save energy by eating one large baitfish instead of several smaller ones.

# The TECHNIQUE for Walleyes

by Dick Sternberg

*Dick Grzywinski's unique snap-jigging technique catches walleyes that ignore the usual methods*

*Ripping a jig through the weeds using the Technique*

Dick Grzywinski deftly steered his boat through a dozen others scattered along the edge of a reef on Lake Winnibigoshish. "'Nuther one," he grunted as he set the hook on a chunky 3-pound walleye. It was his fifty-sixth of the day, and the time was only 11 a.m.

Every once in a while somebody in one of the other boats landed a walleye, but "the Grz" and his customers were hauling in five for every one they caught.

This scene has become a regular occurrence on "Big Winnie" in northern Minnesota. Baffled fishermen follow the Grz around and watch in amazement as he continues to reel in fish.

"It's the Technique," he'll tell you. Notice the capital *T*. That's because he considers it the *only* technique, at least on Big Winnie. And it's difficult to argue the point — it's not unusual for him to boat 100 or more walleyes a day on his guide trips.

The Technique is a fast jig-trolling method originated by the Grz, and practiced by him and a select group of his sidekicks. Most walleye experts advocate slow jigging, but the Grz has found that a fast, erratic jigging action will trigger walleyes that ignore slower offerings. Many envious anglers have studied the Technique and tried to duplicate it, but most have had only limited success. For a while, the would-be copycats were causing problems by following his boat too close and getting in the way, but most of them soon gave up out of frustration or embarrassment.

Despite his confidence in the Technique, the Grz isn't a one-method fisherman. In early spring, when the walleyes are up on shallow, rocky reefs, he cleans up by dropping anchor and pitching a slip-bobber rig baited with a lively ribbon leech. In lakes where the walleyes go deep in midsummer, he gets them by slow-trolling a slip-sinker rig baited with a leech or nightcrawler.

And walleyes aren't his only quarry. The rows of mounted fish on the walls of his living room, and the bulging photo album in his pickup camper, prove he's an accomplished multi-species angler. He spends a lot of time chasing northern pike, largemouth and smallmouth bass, bluegills, crappies, yellow perch, muskies, and even sturgeon. "Had to take down the picture of the wife on the living-room wall to make space for a big chinook salmon," he jokes. "On a cold winter night, I sit back and look at those fish and remember how much fun I had catching 'em."

But on many cold winter nights, the Grz isn't home staring at his walls; he's out ice fishing. In fact, he's an ice-fishing fanatic. He thinks nothing of walking two or three miles onto a lake in a raging blizzard, lugging a bucket of minnows and a 6-gallon pail full of tackle, and toting his Jiffy ice auger over his shoulder. He's been seen trudging off a lake with his beard completely covered with ice and the tips of his ears white from frostbite.

The Grz isn't sure how his nickname originated. It may have resulted from people being unable to pronounce his real name (the right way is *Ja-VIN-ski*), or from his bushy black hair and beard, which make him look like a grizzly bear. In spite of his

fatheads 'cause they're tough. I can keep 'em in my live box for weeks. Best way to hook 'em is through the eyes. I get more bites that way, and they stay on the hook real good. But don't use the black ones with the warts on their head — they're males, and the walleyes just don't like 'em."

The Grz is a master at following structure, which may be the main thing that separates him from the competition. It's one thing to use the Technique, but it's another to use it in the precise depth zone where walleyes are congregated. Along the reef edges in Big Winnie, the zone may be as narrow as 1 foot; the exact depth depends on the time of year. If you fish slightly deeper or shallower, you won't catch a fish.

In a day when most walleye pros backtroll for precise boat control, the Grz trolls forward. "If I backtrolled fast enough to use the Technique, I'd sink my boat," he laughs. "It gets pretty rough on Winnie. The waves would come right over the transom.

"With the Technique, I always troll into the wind," he notes. "If you troll with the wind, you'll go too fast and you won't be able to control the boat. You can't stay on the structure. After I make a pass, I circle back, then make another."

The Grz seems to develop a jigging rhythm that suits the conditions. In shallow water, he trolls a little faster and snaps a little harder than in deep water. When fishing over weeds, he trolls even faster and snaps even harder, to keep the jig from sinking and fouling in the vegetation.

He doesn't have much time for fishing gadgets and short-cut methods. "I get a kick out of the guys that come up here with Color-C-Lectors and pH meters. All those things do is throw 'em off track. Never use scent on my bait either. A walleye doesn't strike because the bait smells good. He sees it trying to get away, and he smacks it. Lotta guys up here use scent — I can smell it a block away. But they're wastin' their time and money."

It's easy to understand why somebody would resort to those means when fishing alongside the Grz. When you're watching him haul in walleyes by the dozen and all you're getting is a suntan, you're looking for a little black magic.

*Treasury of trophies: the Grz's scrapbook, growing thicker by the day*

# Walleye Tips

*Gary Howey*
## Sliding Sinker Stop

Lindy Rigs or other pre-tied slip-sinker rigs are standard in fishing live bait for walleyes. But these rigs have some drawbacks. The leader inevitably gets scuffed up, so you have to cut off the hook and retie, often leaving your leader too short. Most slip-sinker rigs have three knots that are potential weak spots. Gary Howey, a guide and publisher of "The Outdoorsman" newspaper, from Hartington, Nebraska, ties his own rigs using rubber stops made by Northland Tackle. The knot attaching the hook is the only knot required. If the leader gets scuffed, he snips off the hook, reties, and slides the stop a few inches up the line. Another advantage: the leader length can be adjusted to suit different fishing conditions by simply moving the stop.

THREAD on a slip-sinker. Insert your line through the wire ring that comes with the stop, then slide the stop off the wire onto your line. Tie on your hook.

*Jim Crowley*
## Plastic Worms for Walleyes

Jim Crowley, a Hunting and Fishing Library subscriber and resident of Fayetteville, New York, fishes big walleyes in logs and brush using plastic worms. Jim discovered the technique after losing a pile of jigs in a log-strewn Canadian lake. Out of frustration, he tied on an 8-inch worm rigged Texas-style and started catching 5- to 9-pounders. The technique has proven to be a consistent early-season producer in Canadian lakes. Jim's favorite worm colors are blue, lime-green, and purple.

ED IMAN is a well-known Columbia River fishing guide from Gresham, Oregon, and a member of the Mariner National Fishing Team. Ed used his diving worm harness to take this 17 pound 5 ounce walleye, only 3 ounces shy of the Oregon state record.

*Ed Iman*
## Diving Worm Harness

Spinner-nightcrawler rigs are one of the top walleye producers, but the sinkers normally used to get them deep snag easily on a rocky bottom. Ed Iman solves the problem by using deep-diving plugs to pull the spinner rig down. He attaches the spinner rig to a bright-colored plug with the hooks removed. The plug will reach depths of 15 to 25 feet and will seldom snag. The bright color of the plug attracts fish to the spinner rig.

REMOVE the hooks from a deep-diving plug such as a Hot Lips (shown), attach a snap-swivel to the split-ring on the front hook hanger, then clip the spinner rig into the snap. This way, you can easily change spinners.

## Go Light After a Cold Front

Walleyes and saugers don't feed much following a cold front. But they may nip at a small, slow-moving bait. Here's a trick that can put a few walleyes in your boat when fishing really gets tough.

Spool a light spinning outfit with 2- to 4-pound mono, tie on a 1/16- or 1/32-ounce jig and tip it with a small minnow or leech. Use a trolling motor to keep your boat over a spot where you suspect fish are holding, then drop the jig to bottom. Lift and lower it slowly, move it in very short hops or just hold it steady; set the hook if you feel a tap or the line tightens. One problem: light jigs are tough to fish in windy weather.

## Double Bait for Big Fish

If you're catching only little walleyes and saugers, you may be using minnows that are too small. Bigger fish often want bigger bait. If you run out of big minnows, here's a way to save the day:

HOOK two small minnows on a jig or split-shot rig. Don't bury the hook too deeply or the minnows will jam up in the bend of the hook and won't trail naturally.

## Jigs for Weed Walleyes

Stocked walleyes spend a lot of time in the thick vegetation usually associated with largemouth bass. You can catch these walleyes by casting jigs into this heavy cover. But ordinary walleye jigs don't work well; the exposed hook point and attachment eye on top of the jig head snag weeds. And most weedless bass jigs are too big.

Try a 1/8-ounce weedless jig with the attachment eye at the front of the head, which lets the lure slip through weeds easily. Some of these jigs also have a flattened head to slow the sink rate, so you can swim them over very dense weeds. (These special weedless jigs are available from J. M. Tackle, Route 4, Hayward, WI 54843.)

WIND

## Check the Downwind Side ↑

On a windy day, walleye anglers normally fish the wind-ward side of an underwater hump or point. But there are also times when fish feed on the downwind side. On a shallow hump or point, strong wind whips up a great deal of turbulence, causing various kinds of in-vertebrates to drift off the downwind side of the rocks. Baitfish gather to feed on the small organisms. Then gamefish, including walleyes, largemouth bass and muskies, move in to feed on the baitfish.

## A Long Reach Means Fewer Snags

Submerged boulder piles and rocky reefs are top spots for walleyes. But it's nearly impossible to fish a jig or slip-sinker rig in the rocks without getting hung up. You can minimize snags by keeping your line straight up and down, but even then, you'll hang up once in a while. Here's how to improve your chances of freeing

## Slip in on Walleyes

The sound of an outboard, the whir of an electric troll-ing motor, or the clunk of an anchor can spook walleyes off a shallow reef. To approach such a spot silently, anchor at least 50 feet upwind, and pay out rope until you're within casting range. If you need to check the reef with your depth finder, let your boat blow right over the spot, take your readings, and then move slightly upwind by taking in anchor rope.

a lure if you do get snagged. Use a longer rod so you can reach out farther to change your angle of pull, making it possible to dislodge the hook without repositioning the boat. Some anglers use specially designed spinning rods up to 8 feet long or they rig a fly rod with a spinning reel.

## Free-Standing Stinger ↑

Walleyes often nip at a jig and minnow without getting hooked. Many anglers tie a small treble to the bend of the jig hook and imbed this "stinger" in the minnow's tail. But even light mono between the jig and treble inhibits the action of the bait. And the line often wraps around the minnow, cinching it into a half-circle and ruining its action. Here's a better way.

Tie a size 14 or 16 treble hook to the bend of the jig hook with a short length of stiff line, such as Mason hard mono, 15-pound test or heavier. The stiff line holds the treble straight out behind the jig, so you don't need to hook it in the minnow. The bait moves freely, as if the stinger weren't there at all. Yet when a fish nips the tail, it gets hooked.

## Cut Through Stringy Weeds

Walleyes are sometimes found in stringy weeds, such as coontail. The weeds catch on your line, slide down and foul your lure. Sometimes you can shake them off during the retrieve, but more often you have to reel in the lure and remove the weeds by hand. Here's an easier way.

Add a short leader of thin multistrand wire, such as 12-pound-test Sevenstrand, between your line and lure. When you feel resistance from a weed, jerk the rod. The thin wire will cut through the stem, and the weed will fall off the line. The wire leader also ensures that sharp-toothed fish such as northern pike won't bite off your lure.

# Pike & Muskie

"...he weighed upwards of 170 pounds, and is thought to be the largest [pike] ever seen. Some time ago, the clerk of the local parish was trolling...when his bait was seized by this furious creature, which by a sudden jerk pulled him in, and doubtless would have devoured him also, had he not by wonderful agility and dextrous swimming escaped the dreadful jaws of this voracious animal."

*from Sir Izaak Walton's* The Compleat Angler - 1653

A sea of misinformation surrounds the northern pike and muskellunge. Even today, we hear stories of huge pike or muskies attacking swimmers or charging outboard motors. Such tales make good copy in magazine articles, but only serve to perpetuate the "evil" image of these fish.

Of course, pike and muskies are the top predators in any body of water, and they'll eat larger prey than most other freshwater fish. But they're not the ruthless killers they're commonly portrayed to be.

To become a proficient pike or muskie angler, one must put aside the backlog of misinformation about these fish and learn more about their behavior and biological requirements.

Northern pike and muskellunge, along with pickerel, are sometimes referred to as Esocids; they belong to the pike family, whose technical name is Esocidae.

Pickerel, because of their smaller size, are much less popular with anglers. Chain pickerel seldom exceed 5 pounds; redfin pickerel, 1 pound. Although this book features pike and muskies, many of the techniques (on a smaller scale) will work equally well for pickerel.

Northerns hybridize with all other Esocid species. The best-known hybrid, the *tiger muskie*, is a pike-muskie cross. Tiger muskies, which get their name from their distinct vertical bars (p. 134), are rare in nature because pike spawn so much earlier than muskies. But fish hatcheries can easily produce hybrids, and the fish have been widely stocked in the United States. "Hybrid vigor" makes them grow faster than either parent, at least for the first several years of

North American Northern Pike Range

Muskellunge Range

life. Tigers do not reach the ultimate size of purebred muskies because their life span is shorter.

Although pike and muskies have a great deal in common, their differences far outweigh their similarities. Pike occur naturally at northern latitudes throughout the world. Muskies, however, are native only to North America, and their range does not extend as far north.

Muskies seldom reach the population density of pike. Although they deposit just as many eggs, the hatch rate is lower, and because pike hatch earlier, they prey heavily on young muskies.

Technically, both species are classified as *coolwater fish*, meaning that they prefer lower temperatures than warmwater fish such as bass, but warmer than coldwater fish such as trout. In reality, however, their temperature preferences differ considerably.

Muskies prefer water in the 67- to 72-degree range; small pike, about the same. But large pike (30+ inches) could almost be classed as coldwater fish, favoring water temperatures from 50 to 55 degrees. Pike also spawn and feed at lower temperatures than muskies. Another difference: pike bite throughout the year, muskies are seldom caught in winter.

Compared to pike, muskies are more selective as to what they eat. They're known for their habit of following a lure, then turning away at the last second. But muskies can afford to be choosy; pike can't. Since muskies aren't as numerous, they face less food competition from other members of their breed. Pike must eat whatever they can whenever they can or be outcompeted.

Due to their finicky nature, muskies are commonly billed as "the fish of 10,000 casts." Stories often describe how an angler fishes for years to catch a

single muskie. Such tales discourage many anglers from trying for muskies. It's true that muskie fishing can be tough, but it's not nearly as difficult as many writers would lead you to believe. Some muskie specialists land over 100 each season.

Because pike aren't as selective, they're much easier to catch. In a creel survey conducted on a Wisconsin lake, anglers removed 50 percent of the pike crop in a single season. Another reason pike fishing is easier: the fish don't seem to learn from past mistakes. Many anglers have caught a pike with a distinctive marking, released it and then caught it again the same day. Rarely does this happen with muskies.

The relative ease of catching pike makes them extremely vulnerable to overfishing. In most heavily fished waters, pike over 10 pounds are unusual. But in remote areas, they commonly exceed

25 pounds. Muskies are less affected by fishing pressure and frequently reach weights of 35 pounds or more, even in waters pounded by anglers.

Currently, the world-record pike is a 55-pound, 1-ouncer caught in Lake Grefeern, Germany, in 1986. The muskie record is 69 pounds, 15 ounces and was taken in the St. Lawrence River, New York, in 1957. The record hybrid weighed 51 pounds, 3 ounces and was caught in Lac Vieux Desert on the Wisconsin-Michigan border in 1919.

All Esocids are excellent food fish, with lean, white, flaky, mild-tasting meat. They're often belittled because of the Y-bones in the meat, but the bones can easily be removed (refer to *Cleaning & Cooking Fish* and *Fishing Tips & Tricks*, both from The Hunting & Fishing Library). Muskies, however, are too scarce to kill for the meat. Release them to fight another day.

## *Mutants and Hybrids*

SILVER PIKE. A mutant form of northern pike, the silver pike occurs throughout the pike's native range. The sides vary from bright silver to metallic blue or green and have no markings except silver or gold flecks on the scales.

TIGER MUSKIE (pike-muskie hybrid). Sides with irregular, narrow bars, often broken into spots, on a light greenish to brownish background. The tips of the tail are rounder than a muskie's. Usually has 12 to 13 jaw pores.

## The Muskie Triangle

Muskie literature, both popular and scientific, commonly refers to three distinct color phases – clear, spotted and barred. But anglers who catch lots of muskies know that many of the fish don't quite fit into any of these categories. The muskie triangle demonstrates just how variable muskie coloration can be. At the points of the triangle are each of the distinct color phases; along the sides, intergrades between two color phases; in the center, a combination of all three. The intergrades are considerably more common than the distinct color phases.

CLEAR. The sides and fins have no spots or blotches.

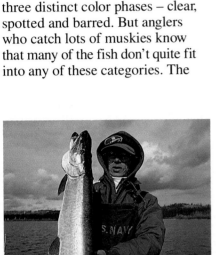

CLEAR/SPOTTED. The front of the body is mostly clear; spots become more prominent toward the tail.

CLEAR/BARRED. The sides have dull bars that get progressively darker toward the tail.

SPOTTED/CLEAR/BARRED. The sides are almost clear at the front, but grade into a mixture of bars and spots that get darker toward the tail.

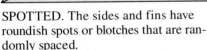

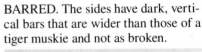

SPOTTED. The sides and fins have roundish spots or blotches that are randomly spaced.

BARRED. The sides have dark, vertical bars that are wider than those of a tiger muskie and not as broken.

SPOTTED/BARRED. The sides have a combination of spots and bars; spots are more prominent toward the rear.

# Pike & Muskie Habitat

The circumpolar distribution of northern pike reflects their ability to adapt to a wide variety of habitat. Their North American range extends from 40 to 70° N, well above the Arctic circle. They've been widely stocked throughout the Great Plains and Rocky Mountain States.

Pike exist in practically every type of water, from warm, shallow ponds, to deep, cold lakes, to muddy rivers. They even live in brackish areas of the Baltic

Sea. Their broad tolerance range for water temperature, water clarity and dissolved oxygen content makes them one of the most adaptable freshwater fish species.

Although pike, especially good-sized ones, prefer cool water, they can endure temperatures into the low 80s. But if they cannot find cool water in summer, they grow slowly and don't live long. Pike can tolerate very low clarity and oxygen levels and are among the last gamefish to die when a lake winterkills.

Muskies also inhabit a variety of lakes and rivers, but they're not nearly as versatile as pike. Found

only in North America, their native range extends from 36 to 51° N, barely reaching into Canada.

Like pike, muskies can survive in a wide range of water temperatures. But they're seldom found in waters with a maximum summer temperature below 68° F. They can tolerate water temperatures up to the mid 80s. Muskies prefer clear water and cannot adapt to water that stays turbid most of the time. They require considerably higher oxygen levels than pike.

Another important difference: muskies have a well-defined home range; pike don't. Several radio-tagging studies have shown that muskies seldom leave their home range, except to spawn, although they roam

about within it. The larger the body of water, the larger the home range.

Both species prefer shallow, weedy water (less than 20 feet deep) during their early years of life. But as they grow larger, they spend more of their time in deep water. This tendency is stronger in pike than in muskies.

Pike and muskies will not tolerate fast current, so they're seldom found in rivers with a gradient (drop) of more than 10 feet per mile. If there are backwater areas where they can get out of the moving water, however, they'll live in rivers with higher gradients and faster current.

# Pike- & Muskie-Fishing Fundamentals

When a pike or muskie decides to take your bait, nothing will change its mind. These fish have been known to ram the boat when an angler lifts a lure from the water.

Because of their aggressive temperament, there's no need for a subtle presentation. You can use heavy line, a thick wire leader and big hooks. And if you splash your bait right on top of them, it's more likely to kindle their interest than to spook them.

Not that they're always willing biters. Pike rank among the easiest gamefish to catch, but muskies may well be the toughest. Even if you locate one, getting it to hit is another matter. They're notorious followers; some days, you'll see a dozen for every one that strikes. The best way to turn followers into biters is to perfect your figure-eight technique (p. 140).

Pike and muskies have bony mouths, so sharp hooks are a must. But hooks large enough for these fish are usually quite dull when you buy them. It pays to carry a good sharpening device that will handle big hooks.

Landing a large Esocid requires the right tools and extreme care. If you stick your hand into its mouth or gills to free your hook, you risk serious injury from the teeth or gill rakers should the fish start thrashing.

Always carry jaw spreaders, a needlenose pliers and sidecutters for clipping off hooks. You can hand-land small pike and muskies (opposite page), but for big ones, you'll need a large net or, better yet, a cradle.

The strong catch-and-release ethic among dedicated muskie anglers has had a major impact in preserving quality muskie fishing. Carry a camera to document your catch, and keep a fish only if you plan to have it mounted. If you want fish to eat, take small pike.

## How to Land Pike and Muskies

LAND a small pike or muskie by grabbing it firmly across the back, just behind the gill covers.

GRAB the tail of a played-out pike or muskie at boatside to prevent it from thrashing while another person frees the hooks. Never attempt to grab the tail if the fish is still "hot."

SLIDE a good-sized pike or muskie into a cradle if you plan to release it. A cradle restricts the fish's movement, preventing it from injuring itself and protecting you while you unhook it.

NET fish only if you plan to keep them. They may bruise themselves or split their fins in an ordinary landing net.

## How to Unhook and Release Pike and Muskies

FREE hard-to-reach hooks with a long-handled hook remover. This way, you won't have to put your hand in the fish's mouth.

CUT the points off deeply embedded hooks using sidecutters. Then, you can get the fish back in the water quickly without injuring it.

HOLD the fish upright and gently rock it back and forth to revive it. Don't let the fish go unless it can remain upright on its own.

## Figure-Eighting

WATCH carefully for follows when retrieving your lure; polarized glasses and a long-billed cap are a must. If you're not paying attention, you may pull your lure away from a fish only inches behind it.

Figure-eighting works with most any kind of artificial lure, even top-waters and jerkbaits. Some muskie experts take up to 40 percent of their fish this way. The technique is effective for reluctant pike, too.

The idea behind the figure-eight technique is to keep the lure moving and try to keep it away from the fish by speeding it up. Most beginners use the opposite tactic; when a fish follows, they slow their retrieve or stop reeling altogether, causing the fish to lose interest.

Watch carefully to determine whether or not the fish is hot. If it's right on the lure and appears to be nipping at it, keep figure-eighting. But if it's swimming slowly and seems only mildly interested, leave it alone, mark the spot and come back a couple of hours later or when the weather changes. Or try again at dusk.

Figure-eighting is especially important in low-clarity water or at night, because you probably won't see your follows. In these situations, the best policy is to figure-eight, or at least make an L-turn, after every cast, just in case a fish is eyeing your lure.

It pays to figure-eight every few casts in clear water too; sometimes fish hang 3 or 4 feet beneath the boat and are tough to see.

*The Figure-Eight Technique*

EASE your rod tip under the surface when a fish follows. Draw the lure to within a foot of the tip, press the free-spool button and thumb the reel.

SWEEP the rod in a wide, smooth, figure-eight pattern, keeping the tip well below the bottom of the boat. If your pattern is too tight, a good-sized fish won't be able to turn sharply enough to follow the lure. If the fish won't come up for the lure, push the lure deeper.

TRIGGER a strike from a half-interested fish by drawing the lure across its snout. Do not use this technique if the fish is hot.

SET THE HOOK when you feel the weight of the fish. Your hooking percentage is best when you set upward or back into the fish.

# Fishing Pike & Muskies with Artificial Lures

When you see a big, shadowy form inches behind your lure, you'll understand why so many anglers fish pike and muskies with artificials. Bait fishermen rarely experience the thrill of seeing a follow, then figure-eighting to make the fish strike.

Almost anything with a hook attached will catch pike and muskies – when they're in the right mood. But when they're not, lure selection becomes critical. Following are the main considerations in deciding what artificials to use:

SIZE. In regard to food habits, it is said that pike and muskies prefer baitfish at least one-fourth their own length. If you follow this line of reasoning, a 48-inch muskie, which weighs about 30 pounds, would be more likely to strike a foot-long lure than the 4- to 6-inchers used by most anglers.

But 30-pounders are scarce in most waters; if you relied solely on foot-long lures, you wouldn't get many strikes. Gauge the size of your lure to the size of the fish you expect to catch. If your lake has plenty of 5-pounders, for instance, but seldom produces a 10, a 7- to 8-inch lure would be a better choice. Go a little smaller in spring or after a cold front, a little larger in fall.

RUNNING DEPTH. Being aggressive predators, pike and muskies may swim up 10 to 20 feet to take a lure. But when they're not in the mood to feed, you'll have to put it right in their face. It's a good idea to carry a selection of lures that run at different depths, from the surface down to 30 feet.

Another suggestion: carry a variety of pinch-on or twist-on sinkers so you can weight your lures to go deeper. With some, such as bucktails and spinnerbaits, you can add weight to the lure itself; with others, you'll have to attach the weight just ahead of the lure.

If you're not sure how deep a lure runs, find an area with a clean, gradually sloping bottom. Then make a long cast and retrieve the lure at normal speed. If you don't feel it hit bottom, move shallower until

you do. Write the running depth on the lure with waterproof ink.

Many pike and muskie anglers make the mistake of using line much heavier than what's really needed.

The water resistance of thick-diameter line lifts the lure, preventing it from reaching its depth potential. Thus a lure that runs 8 feet deep with 30-pound mono may run 12 feet deep with 17-pound.

ACTION. As a rule, the intensity of the action should increase as the season progresses. In spring, lures with a tight wobble or subtle action usually work best. By fall, however, the fish seem to prefer lures that have a wider wobble or more erratic action, those that make lots of noise and splash or those with hard-thumping blades. Lures with high-intensity action also work well in low-clarity waters.

When casting, it pays to vary your retrieve to change the lure's action. Speed up, slow down, give it a twitch now and then and switch your rod from side to side to change direction. When trolling, sweep your rod forward every few seconds, then drop it back. If a fish is following, the hesitation often draws a strike. But at night or in murky water, use a steady retrieve; it's harder for the fish to home in on a lure moving erratically, so they'll often miss it.

COLOR. For decades, the accepted color for pike was red-and-white; for muskies, black. And no doubt those colors produced the most fish since few anglers used anything else. Today, serious fishermen carry a large assortment of different-colored lures for waters of different clarity and different weather conditions. The chart at right provides some general guidelines to color selection for pike and muskie fishing. There's no need to make a distinction between the two species. Following these recommendations will improve your odds – most of the time.

But remember that there are no hard-and-fast rules. Stick with colors that you know have produced in the body of water you're fishing, but don't hesitate to experiment if they're not working.

*Color-Selection Chart*

|  | **CLEAR TO MODERATELY CLEAR WATER** | | **LOW-CLARITY WATER** (visibility of 2 feet or less) | |
|---|---|---|---|---|
| Spinner-blade Color | Nickel (C, O)<br>Gold or Brass (C, O)<br>Fluorescent Orange (O)<br>Fluorescent Chartreuse (O) | | Gold or Brass (C)<br>Copper (C)<br>Fluorescent Orange (C, O)<br>Fluorescent Chartreuse (C, O) | |
| Lure or Bucktail Color | Black (C, O)<br>Brown (C, O)<br>Purple (C, O)<br>Gray (C, O)<br>White (C, O) | Silver (C, O)<br>Gold (O)<br>Red (O)<br>Fluorescent<br>Chartreuse (O) | Black (C, O)<br>Yellow (C, O)<br>White (C, O)<br>Fluorescent Orange (C, O)<br>Fluorescent Chartreuse (C, O) | Gold (C)<br>Copper (C) |

COLOR SELECTION depends on water clarity and cloud cover. Good colors for waters of high to moderate clarity are listed in the left column; low clarity, in the right. Spinner-blade colors are listed at the top; lure-body or bucktail colors, at the bottom. The letter "C" signifies a good choice for clear skies; "O," overcast skies.

## Fishing Pike and Muskie with Bucktails and Spinnerbaits

The big, thumping blades on these spinners produce enough vibration to attract pike and muskies from a distance, even in low-clarity water where they can barely see.

Though generally consided to be warmwater lures, spinners will catch fish in cool water too, if you slow down your retrieve.

Spinners can be retrieved quite rapidly, so they enable you to cover a lot of water in a hurry. They're most often used for casting, but also work well for trolling.

Circumstances dictate whether to use a bucktail or a spinnerbait.

BUCKTAILS. The term *bucktail* has been applied loosely to any large in-line spinner, regardless of the type of tail dressing. But the best bucktails are actually dressed with hair from a deer tail. Because deer hair is hollow, it is very buoyant and has an attractive billowing or breathing action in the water. The deer hair is usually tied around the base of a treble hook at the rear. Some baits have two or even three dressed trebles in a line.

In water with few weeds or other obstructions, a bucktail is a better choice than a spinnerbait. Normally, you fish this lure with a straight retrieve, so pike and muskies have no trouble zeroing in on it. This quality, combined with the exposed treble(s) at

BUCKTAIL models include: (1) single-blade, such as Windel's Harasser, by far the most common type; and (2) tandem-blade, such as the Com Boo, which has more flash and better lift.

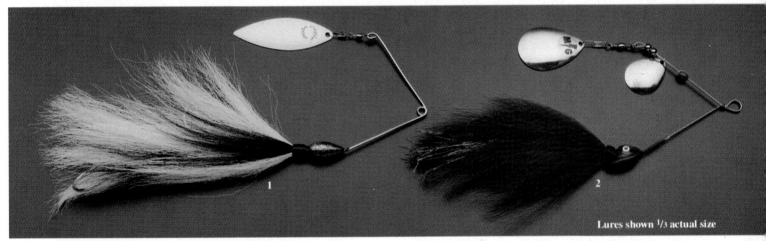

SPINNERBAIT models include: (1) single-blade, such as the Eagle Spin, best for fishing in deep water and helicoptering; and (2) tandem-blade, such as the M-G spinnerbait, best for bulging because of the extra lift.

the rear, results in a hooking percentage higher than that of most other lures.

When casting bucktails, start reeling just as the lure hits the water. If you let it sink, the hook may foul on the line. Reel rapidly at first to get the blade spinning. If it starts, you'll feel the vibrations. If it doesn't, give the lure a sharp twitch. Then slow down; the blade will keep spinning.

The main considerations when selecting bucktails are size and running depth. In spring, when the water is below 60° F, use a 3- to 5-inch-long bucktail. Later, use 6- to 10-inchers. Bigger bucktails also seem to work better in low-clarity water and at night. For trophy fishing, or when hammer-handle northerns are a problem, don't be afraid to try bucktails as long as 12 inches.

How deep you want your bucktail to run depends mainly on the water depth or the depth at which the weeds top out. As a rule, if that depth is less than 5 feet, use a shallow runner; greater than 5 feet, a deep runner.

Running depth can be gauged as follows: the lighter the body, the more hair or soft-plastic dressing, and the larger and rounder the blade, the shallower the lure will track (p. 146). Also, a tandem-blade bucktail will run shallower than a single.

You can regulate the depth at which a bucktail tracks by simply changing your retrieve speed. When you speed up, the blade spins more rapidly, creating more "lift" and making the lure run shallower. If you hold your rod tip high and reel fast, even a deep runner will "bulge" the surface, making a wake that often draws the fishes' attention.

SPINNERBAITS. Because the safety-pin shaft "runs interference" for the single upturned hook, a spinnerbait will go through most heavy weeds without fouling. The blade is attached to a swivel, so it spins not only when the lure is pulled forward, but also when it sinks. The lead head makes the lure sink rapidly and acts as a keel, preventing line twist. But spinnerbaits have one drawback: the single hook reduces your hooking percentage. If you'll be fishing in open water, it pays to use a spinnerbait with a treble-hook trailer.

A spinnerbait is one of the most versatile pike-muskie lures. You can cast or troll it over shallow, weedy flats, "helicopter" it into holes in or alongside the weeds, jig it along bottom, bulge it on the surface as you would a bucktail or count it down to reach suspended fish.

Like bucktails, spinnerbaits come in single- or tandem-blade models. Singles run deeper, helicopter better and have less wind resistance, so they're easier to cast. But tandems produce more vibration, an advantage in murky water or at night. Spinnerbaits with willow-leaf blades are most weedless because the blade spins closest to the shaft. Most good spinnerbaits have thick wire shafts; those with thinner wire bend easily but vibrate more.

In spring, use ¼- to ⅜-ounce bass spinnerbaits. In summer and fall, you'll probably do better on ½- to 1-ounce sizes. Weight, dressing and blade size affect the running depth of spinnerbaits in the same way they do bucktails.

Lures shown ¾ actual size

RUNNING DEPTH of bucktails is determined by blade type, body weight and tail bulk. The top lure runs shallowest because it has a fluted Indiana blade, a body made of hollow beads and a bulky tandem tail. The middle lure runs deeper due to the French-style blade, the bullet-type body and the thinner tandem tail. The bottom lure runs deepest because of the willow-leaf blade, the solid-brass body and the single tail.

## Spoon Fishing for Pike and Muskie

Only a few decades ago, spoons were about the only lure anyone tossed at pike and muskies. And even though spoons play a lesser role in Esocid angling today, they still catch plenty of fish.

The usual way to fish a spoon is simply to retrieve or troll it at a steady pace. But spoon-fishing experts know that's not the whole story. Spoons can also be fished with an erratic stop-and-go retrieve, ripped over the weed tops, fluttered into pockets or along edges of the weeds, vertically jigged in deeper water and even skittered across the surface like a topwater.

Most pike-muskie spoons measure from 4 to 6 inches long. A wide assortment is available, ranging from thin models for maximum wobble to thick models for distance casting and vertical jigging to weedless models for thick cover. Weedless spoons work best when coupled with a pork strip, plastic curly tail or other attractor.

You don't need expensive spoons to catch pike and muskies. Any spoon will work, as long as the hooks are strong and sharp.

For the best action, clip the spoon to a thin, braided-wire leader. A stiff leader restricts the wobble too much. Many anglers prefer a single Siwash hook (p. 151) to a treble because it provides more positive hook sets and makes it easier to release fish unharmed.

### Spoon-Fishing Tips

STORE your spoons in a soft pack for longer life. Stacking them in the trays of an ordinary tackle box chips the paint and dulls the metal.

SKITTER a spoon on the surface by keeping your rod tip high as you retrieve. The spoon should ride with the convex side down.

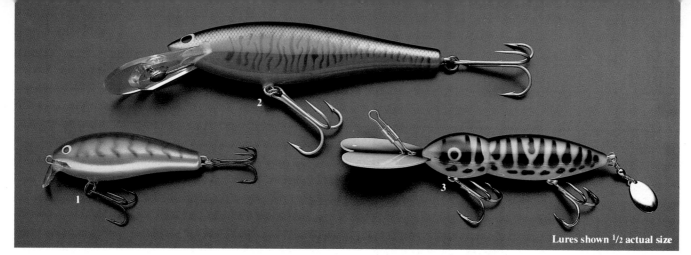

CRANKBAITS for pike-muskie fishing include: (1) shallow runners, such as the Rapala Fat Rap; (2) deep runners, such as the Bagley DB-06; and (3) extra-deep runners, such as the Whopper Stopper Hellbender.

## Fishing Pike and Muskie with Subsurface Plugs

Practically every longtime pike or muskie hound has an old, beat-up plug that is perforated with teeth marks, a reminder of past Esocid encounters.

The following categories of subsurface plugs differ considerably in action, but all are effective for pike and muskies. These plugs differ from jerkbaits (p. 153) because they wobble or vibrate when retrieved.

CRANKBAITS. The front lip gives these lures an intense wobble. Most crankbaits float at rest, which is a definite advantage when you're fishing over weeds or logs. When you feel the lure bumping an obstruction, stop reeling and it will float back up. If you hook a weed, a sharp jerk of the rod will often rip the lure free.

How deep a crankbait runs depends on the size and angle of its lip. Some dive only a few feet; others, as much as 30. As a rule, a crankbait will run twice as deep when you're trolling as when you're casting. Some crankbaits sink, so you can count them down to fish in deep water.

MINNOW PLUGS. The effectiveness of these lures is partly due to their shape. Esocids and most other predator fish prefer long, slim baitfish because they're easy to swallow.

Minnow plugs work well for casting or trolling. They have a tighter, more lifelike wobble than crankbaits. But many anglers prefer to retrieve them in jerkbait fashion to create a tantalizing stop-and-go action. When the fish aren't aggressive, try twitching a minnow plug or crankbait on the surface (p. 151).

Like crankbaits, minnow plugs come in floating and sinking models. Floaters run anywhere from a few to more than 15 feet deep. Sinkers can be counted down to any depth.

MINNOW PLUGS include: (1) shallow-running floaters, such as the Bagley 8" Bang-O-Lure; (2) deep-running floaters, such as the Bomber Diving Long A; and (3) sinkers, such as the Countdown Rapala Magnum.

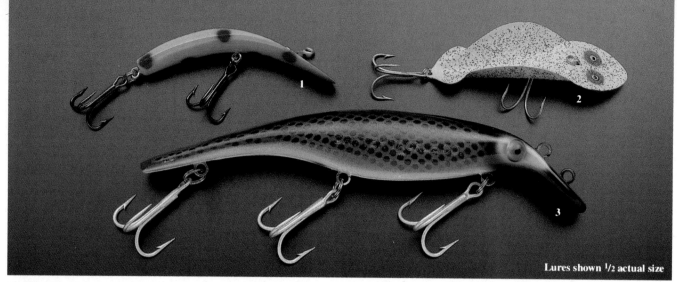

TROLLING PLUGS include: (1) shallow runners, such as a Flatfish, with the attachment eye near the snout; and (2) deep runners, such as a Spoonplug, with the attachment eye farther back from the snout. Some plugs, such as a (3) Believer, have separate attachment eyes for deep and shallow running.

Most minnow plugs are plastic, but many anglers prefer those made of balsa wood because their wobble is more intense. However, some balsa plugs are too light to cast well, especially against a stiff wind, and they won't stand up to the sharp teeth of Esocids.

When selecting balsa minnow plugs for pike and muskies, make sure the hooks are anchored well to the plug body. Some models have an internal wire that prevents the hooks from pulling out of the soft wood.

TROLLING PLUGS. These lures have a flattened or scooped-out forehead that makes them difficult to cast but produces an extra-wide wobble. Different models run at different depths, from 2 feet to 20.

Trolling over large, shallow flats or along lengthy weedlines is a good way to locate pike and muskies. Once you find them, switch to casting to cover the area more thoroughly.

Some plugs are designed for slow trolling, others for speed trolling. If you troll too fast with a slow-trolling plug, it spins or skates to the surface. Speed-trolling plugs, on the other hand, don't have much action at slow speed. To find the right speed for the plug you're using, let out a few feet of line and run the plug alongside the boat.

VIBRATING PLUGS. With the attachment eye on the back, these lures have a tight wiggle and produce high-frequency vibrations that fish can detect even in muddy water.

Most vibrating plugs sink, but some float. Sinkers are most versatile because you can cast them and count them down to the desired depth or troll them, increasing depth by letting out more line. Floating models work well over shallow weed flats. All vibrating plugs catch fewer weeds than plugs with lips.

For the best action, attach all subsurface plugs with a round-nosed snap or clip on a thin, braided-wire leader. A heavy snap-swivel or thick-wire leader will restrict the wobble too much.

To achieve maximum depth, all subsurface plugs must run perfectly straight. If they veer to one side or the other, they're "out of tune." To tune them, simply bend the attachment eye or the wire attachment arm to the opposite side.

Line diameter also affects the running depth of subsurface plugs. Thin line has less water resistance, so your lure will track deeper than with thick line. The smaller the plug, the more line diameter affects its running depth.

VIBRATING PLUGS include: (1) floating models, such as a Rat-l-Trap Floater, and (2) sinkers, such as a Rattl'n Rap. Most of these lures have internal lead shot that makes a rattling noise in addition to adding weight.

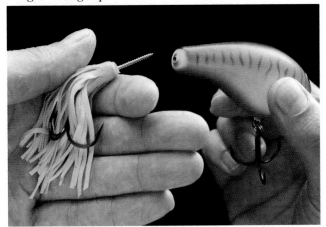

ADD a rubber skirt to a plug for more action. Remove the rear hook, thread on the skirt and replace the hook.

REPLACE the rear treble with a single Siwash hook and remove the front treble when you're catching lots of fish. You'll be able to unhook them much faster, and you're less likely to injure them.

SELECT plugs with sturdy lips such as the (1) Grandma, which has an extra-thick, strongly anchored Lexan lip, and the (2) Bagley DB-06, which has a wire connecting the lip to the body.

PAUSE a few seconds after twitching a floating minnow plug or crankbait, allowing it to float back to the surface. Then twitch it again to make it dive. A half-interested fish usually strikes when the lure is at rest.

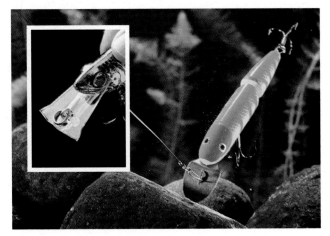

USE a metal-lipped plug when fishing on a rocky bottom. Rocks may break thin plastic lips (inset) or knock them completely off. Even if the lip stays intact, the rocks will gouge it, causing the lure to track to the side.

# Jerkbait Fishing for Pike and Muskie

These big wooden plugs have no built-in action. They do only what you make them do. When retrieved with a series of sharp jerks, they dart erratically, like an injured baitfish. This action often appeals to pike and muskies more than a regular wobbling action.

Although jerkbaits vary widely in size, shape and action, they fall into two main categories: divers, which dart downward when pulled forward; and gliders, which swing from side to side with each pull.

Divers run 2 to 4 feet deeper than gliders, so they're a better choice for working deep water. They also work better in dense weeds. They have very little side-to-side movement, so you can thread them through narrow slots in the vegetation. But there are times when the fish prefer the erratic lateral action of a glider.

Most jerkbaits float at rest, but some anglers add weight to make the lures less buoyant (p. 155). Extra weight not only makes a jerkbait run deeper, but also allows you to work it more slowly. Because it takes longer for the lure to float up after each jerk, you don't have to retrieve as fast to hold the depth.

Missed strikes are a common problem when fishing jerkbaits, especially gliders. Because of their erratic action, the fish have a hard time zeroing in on them. And when a fish grabs a jerkbait, it sometimes sinks its teeth into the wood, making it difficult to move the plug enough to set the hook.

Despite their large size and lack of built-in action, jerkbaits can be figure-eighted in much the same manner as bucktails, spoons or crankbaits. Just add some short twitches while you make the figure-eight pattern.

**Lures shown ²/₃ actual size**

GLIDERS include: (1) flashbaits, such as the Bagley B-Flat, which have an erratic action; and (2) true gliders, such as the Eddie Bait, which have a regular side-to-side gliding motion.

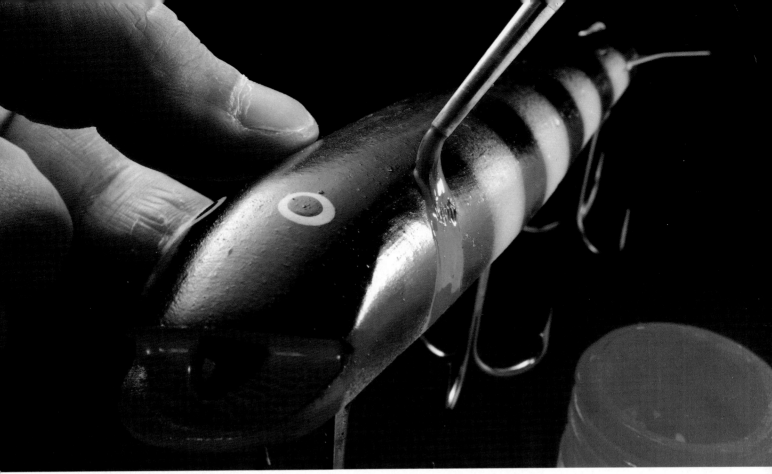

*A touch of color can make a difference*

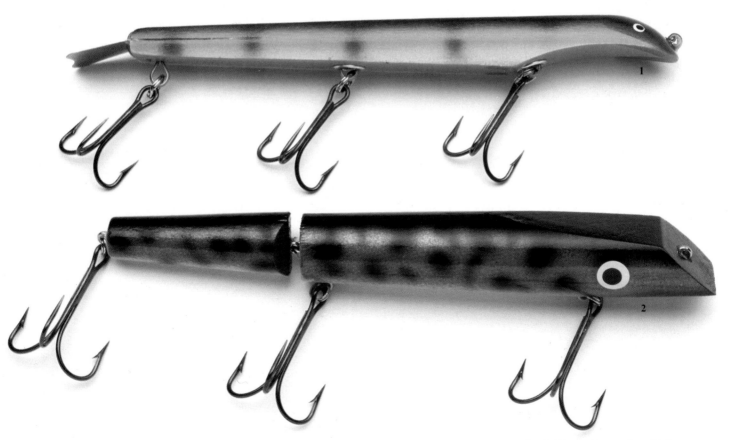

DIVERS include: (1) tailbaits, such as the Suick, which have a metal tail that can be bent to change the dive angle; and (2) true divers, such as the Stidham Sensor, in which the angle of the head determines how it dives.

DIVER. Point your rod at the lure and sweep it smoothly downward to make the lure dive (inset). Stop the rod at 6 o'clock. Reel up slack while returning the rod to the origi-nal position. Continue retrieving with a series of sweeps; how long you hesitate between sweeps determines how deep the lure will track.

GLIDER. Point your rod tip at the lure and make a 6- to 18-inch downward twitch. The lure will glide to one side (inset). Reel up the slack and twitch again before the lure finishes its glide to make it veer the other way. If you wait too long, the lure may not change direction. Continue retrieving with short, rhythmic twitches.

## How to Weight a Jerkbait

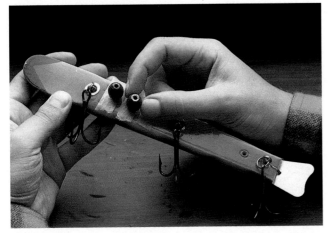

1. ATTACH several egg sinkers to the bottom of a jerkbait using small pieces of carpet tape, which has adhesive on both sides.

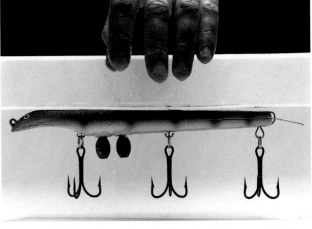

2. TEST the lure's buoyancy by floating it in water. Add enough sinkers so the lure barely floats. It should ride in a horizontal position.

3. DRILL a sinker-size hole at the exact spot each sinker was taped. Wrap masking tape around the drill bit to serve as a depth gauge.

4. INSERT the egg sinkers into the holes, then fill the holes with epoxy glue. Allow the glue to dry for at least an hour before submerging the lure.

## Quick Weighting Methods

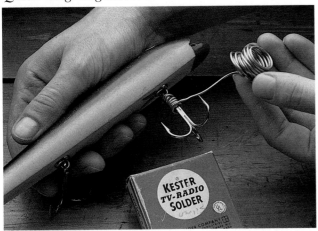

WRAP lead solder through the eye and around the shank of your jerkbait hooks until the lure floats with its back just out of the water.

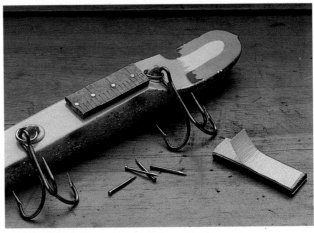

USE model weights, available at hobby shops, to weight a jerkbait. They have adhesive on one side, so you can move them to achieve the right balance. Tack them in place.

**Ted Jowett**

**Home:** *Winnipeg, Manitoba*

**Occupation:** *Fishing and hunting guide*

*Ted Jowett fishes and hunts — and helps others to do so — some 300 days a year. He starts in the long Manitoba winters, dangling lines through the ice for pike and walleyes. Springtime is bear season: he's busy preparing and setting out forty baits, big oil drums filled with fish, bread, and honey. He also schedules in some early walleye trips — fishing in the morning, hunting in the afternoon. June is for pike and for big channel cats, 20 pounds plus, in the Winnipeg River. July and August finds him guiding in northern Manitoba, beyond the tree line, where pot-bellied lakers hang near the surface and pike grow as long as church pews.*

*Come autumn, the pace really picks up. In September, Jowett fishes walleyes; by October he's hunting geese, while continuing with the walleyes — leaving home at 3 in the morning, returning at 11 at night, seven days a week. He guides bow hunters for deer from late October through November; mercifully, the goose guiding*

# The One-Two Punch for Pike

by Nat Franklin Jr.

*Ted Jowett uses European dead-bait methods and big artificial lures to outwit Canadian monster pike*

On a morning early in June, Ted Jowett launches his boat at a ramp in the heart of Whiteshell Provincial Park, in southeast Manitoba. Daybreak came at 4 a.m.; and now, only 9, it feels like lunchtime. The temperature has wasted no time hitting the mid-90s. The past two weeks have been record-breakers, nearly 100 degrees every afternoon — a condition Jowett says will make the pike fishing a real challenge, since mature northerns are cold-water fish by nature.

A bush plane floats at a dock nearby; and beside it, incongruously, a swimmer dog-paddles in almost tropical water. Jowett's water thermometer registers

*halts with the first big freeze around November first. Finally, sometime in November, the ice is solid enough for him to head out with his frostbite angling customers again.*

*"I guess it's a little hard on my system," Jowett says. "If I ever get tired of it, I'll just quit and go back to the machine shop. But I'll never get tired of it."*

*The machine shop: before becoming a guide, he worked ten-hour shifts on a 100-ton punch press. He also did stints as a farm worker, landscaper, construction worker, and delivery-truck driver. But he'd grown up fishing and hunting with his father and wanted to make a career of it, so eventually he got a sales job at a tackle shop in Winnipeg. There, he started to sign up customers for guide trips on his days off.*

*In eight years of guiding, Jowett and his parties have taken seventy pike over 20 pounds and hundreds in the teens. The biggest was just over 27 pounds. In 1987, Jowett competed in Manitoba's first pike tournament ever, a two-day event on Paint Lake. Out of a crowded field of 400 entrants, both amateur and professional, he finished in first place.*

80 at the surface — with the calendar start of summer still more than two weeks away. This will be his first pike trip since the end of bear season, and the fishing conditions could scarcely be more unusual, the pike behavior harder to predict. But Jowett is prepared for almost any eventuality. In the boat he's got a styrofoam-lined box prickling with jerkbaits, spinnerbaits, and standard bucktail spinners, plus a big cooler packed with dead smelt and other baitfish on ice.

*Jowett displays his lures and baits*

Dead bait? In this instance, it's not the result of overcrowding or bad water in a minnow bucket, but deliberate choice. Though Ted Jowett is an all-around pike angler, a pragmatist who gives stubborn fish whatever they want on a given day, his specialty is tempting them out with stone-cold, stiff-as-a-board dead bait. To the uninitiated, fishing with any baitfish that isn't alive, well and wriggling might seem a form of madness. But not to Jowett, nor to any of his pike-fishing clients. Jowett has been one of the first North American anglers to adopt the deadly dead-bait techniques imported from Europe and the British Isles.

One reason for bringing dead bait along today is purely regulatory: here in the Whiteshell Park, live bait isn't allowed. If you want to feed the northerns real meat — and there are times when this will work much better than any artificial — then your only option is a dead "live" bait.

But even if given a choice, Jowett would still do his trophy-pike fishing with dead bait, at least in the early season. Northerns are far more inclined to take a dead bait than a live one during those initial weeks of fishing after the opener. Tons of baitfish die in winter when lakes and rivers are shrouded with ice, and the pike get in the habit of scrounging — *scavenging* — these inert, easy meals. Come spring, the bottom is a veritable smorgasbord of dead bait-fish, and pike continue to feed on them well past the spawning period. Artificials? Until the water warms more and the larder of dead protein runs low, few trophy northerns are about to go chasing any zippy chunks of chrome or polystyrene.

On this late-spring day, the spawn is only three weeks past; but since then, the water has warmed much faster than normal. Jowett makes a final check of his bait and lure supplies, then cranks up and heads across Big Whiteshell Lake.

His boat is a Lund Alaskan, an 18-footer built of heavy .100-inch aluminum. Three pedestal seats for his clients form a row along the centerline; he takes out a seat or two on days when he's guiding fewer fishermen. Aft is a fourth seat, offset to one side, where he sits to operate the electric motor and the tiller-control outboard. Along each side of the hull is a large rod locker. Jowett helped Lund design this particular layout, so it's ideal for his style of fishing. His 70-horse tiller-operated outboard is more powerful than any tiller model available in the U.S.

The lake this morning is utterly flat, not a whisper of breeze. The water is clear, visibility several feet, with a thin saffron layer of pollen adrift on the surface. The sun beats down brighter and brighter; for dead-baiting, Jowett would favor wind and clouds. He sets his jaw.

"I have to be on a high note all the time" — so goes his credo of successful guiding — "a positive note. If I wake up thinking I can't catch fish, I've still got to cheer you up. So I think: just one fish, that one big trophy. If we can just present the bait properly, we might tag that one big fish."

Out comes the tackle. His rods are 6½-footers, baitcasting, medium-heavy action. The length is a compromise, a reasonably happy one: he readily acknowledges that a longer rod, 8½ feet, would be the ideal for lobbing dead-bait rigs, while a shorter rod, 5½ feet, would be handier for "throwing wood." He supplies all the tackle for his fishermen, and the compromise rods reduce the clutter on deck. He spools his reels with 17-pound mono. Artificials are rigged on 30-pound wire leaders with sturdy cross-lock snaps. For dead bait, he assembles quick-strike rigs — European devices, to his mind "the greatest invention since the telephone."

Big Whiteshell has a maximum depth of only 20 feet, so the pike cannot go deep to escape the heat. Jowett believes he will find them at a depth of 8 to 12 feet. The spot he's picked now is an extensive bed of cabbage; in places it's already grown to the surface, but most of it remains at least a few inches below, leaving plenty of room to slip a lure over it.

He starts with a big jerkbait, a Teddie, heaving it with thick forearms into openings on the outside edge of the weedbed. On the retrieve, he points the rod straight ahead and makes the lure dart a foot or so at a time, by jerking the rod tip downward until it almost touches the water. The rod stays below horizontal at all times. Because of the longer rod, he stands on one of the rod lockers to gain extra height above the water.

*Jowett keeps rod aimed at jerkbait on retrieve*

Sometimes he makes short jerks to the side. The big mistake he sees most anglers commit is sweeping the rod so far to the side they can't set the hooks when a pike hits. It takes a good hard jab, or a series of them, to pull the wood through a trophy pike's teeth and sink the barbs. When a fish hits, Jowett hauls the rod up high and hard, rather than trying to set the hook by jerking farther down or sideways.

Several pike slam his Teddie, then whip and buck through the water like overloaded leaf springs on a potholed road. A few 5-pounders, a 6, plus any number of smaller fish. He releases each one of them carefully, bending low over the side of the boat with his pliers.

Jowett is a forceful advocate of catch-and-release pike fishing. His stern pronouncements on putting trophy fish back would win the admiration of any no-kill trout nut. "Up at Nejanilini [in far northern Manitoba, where he guides in midsummer] everyone wants to take home just one trophy pike. But I say, look, pike grow slow up here, they put on maybe a pound a year. If 50 guys come up in a season and take out a 20-pound fish, you're knocking off a thousand years of growth, just like that. Pretty soon, you're going to have no trophies left in the lake."

To avoid injuring pike, he unhooks them without lifting them fully out of the water. If a picture is to be taken, he waits until the camera is ready before pulling the fish up. He weighs a trophy pike without harm by slipping a special weighing sack under it in the water, then lifting the sack out and attaching it quickly to the scales. The sacks are available commercially; they're actually fine-weave slings with a pocket at each end to keep the head and tail of the fish from slipping out. Landing nets should not be used for this purpose, since the coarse mesh will cut into a fish and scrape off the slime.

*Sack permits weighing and releasing pike unharmed*

In search of bigger game, Jowett switches to a spinnerbait for casting way back in, right over the cabbage. He likes to fish this type of lure just under the surface, so it makes a bulge on top as it travels along. His preference is a tandem-blade spinnerbait, which has two blades on a single arm, one behind the other. This design has greater lift than a single-blade model, because of the double water resistance; it's much easier to fish on the surface.

*Jowett's favorite warm-weather hardware*

He holds his rod high and reels just fast enough to keep the lure from falling into the cabbage. When it reaches an opening, he slows the retrieve to let it drop a short way beneath the surface.

*"Unbelievable"*: Jowett's terse reaction when his first spinnerbait pike of the post-bear hunt season clobbers the burbling lure. A few others take a swipe at it too, though not as many as hit the jerkbait. Jowett decides to cover more water, and trolls for a while along the outer edge of the weedbeds. He trails a big bucktail spinner about 20 yards behind the boat.

A half hour of this, with no sawlog pike to show for it, and Jowett decides to pack it in. The heat has definitely soured the fishing. A couple of years ago these same waters produced pike of 25½, 23½, 22 and several in the teens in one day of fishing.

Reasoning that the effects of the heat wave may not be as great in moving water, Jowett loads the boat and hits the road northward. On the way through Whiteshell Park, birches and aspens glow in early pale-green leaf; broods of newly hatched teal and mallards swim in ditches along the berm. Everywhere in the park, water is low: rain has been scant, and forest fires blackened some areas in the middle of May, several months earlier than the usual fire season. "Spots that used to have good cabbage with water on top are dead," says Jowett. He's discussing the river, the Winnipeg, as he gestures toward its flat, lakelike waters at a launch ramp. "This low water has really been messing us up the last few years."

The boat skims upriver to a narrows bounded by huge mounds of pink granite. The river stays flat here, no whitewater, but through the constriction a visible flow powerfully uncurls. "When the water was normal, I used to make guys get out of the boat before I went through," he explains. "The water was so fast it was a tough run." He snakes smoothly through, and then up several more miles to a dam with a brick powerhouse on top.

Surprisingly strong currents thump from a series of gates beneath. A hundred yards downstream, a necklace of oil drums strung on a thick steel cable keeps boats from running any closer. Jowett's motor churns upcurrent, blaring like a mandrill. He zips across the cable, having raised the lower unit at the last instant, pressing a button at the tip of the tiller, timing it perfectly. The button is normally the kill switch but Jowett rewired it, to avoid turning around backward to operate the tilt switch on the engine itself.

"I know these people here," he points out. Up on the dam, a worker in a hardhat gives him a high sign.

With his electric motor, Jowett maneuvers near the last gate, where the current eddies out in a slack pocket beside a natural outcrop of granite. Once in position, he sets to work with the tackle.

Jowett's version of the quick-strike rig consists of 18 inches of Sevenstrand braided-steel wire, 30-pound test, with two treble hooks attached. The hook on the front tip of the wire is a size 6 or 8; the other one, which slides along the wire, is a size 10. Jowett prefers bronzed trebles, not stainless, since they'll rust out of a fish's jaw if a break-off should occur. The wire is connected to his line with a large swivel. On the line itself, a slip-bobber is rigged.

The dead bait is usually a mooneye, smelt, tullibee or sucker. It should measure 6 to 12 inches long; big pike generally go for the bigger baits within this range.

Jowett inserts the front hook first, on the top side of the baitfish straight above the gill opening. The rear hook is inserted into the body at the front of the dorsal fin; since the hook slides on the wire, the rig adjusts to baitfish of any size.

Rod inclined to the rear, both hands on the grip, Jowett takes a long, hard look at the rolling water. The hook-studded baitfish hangs in air, slowly revolving: on lighter tackle, it wouldn't be a half-bad catch.

He launches it smoothly toward the edge of the current emerging from the gate. The throw is short, an easy lob that won't separate the bait from the hooks. The bait sinks until the bobber stop on the line draws snug against the bobber; Jowett feeds a bit of line as the rig drifts on the current, so the bobber has just enough slack to stand up straight. The rule on setting bait depth, he says, is to put it either halfway to the bottom or within 2 feet of the bottom. In winter and early spring, he gets 90 percent of his pike close to the bottom, but once the water warms up he varies his depth more.

Another tip: don't let your bobber get farther than 35 feet from the boat, or hook-sets will be tough because of the sharp angle formed in the line at the bobber. When the rig starts to drift too far away in the current, he reels in a few yards of line and lets it drift again. Occasionally he starts over with a new cast, though casting is best kept to a minimum so the bait isn't torn loose.

"I usually set the hook within a few seconds after the bobber goes down and moves off," says Jowett. "If the bobber's moving toward me, I wait a little longer. Your hooking percentage is best when the fish is swimming away.

"A pike will take a bait in its mouth crosswise, and the idea is to set the hook before it gets the bait aimed down its gullet and starts to swallow." With a single-hook rig, you miss too many fish if you strike early: the hook may not be in the fish's mouth till the bait is swallowed, or nearly so. But with the quick-strike rig, one hook or the other will generally be in striking position whenever the pike picks

*How to Tie and Fish a Quick-Strike Rig*

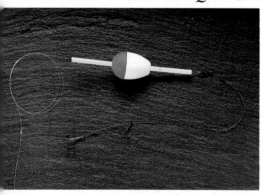

THREAD on slip-bobber, add swivel and wire leader, slip on size 10 treble, crimp on size 6 or 8 treble.

HOOK the baitfish with main treble above the gill opening; sliding treble at the front of dorsal fin.

LOB-CAST with a smooth sidearm motion to avoid snapping the bait off the hook.

160

up the bait. If you wait too long to strike, the fish will get the hooks deep. That means it usually won't give you a great battle; nor will you be able to turn it loose uninjured.

A flutter of the bobber, then it heels over and abruptly vanishes. For a moment, the eggshell color of the sunken float shines up through the scum and bubbles drifting on the surface. Jowett holds off, rod pointed low, but not for long: the period of grace seems five or six seconds, at most.

He sets the hooks with a flick of the wrists. With a quick-strike rig, a powerful hook set is not necessary and may even rip the hooks out. The fish affixes itself to the current, heading for the oil drums and deep realms beyond. In five minutes or so, the stiff rod and Jowett's thumb on the spool take a toll. Fifty yards out, the fish starts to tire, thrashing on the surface and allowing Jowett to work it back to the boat.

Jowett goes after the hooks with his pliers. One treble is caught in the acute angle of the jaw; the other hangs unattached. Frequently, Jowett says, both hooks will be in the fish, one on each side of the mouth. A hook may have ripped loose in this case: the pike is a fine one, close to 15 pounds.

In the course of this scorching northern day Jowett catches — and releases — at least a score of good-sized pike from the chutes and eddies below the dam. Most fall to his quick-strike rig, but several hit jerkbaits and spinners. "You get the more aggressive fish with the jerkbait," he says. "But the bigger ones go for the dead bait."

He recalls the time when he was guiding for catfish on the river, and his client decided he wanted to catch a pike. Jowett rigged him up with a quick-strike rig and a dead bait, and tossed anchor below the powerhouse. The anchor was necessary because he didn't have his electric motor along — he doesn't ordinarily use it when catfishing. Within seconds, the client's bobber shot under the surface and he set the hook. "How does it feel?" Jowett wanted to know, as the fish ran with the rig. "Like a 20-pounder," said the client, who'd been hauling in catfish about that size.

At that instant, a sudden release of heavy water rumbled from the dam gates, washing the pike right under the boat. Jowett got a glimpse of the fish and saw it would go far more than 20 pounds — maybe 15 pounds more, in fact. But on its way past the anchor rope, one of the trebles snagged; the other tore loose from the fish. Finale of saga — or so Jowett figured. Only minutes later, the former catfisherman tied into another pike. This one came aboard: all 21 pounds of it.

*Jowett lands hefty pike below Winnipeg River dam*

Besides dams, Jowett's favorite springtime spots for fishing dead bait are the mouths of creeks and backwaters, and openings into shallow bays where the pike have spawned. Dead bait will take fish in summer too, though the fish generally like something that moves faster then, and artificials are more productive in most cases. Also, weeds are a problem when fishing in summer; to avoid snags with a dead bait, you're limited to fishing the edges of the beds. If you do fish dead bait in the warmer months, Jowett recommends the "high-percentage spots — rocky points or any place along shore where pike might concentrate or funnel past." Fall is good for dead bait, though he's less likely then to use a quick-strike rig than a big bucktail jig baited with a dead sucker.

Toward the end of our trip, the heat finally breaks. A cold rain falls briefly in the morning. The midday air temperature is 40 degrees lower than the day before; the river temperature plummets to 66. But when Jowett is fishing for pike, cold fronts don't bother him. "We're after one fish," he announces. "We can get him anytime. We just put the bait right in front of a fish."

He puts it there, and he catches plenty.

# Northern Pike & Muskie Tips

## Spokes for Spinners

A lot of muskie and pike fishermen make their own spinnerbaits and in-line spinners. Most of the components are readily available from specialty fishing tackle stores and mail-order firms. But you may have trouble finding the stiff, heavy stainless steel wire (at least .060 inch) you need to make really large spinners and spinnerbaits. If the wire is too light, fish will bend it and the spinners won't spin properly. A ready source of heavy wire: bicycle wheel spokes. The rustproof spokes are available in any bicycle shop.

## ← Add Flash to Muskie Lures

Muskies are notorious for following lures to the boat and turning away at the last minute without striking. If you are getting follows but no strikes, try dressing up the lure with a small spinner. The added flash and vibration is often all it takes to trigger a strike. Here's how to add spinners to three different kinds of lures:

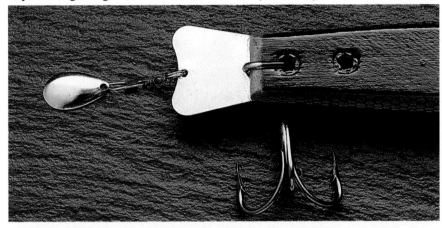

JERKBAITS with metal tail blades, such as Suicks, can be modified by drilling a small hole at the center of the rear edge of the tail blade. Add a split ring, a snap-swivel and a size 0, 1 or 2 spinner. The greater drag of sizes larger than this inhibits the lure's action. The snap allows you to easily remove or change the spinner blade.

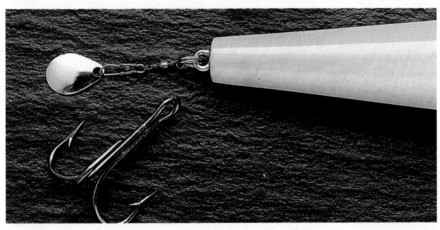

GLIDEBAITS and other jerkbaits without metal tail blades, such as Reef Hawgs and Eddie Baits, can also be fitted with a spinner blade. Remove the rear treble hook. Then replace it with a split ring, a snap-swivel and a size 0, 1 or 2 spinner blade.

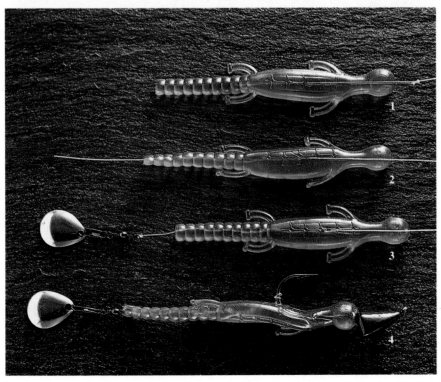

CREATURES, such as big soft-plastic waterdog imitations, can be modified by threading a long needle with 10-pound mono (1) into the "chest" of the creature and out the tail. If you can't find a needle long enough to do the job, use a piece of stiff piano wire with a loop in one end. (2) Pull the needle and line out the tip of the tail. (3) Tie line to a snap-swivel and number 1, 2 or 3 spinner. (4) Pull the swivel snug to the end of the tail. Insert a large jig with a stout hook into the head of the lure; tie off the line on the bend of the hook.

## Weed-Resistant Pike Plugs

Pike are suckers for big, metal-lipped plugs such as Pikie Minnows, but when the fish are lurking in shallow weeds, these plugs are impossible to use. They run too deep, and the lip collects weeds.

Here's a way to modify these plugs so they run shallower and don't pick up as many weeds:

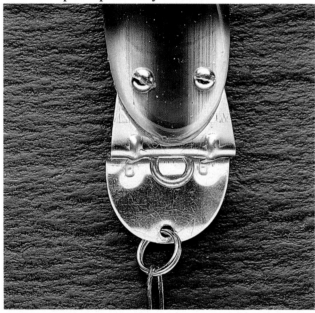

DRILL a hole near the end of the lip and insert a split ring; attach your leader. The plug will run just under the surface. And weeds will slip down the line and pass under the plug, rather than hang up on the lip.

## Muskies After Dark

Boat traffic and fishing pressure can force muskies to feed at night. Successful fisherman change their habits, too. Fish the same areas you would during the day, and try shallower areas as well. Use bucktails or jointed plugs, working them with a steady retrieve so the fish can easily home in on them.

## Go Deep for Big Summertime Pike

Fishermen catch plenty of good-sized pike in shallow weedy bays in spring, but when the water warms up, they get nothing but "hammer handles" in these areas. The lack of big pike in summer had led to the mistaken belief that big pike lose their teeth or have sore mouths in summer and don't feed. But in reality, they're feeding more than ever.

The main reason for the scarcity of big pike in summer is that anglers aren't fishing deep enough. As pike get larger, they prefer cooler water. In some cases, they'll stay in shallow water and congregate around spring holes, artesian wells, the mouths of trout streams, or other specific point sources of cold water. But if there are no point sources, pike have no choice but to go deep.

If there is adequate oxygen in the lake depths, they'll go as deep as 50 feet and occasionally down to 100. Lake trout anglers sometimes catch big pike. At these depths, they're generally feeding on good-sized baitfish, such as ciscoes and whitefish, and you'll have to use similar-sized baits to catch them.

## Improve Glidebait Action

A wire leader deadens the action of a glidebait, such as an Eddie Bait or Reef Hawg. But you can increase the glide and the side-to-side motion by inserting a split ring (arrow) between the leader and the bait. The ring allows freer play between the steel leader loop and the eye of the plug.

If you're using a heavy line and are concerned about the strength of the connection, solder the ring, making sure to file all rough edges that would inhibit movement of the lure. Or you can fit a small split ring inside a larger one.

## Weight Bucktails Quickly

Fishermen often weight bucktails to make them run deeper or to cast farther into a stiff wind. But sinkers added to the line makes casting awkward; the sinker and lure twirl like a bolo. You can eliminate tangles by adding weight directly to the lure. Here's how:

ATTACH a Snap-Loc bell sinker of the appropriate weight to the split ring or wire loop that holds the treble hook. These sinkers make changing or removing weight easy.

## Protect Hands From Sharp Teeth

The needle-sharp teeth of pike and muskies, and the large hooks you use to catch these fish, are a constant danger and can inflict serious wounds in an instant. Protect your hands with heavy buckskin gloves while landing and unhooking these fish. The hooks aren't likely to penetrate the thick leather.

## Split Rings Improve Hooking

Muskies and big pike often manage to throw the hook by twisting and thrashing against the weight of a plug. Improve your chances of landing the fish by inserting split rings between the lure and trebles. The rings allow the hooks freer play so big fish can't twist free or bend hooks as easily. Here's how to add them:

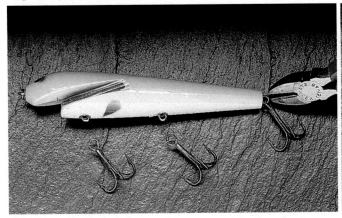

CUT off the old treble hooks or remove them by opening the eye of the hook hanger.

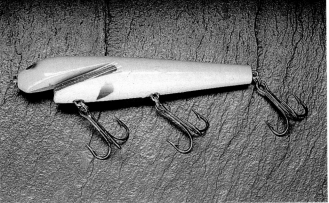

ADD split rings or double split rings and new trebles; close the eye of the hook hanger.

Panfish

# Fishing for Crappies

Catching crappies can be ridiculously easy; or it can be next to impossible. In spring, when crappies school in shallow bays, youngsters with cane poles take home heavy stringers. But when the fish suspend in open water, even expert anglers have trouble catching them.

Unlike sunfish which are naturally curious, crappies shy away from any unusual disturbance, especially in clear water. Even experienced scuba divers can seldom approach crappies. This fact has a bearing on your angling techniques. Keep your distance, avoid unnecessary movements or noise, and use the lightest line possible for the conditions.

The standard crappie rig consists of a small float, split-shot, and a plain hook baited with a minnow. Most fishermen in the North use #4 or #6 hooks. But southern anglers often use much larger hooks.

Many southern fishermen *tightline* for crappies. They lower the bait to bottom on a tandem hook rig tied with 2/0 to 4/0 light-wire hooks and a 1-ounce sinker. With the line nearly vertical, they bounce the sinker off stumps, logs or other snaggy cover. The heavy weight allows them to feel the cover without snagging the hooks. If a hook should become snagged, a strong pull will bend the light wire enough to free the hook.

When tightlining, most anglers use bait-casting gear or medium power spinning tackle. You can get by with ultralight spinning gear and 4-pound line in snag-free water. Veteran anglers prefer cane or extension poles with 15- to 20-pound line for fishing tight spots.

Fly-fishing for crappies has not gained widespread popularity, but it can be extremely effective, particularly at spawning time. Subsurface flies take more fish than poppers or floating bugs.

Crappies strike less aggressively than most other panfish. At times, they barely move the bobber. Or the float may start to move against the wind. With an artificial lure, the only sign of a strike may be a slight sideways movement of the line.

A slow retrieve will usually catch the most crappies. They seldom strike a fast-moving lure. Keep your line tight after setting the hook. A crappie's soft mouth tears easily, so the hook can fall out if the line goes slack.

# Where to Find Crappies

Crappies are nomads, roaming throughout natural lakes, reservoirs and large river systems. They sometimes ignore structure and cover. In one study on a Tennessee reservoir, crappies were recovered as far as 18 miles from the site where they were tagged.

The whereabouts of crappies depends on the season and weather. Movement patterns in natural lakes differ from those in reservoirs.

NATURAL LAKES. Crappies begin to bite shortly after ice-out or when the water warms to the mid-40s. The fish move into shallow, black-bottomed bays or channels connecting lakes. These waters warm faster than other areas and have the earliest crops of plankton.

In lakes that lack shallow bays or channels, look for crappies just outside weedlines. Finding them can be difficult because they may be scattered.

When temperatures rise to the mid-50s, crappies begin moving into the vicinity of their spawning areas. Black-bottomed bays often lack nesting habitat, so crappies move to areas with harder bottoms.

The best spawning areas have sand, gravel or rock bottoms. They have a moderate growth of submerged or emergent vegetation and are seldom deeper than 5 feet. Many crappies move into bays or

*Crappie Locations in Natural Lakes*

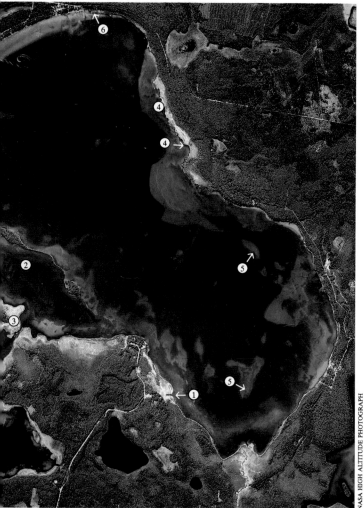

EARLY SPRING-EARLY FALL locations include: (1) dead-end channel, (2) shallow isolated bay, (3) channels connecting lakes, (4) weedy shoals, (5) shallow rock piles and sunken islands, (6) docks in shallow water.

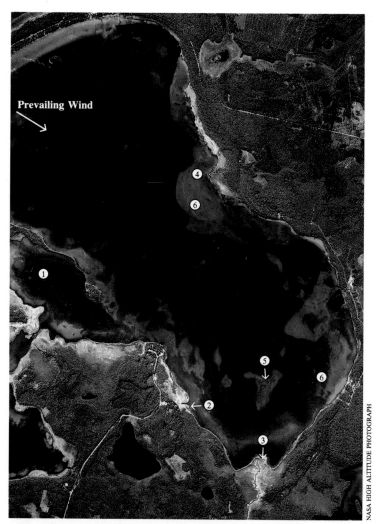

SPAWNING AREAS in natural lakes include: (1) sheltered bays, (2) dead-end channel, (3) mouth of inlet, (4) points with emergent weeds, (5) shallow humps with emergent weeds, (6) shallow flats with emergent weeds.

canals sheltered from prevailing winds, but the largest fish generally spawn on main lake shoals, points, humps and rock piles. Some crappies nest near inlets and outlets.

Crappies in bays and canals spawn earlier than fish in the main lake. Mid-lake humps warm more slowly than inshore areas and are the last to hold spawning crappies.

During the early stages of the spawning period, crappies filter into deep, sparse edges of weedbeds. At the peak of spawning, shallower, thicker parts of weedbeds hold more fish.

After spawning, crappies that nested in bays and canals return to the main lake. They often suspend just off breaklines near entrances to the bays and canals. Main lake spawners frequently scatter over a weedy flat between the spawning area and the drop-off. In lakes without weedy flats, crappies cruise along drop-offs.

In summer, look for crappies in deeper water. Prime locations include rock piles and humps that top off at 12 to 20 feet and have some weeds.

Crappies also hang along shoreline breaks and edges of gradually tapering points. Some of the best slopes have cabbage. Although crappies usually relate to some type of structure, they may suspend over a featureless bottom.

In early fall, crappies begin moving toward the shallows. They form tight schools along weedlines or just inside them. When the weeds begin to die off, the fish school around rock piles and sunken islands in deeper water. In late fall, they move away from structure and suspend over deep water. Some fish gather near spring holes where the temperature is

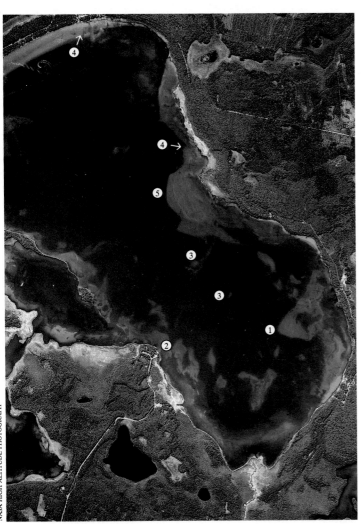

SUMMER locations include: (1) submerged point, (2) gradually tapering shoreline points, (3) deep rock piles and sunken islands, (4) irregular weedlines, (5) deep edges of weedy flats.

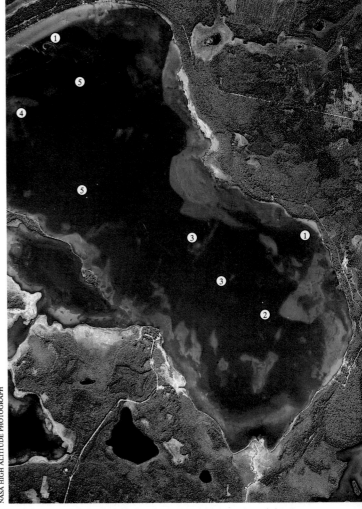

LATE FALL-WINTER locations include: (1) deep weedlines, (2) deep water off submerged point, (3) deep rock piles and sunken islands, (4) deep flats, (5) deep areas in open water.

warmer than the surrounding water. They remain in these areas through winter.

RESERVOIRS. Prior to spawning, crappies congregate around entrances to creek arms. The best arms have dense stands of timber, active streams flowing in, and maximum depths of 20 to 35 feet. As the water warms, the fish begin moving up the creek channels toward their spawning grounds. Look for them along creek channel drop-offs or in secondary coves just off the main creek arm.

Crappies usually spawn near woody cover in the back half of a cove. Check for spawning activity at the extreme back end, on shallow points, on shoreline flats or near small inlet streams. Shallow, timbered coves off the main lake will also attract spawners. Large crappies generally nest at 3 to 4 feet; smaller fish spawn shallower.

After spawning, crappies begin filtering toward the main body of the lake. The best post-spawn locations include drop-offs along the creek channel and near standing timber, stumps, brush and fallen trees close to the channel.

Most crappies move to the main lake by summer, but some remain near creek arm entrances. Prime summertime areas also have dense, woody cover. Look for steep points near deep water, drop-offs along the main river channel, and plunging shorelines near the dam.

*Crappie Locations in Reservoirs*

EARLY SPRING-EARLY FALL locations include: (1) points at mouths of creek arms, (2) edges of creek channel (small dashes), (3) secondary creek arms, (4) marinas, (5) bridges, (6) shallow main lake cove.

SPAWNING AREAS include: (1) woody shallows in the back ends of coves, (2) stream inlets, (3) shallow points, (4) large flats. Some fish spawn in (5) shallow coves on the main lake.

In early fall, crappies return to the entrances of creek arms. When the water temperature drops to the mid-60s, the fish begin moving up the creek arms toward pre-spawn locations. They feed heavily along the way.

When the water falls into the mid-40s, the fish start moving back toward the main lake, stopping at post-spawn locations along the way. As winter approaches, crappies migrate to deep water near their summer haunts. They form tight schools at depths of 20 to 40 feet. Some move to depths exceeding 60 feet, but these fish are seldom caught.

DAILY MOVEMENT. Crappies usually head deeper in response to bright light. Anglers catch most fish in morning and evening, and on overcast days when fish are in shallow water. In late fall, winter and early spring, crappies frequently move into the shallows in mid-afternoon. They feed heavily once the sun has warmed the water.

Crappies commonly suspend during midday, but may suspend at any time. On dark days, they sometimes move to within a few feet of the surface.

Cold fronts have a dramatic effect on daily movement, especially before spawning. If the temperature drops in a shallow bay, crappies move to deeper water. They feed very little under cold front conditions, but fishermen who locate a concentration usually catch a few fish.

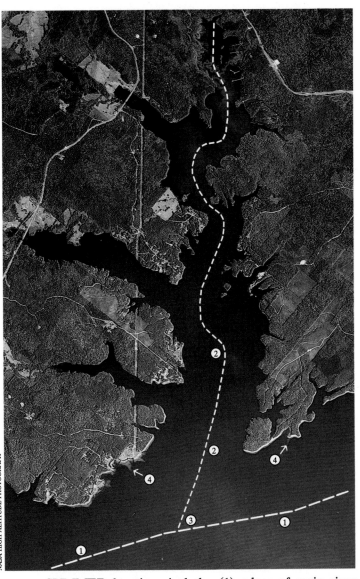

SUMMER locations include: (1) edges of main river channel (large dashes), (2) edges of creek channel, (3) intersection of main channel and creek channel, (4) submerged points in the main body of the reservoir.

LATE FALL-WINTER locations include: (1) the main river channel, (2) deep sections of the creek channel, (3) sharp-breaking shorelines, (4) deep shoreline points on the main lake, (5) deep coves on the main lake.

# How to Catch Crappies

Most crappies are caught on minnows or lures that resemble minnows. A slow, erratic retrieve is best, although crappies occasionally strike fast-moving lures. Twitching the lure, then allowing it to settle back, entices stubborn crappies to bite. They are likely to grab the lure as it falls.

Choice of lures depends on the depth of the crappies. Jigs and small, deep-diving plugs are good for deep water. When crappies are shallow, use floating-diving plugs, spoons or spinners.

The *countdown* method is used when casting jigs for suspended crappies. To find the right depth, cast the jig, then count as it sinks. After several seconds, begin the retrieve. Vary the count on successive casts until a crappie strikes, then stay with that count.

Light tackle is popular among crappie fishermen. Most use 2- to 6-pound test line, but 12- to 20-pound test may be necessary when fishing in thick cover, such as stumps or brush piles. If a bobber is used, it should be small enough so a crappie can pull it down easily.

The crappie nickname, papermouth, is derived from the paper-thin membrane around its mouth. Once a crappie is hooked, do not reset the hook or pump the rod. While these techniques may be necessary for other gamefish, they could tear the hook from the crappie's mouth.

HOOK minnows according to the angling technique. For bobber-fishing, hook the minnow behind the dorsal fin. When trolling, hook it through the lips. For jigging, hook the minnow in the head or through the eye sockets.

## *How to Tightline for Crappies*

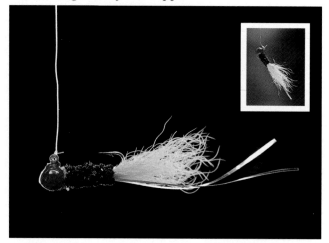

1. TIE on a 1/16- to 1/48-ounce jig and slide the knot to the top of the eye so the jig hangs horizontally. Adjust the knot often; if it slips to the front of the eye (inset), the jig rides vertically and looks unnatural.

2. SCULL with a short paddle to slowly move the boat through likely crappie water. You can best control the boat by sculling from the front end. Sculling allows precise boat control and is even quieter than an electric motor.

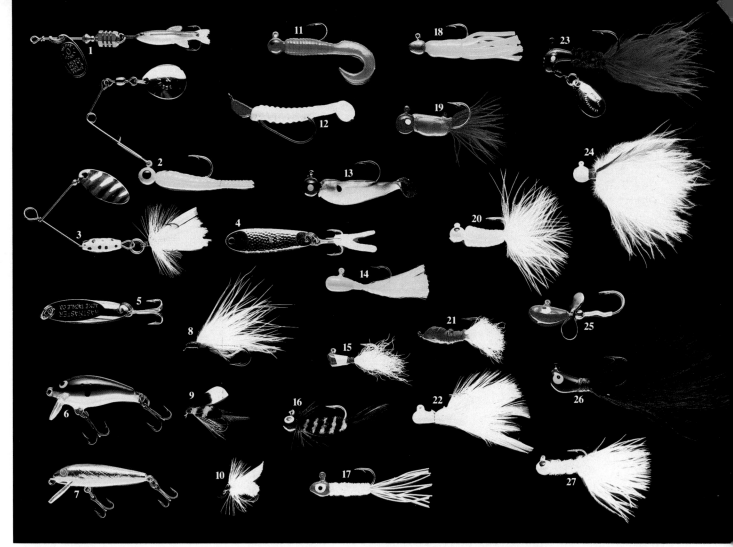

LURES for crappies include: (1) Comet®-Mino, (2) Beetle Spin™, (3) Super Shyster®, (4) Hopkins Shorty® with pork rind, (5) Kastmaster, (6) Fat Rap®, (7) Minnow/Floater, (8) streamer, (9) McGinty, (10) White Miller, (11) Twister® Teeny, (12) Crappie Slider, (13) Sassy® Shad, (14) Quiver® Jig, (15) Dart, (16) Bumblebee Jig, (17) Lightnin'™ Bug, (18) Tiny Tube™, (19) Hal-Fly®, (20) Fuzz-E-Grub®, (21) Crappie Killer, (22) No-Alibi, (23) Road Runner®, (24) Maribou Jig, (25) Whistler®, (26) bucktail jig, (27) Crappie Jig™.

3. HOLD your rod steady as the boat moves along. Crappies often prefer a steady swimming motion to an erratic jigging action. Fish can be at different depths, so you'll have to experiment to find the right depth.

4. COMPARE depth settings when one angler starts catching crappies. Other anglers in the boat should adjust their lines to fish at exactly the same depth. Sometimes a few inches can make a big difference.

# World's Best Crappie Bait?

by Frank Sargeant

*Tom Floroski catches plenty of giant crappies on his paddletail grubs, but …*

**Tom Floroski**

**Home:** *Milford, Connecticut*

**Occupation:** *Medical electronics technician*

*Tom Floroski grew up in Connecticut and spent a good share of his youth fishing for panfish and bass. He still pursues those species with a passion. In the early 1980s, Floroski started fishing in bass tournaments at the urging of Russ Hall, winning the first two tournaments he entered. But he especially likes fishing for crappies. "I love crappies of any size," he says, "and catching the big ones is as much a challenge as catching a 10-pound bass." On a recent trip, Floroski boated several crappies over 2 pounds and a pair over 3 pounds, the biggest weighing in at 3 pounds 4 ounces.*

Tom Floroski and Russ Hall are alike in a lot of ways. Both of the bearded giants are prominent names in Connecticut fishing. Between them, they've won the state tournament bass championships ten times running.

Both started fishing at age 5. And both enjoy catching crappies as much as bass. Their specialty is slab crappies, 2- to 3-pounders. They fish together much of the time, and a good deal of their tournament fishing is done as a team. Aside from that, they get out two or three times a week for fun, spring through fall; and in the winter they team up on a few ice-fishing trips.

They even operate the same type of boat, a vintage Ranger, and they

*... Russ Hall, his fishing partner, says that kellies are the world's best crappie bait*

use many of the same angling techniques. But when it comes to crappie fishing, they go about things a little differently.

Floroski prefers to fish fast and cover a lot of water, so he relies heavily on small jigs tipped with plastic grub bodies. His favorite design is a simple paddletail — no wriggling tail or octopus legs to help attract attention. "I can locate the fish with jigs a lot faster than with minnows," he explains.

Hall's philosophy: "Nothing imitates live bait like live bait." Most of the time, he knows where the fish are, so it's just a matter of giving them a bait that they like. And, according to Hall, "The world's best live bait for crappies is kellies."

**Russ Hall**

**Home:** *Orange, Connecticut*

**Occupation:** *Inspector at aircraft-engine plant*

*Russ Hall is the founder of a bass-fishing club in Connecticut, but like Tom Floroski, he'd just as soon fish for crappies. "I love the competition of bass tournaments," he says, "but when I fish for fun and food I'd rather have crappies." Hall takes his fishing seriously, logging the results of every trip, then studying the log carefully to help plan future trips. "A person has to pay his dues and invest a lot of time to become a good fisherman," he says. "When I was growing up, I didn't chase girls or get into trouble — I was too busy fishing."*

*Hall (foreground) and Floroski get started early*

When Hall refers to kellies, he actually means mummichogs, which are members of the killifish family. Mummichogs are extremely hardy baitfish found mainly in brackish waters along the Atlantic coast, particularly in estuaries and salt marshes. Presumably, the name "kelly" is a shortened version of the family name.

Both anglers admit that they'll switch to different baits when their favorites aren't working. Floroski always keeps a few kellies handy, just in case. "What usually happens is you get on the fish with a jig, and you catch four or five, then they seem to get wise to it," he says. "When that happens, you either have to back off the spot and rest it thirty minutes or so, or you have to switch to live bait. I'd rather switch. When you do, you can usually go ahead and catch all you want, as long as you stay well back from the spot and don't run your trolling

motor right on top of them." Similarly, Hall may use a jig when he's prospecting new water.

Recently, I joined the pair for a few days of fishing, so I had a chance to observe their crappie-catching tactics firsthand.

I'd timed my trip just about right. It was late October, and the very best period for lunker crappies, they say, is fall and early winter.

"Crappies are scattered all over a lake or river in summer," Hall explains, "but when the water drops below 50 degrees, they start to school up and feed really strong wherever they can find baitfish concentrations. In the lakes around here, that's usually over offshore humps, water maybe 5 or 6 feet deep next to drops into maybe 20 or 30 feet.

"In the Connecticut River, they move into the boat basins and marinas — again, about the same depth, with plenty of little baitfish hanging around the docks and underwater cover."

The days I was with them, we fished the river, probing a boat basin that covered about two acres. While yachtsmen rushed to pull out their boats ahead of the freeze-up, we eased around the docks in the team's Ranger bass boats and just about wore ourselves out catching fish.

On the first day, I went with Floroski. We fished mainly with 1/32-ounce jig heads rigged with 1/2-inch paddletail grubs in a silver-smoke shade. The tiny lures are tossed up against docks, pilings or other cover.

The trick with either jigs or live bait is to get the offering very close to the spot where the crappies are holding. In the marinas, you have to cast right up to the docks, so the jig or bait falls within an inch or two of the cover.

*Floroski's favorite jigs: (1-4) Cabela's Pro Crappie Jigs; (5-6) Toledo Tackle's Feather Grubs*

"The fish don't want to move much in the cold water," Floroski says. "If you toss it a foot away from the spot where they're at, you won't get half as many hits."

After you cast the jig, you allow it to sink all the way to bottom, then you retrieve it in minute twitches. That is, you *try* to retrieve it in minute twitches. More than half the time, something would eat the jig before we could start to crank. Sometimes it was a slab crappie. And if a crappie didn't take the jig, a yellow perch, bluegill, or junior-sized largemouth did. The basin was stiff with panfish of all types.

Floroski notes that a deft touch is necessary when fishing the small jigs. For maximum sensitivity he recommends a 5-foot light graphite spinning rod, an ultralight spinning reel, and 4- or 6-pound mono. "The fish don't want much motion in the lure. Sometimes a fish just eats it and the only way you know it's there is by feeling resistance, so I set

the hook whenever anything feels the slightest bit unusual. A lot of times when the lure is dropping, you won't feel anything at all. But you might see the line twitch just a bit, the way it will when a bass takes a sinking plastic worm."

Floroski's strategy paid off — during the course of the afternoon, we caught well over a hundred panfish, including several pound-and-a-half crappies.

The next morning, Hall and I went back to the same spot, this time toting a bucket full of kellies.

"When it's cold, kellies will live in wet moss," Hall says. "You don't even have to keep them in water. They're easy to catch, too. You can seine them, or trap them. Put a can of cat food in a wire trap and set it in shallow water in a tidal creek. Next morning, the trap will be stuffed with them. You don't have to aerate the water to keep them alive. They stay calm in the bait bucket so they're not killing themselves by banging the sides like

*How to Catch and Keep Kellies*

TRAP kellies by placing a wire minnow trap in shallow, brackish water in a tidal creek or salt marsh. Bait the trap with a can of cat food.

KEEP the kellies alive in cold weather in a container filled with damp grass or moss. In warmer weather, keep them in water in a bait bucket.

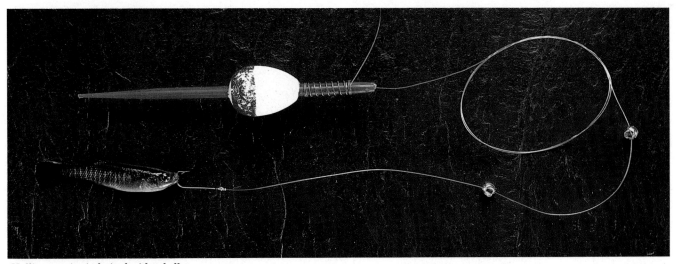

*Hall's crappie rig baited with a kelly*

177

*Crappies hang near marina dock posts in late fall*

shiners do. And they're tough — you can catch two crappies on one bait if you want to."

A little while after he told me this, he managed to catch four crappies on a single 2-inch kelly. When he finally took it off the hook, it still had the grit to swim slowly off.

Hall fishes his kellies on light-wire hooks, size 4 or 6, running the sharpened points through the thin membrane just behind their lips. He uses a spring-lock bobber with a body about the size of a dime and a 3-inch quill. He adds two or three split-shot so the body of the float sinks, leaving only the quill

above water. When a crappie takes, the quill drops like a periscope below the surface — or on occasion, pops to the surface and lies on its side.

"Crappies sometimes take from below, rising up to gulp the bait," Hall says. "When that happens, the bobber flops over instead of dropping, because they're raising the sinkers right up with the bait. That's the time to set the hook."

Hall's tackle includes a 6-foot graphite spinning rod, light power, and a spinning reel spooled with 4- or 6-pound mono. The outfit is not as sensitive as Floroski's ultralight, but sensitivity is not much

*Hall reels in crappie that hit within inches of dock*

of an issue when bobber-fishing, and the longer rod works better for setting the hook.

In just over two hours, Hall and I iced maybe fifty whopper crappies, with a few pushing 2 pounds. We caught considerably fewer small panfish than Floroski and I had taken the previous day, but the difference may have been due in part to a change in the weather. A cold front passed through overnight, and Hall speculated that the chilly weather may have moved the big crappies into the boat basin.

But even if the weather played a role in our success, it's difficult to deny that kellies are a tremendous crappie bait.

It's surprising that a bait so effective hasn't gained popularity in other regions of the country. Although kellies are found only along the coast, other species of killifish are widely distributed and would probably work nearly as well. The banded killifish, for instance, is found throughout the northeastern and north-central states, as far west as the Dakotas.

During my short stay, we did all of our fishing in Connecticut River boat basins and marinas. We didn't have a chance to fish the team's other prime fall and early-winter spots — submerged humps in area lakes. Nevertheless, the team offered some advice on fishing spots of this type. First, they find the right kind of hump using a chart recorder or flasher. If they spot fish, they mark the hump with a plastic float. After that, they back off to sieve it with casts until they home in on a school of crappies.

Once they have a school pinpointed, both anglers prefer to anchor upwind at the edge of casting range, rather than continue drifting or controlling the boat with the electric motor. "The more the boat moves around, the sooner the fish stop biting," Hall says.

Though some anglers contend that crappies and most other fish slow down their feeding as colder weather arrives, Hall and Floroski believe otherwise. "We've had good fishing right into December most years," Hall notes. "In fact, on the days we've caught the largest crappies of the year, we've actually had to use the boats as icebreakers in the marinas, running them up on the ice and cracking the skin. Then we go somewhere else and do the same thing, and half an hour later come back to the first spot and catch big fish."

The ice sets in permanently sometime in late December or early January, depending on whether the power plant up the river is heating the water. Even after ice-up, Floroski says, crappies will continue to bite for those hardy enough to go after them.

The bearded giants are definitely hardy enough.

*Hall lands a "slab" that pushes 2 pounds*

# Fishing for Sunfish

Catching small sunfish is easy. But taking big ones requires more know-how. Small sunfish form large, loose schools near the shelter of shallow weeds, docks, bridges or other cover in shallow water. Even inexperienced fishermen have little trouble finding them. In addition, small sunnies are curious, often swarming around any small object tossed into their midst.

Bigger sunfish tend to be loners, but occasionally collect in small groups. They stay in deeper water and are less inquisitive than small sunfish. They inspect baits carefully, backing off from anything that looks suspicious.

To present a bait or lure naturally, expert panfish anglers use light line and small hooks. Six-pound, clear monofilament works well in most situations. But some fishermen prefer 4-pound line in extremely clear water or when the fish seem reluctant to bite. In timber, brush or dense weeds, many use line as heavy as 20-pound test to free snagged hooks.

Most sunfish have tiny mouths, so #8 or #10 hooks are good choices. Some anglers use even smaller hooks when fishing with insect larvae. A #6 may work better for large sunfish or for species with large mouths, like warmouth and green sunfish.

Sunfish often swallow the bait. Some fishermen prefer long-shank hooks, so they can remove them quickly. But hooking fish is easier with a short-shank hook. You can remove the shorter hook with a disgorger or a longnose pliers.

A sunfish usually swims up to a bait, studies it for an instant, then inhales it by sucking in water which is expelled out the gills. But a sunfish may spit the bait just as quickly, especially if it feels the hook. To avoid this problem, some fishermen cover the point with bait. Normally, you should wait a few seconds before setting the hook. But when the fish are fussy, set the hook at the first sign of a bite.

When you hook a sunfish, it instinctively turns its body at a right angle to the pressure. Water resistance against the fish's broad, flat side makes it difficult to gain line. This trait makes sunfish one of the toughest fighting panfish.

You can catch sunfish with a wide variety of techniques. Most fishermen simply dangle live bait from a small bobber. But fly-fishing, casting small lures, and even slow-trolling or drifting in deep water often produce good catches.

If an area holds sunfish, they will usually bite within a few minutes after you begin fishing, or they will not bite at all. It seldom pays to wait them out. The best sunfish anglers spend only 5 to 10 minutes in a spot if they are not catching fish.

Many panfish anglers make the mistake of using heavy rods, big hooks or large floats. Some even attach thick steel leaders. Although sunfish are strong fighters, you do not need heavy-duty equipment to land them. Heavy tackle reduces the number of bites and detracts from the sport of fighting these scrappy fish.

# Where to Find Sunfish

If you can find sunfish, chances are you can catch them. Sunfish in natural lakes and reservoirs move more than many anglers realize. They change location depending on the season and daily weather patterns, so experts adjust their fishing strategies accordingly. Sunfish in streams, ponds, canals and other small waters do not move as much from one season to the next, so fishermen have less trouble finding them.

NATURAL LAKES. Early in the season, angling remains slow until the water warms to about 60°F. Fishermen willing to work hard for a few sunfish can find them in shallow, mud-bottomed bays. These bays are the first to offer new weed growth and a supply of insects and other small foods.

Fishing improves as spawning time approaches. Sunfish hang in water slightly deeper than their spawning grounds. They move into the nesting area on a warm day, but move out again when the weather cools.

Spawning sunfish prefer shallow, protected bays. If none are available, they will spawn along a sheltered shoreline. Most fish nest on firm sand or gravel bottoms. They rarely spawn over soft mud. Sunfish prefer emergent vegetation, but will nest around submerged weeds if emergents are not available. They nest within loosely-spaced vegetation. In dense weeds, look for them along edges or in pockets. After spawning, sunfish drift back to their pre-spawn locations. Some fish return to the shallows to

*Sunfish Locations in Natural Lakes*

SPAWNING AREAS for sunfish in natural lakes include: (1) shallow bays with sand or gravel bottoms, (2) sheltered shorelines, (3) points with stands of emergent weeds, (4) sandy beach, (5) boat harbor.

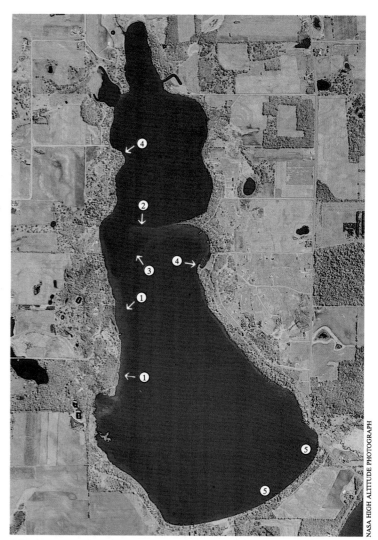

SUMMER locations include: (1) weedlines along drop-offs, (2) submerged extensions of shoreline points, (3) mid-lake ridge or hump, (4) gradually tapering points, (5) docks and boathouses in deep water.

spawn again a week or two later. Others move to summer locations.

Big bluegills and shellcrackers spend most of the summer just outside weedlines. They concentrate near areas where the weedline forms points, notches and inside turns. In a clear lake, they may spend the summer at depths exceeding 20 feet. Pumpkinseeds do not move quite as deep. Small bluegills and shellcrackers, and the smaller sunfish species like longears and greens, remain in the shallows through summer. Sunfish will suspend to feed on plankton, especially on calm, sunny days. The fish often hang just off a weedline, but may suspend in deep, open areas.

As the surface temperature begins to drop in early fall, large sunfish return to shallower water in bays and along breaklines, especially those close to shore. They remain in these areas until the surface water cools to the same temperature as deep water. But as the lake begins to turn over, the fish scatter and become difficult to find. In the North, most anglers stop fishing until freeze-up.

Surface temperatures of lakes in the Deep South range from 50° to 60°F during winter. Fishermen continue to catch sunfish in deep fringes of emergent weeds and in mid-lake holes with weedy or brushy cover.

RESERVOIRS. The same principles govern sunfish movement in lakes and reservoirs, although the types of habitat may differ. Most fish move into the back ends of creek arms, or coves, to spawn. The best coves are at least 20 feet deep at the entrance to

EARLY FALL locations include; (1) shallow bays with submerged vegetation, (2) docks and boathouses in shallow water, (3) shallow shoals with submerged weeds, (4) shallow submerged weedbed off shoreline point.

LATE FALL-WINTER locations include: (1) deep water off sharp drop-offs, (2) deep water off shoreline points, (3) inside turns of shoreline breaks, (4) deep holes, (5) deep bays.

183

the main lake. Shallower coves generally attract only small fish. Sunfish prefer creek arms with clear, inflowing streams. Avoid coves fed by muddy creeks, because the bottom will probably be too soft for sunfish to nest.

Most sunfish spawn on gradually-sloping sand or gravel points, especially those exposed to the sun. But they will spawn on shallow flats adjacent to the creek channel or along straight shorelines. The best spawning areas have some weeds, brush, timber or stumps for cover.

Prior to spawning, sunfish hold in water at least 10 feet deep. Look for them in creek channels or in deep water off points. Like sunfish in lakes, they move into the shallows on warm days and out on cold days.

After spawning, sunfish scatter in deeper water. But some fish remain near the nest areas and return to spawn a second or even a third time. Each successive spawn takes place in deeper water.

Some sunfish remain in deep coves all summer. But if a cove is less than 10 feet deep, sunfish will usually move to the main body of the reservoir. To locate fish, you must find structure with weeds, brush or trees that provide shelter in the shallows. The structure must also be near deep water, because big sunfish will retreat as deep as 30 feet during extremely hot weather.

Prime summertime structure includes creek and river channels, points and flats. Look for edges where channels slope into deep water. Sunfish prefer outside bends and intersections with other channels.

## Sunfish Locations in Reservoirs

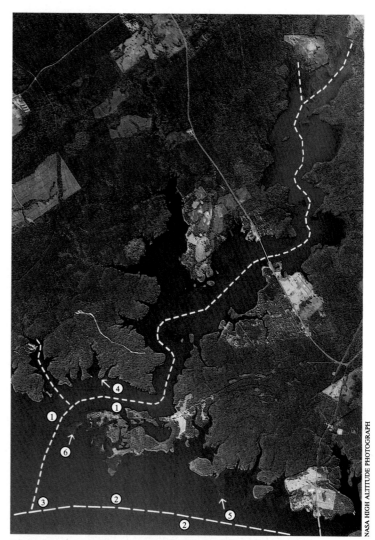

SPAWNING AREAS include: (1) back ends of both creek arms and secondary creek arms, (2) gradually-sloping points, (3) flats near the creek channel (small dashes), (4) shallow humps, (5) wooded main lake coves.

SUMMER locations include: (1) edge of creek channel, (2) edge of river channel (large dashes), (3) channel intersection, (4) deep points in creek arm, (5) submerged points in main lake, (6) sunken island in main lake.

Select main lake points that slope gradually into deep water. Look for flats that top out at 10 to 20 feet. Sunfish congregate in depressions on the flats. Man-made features like fish attractors and docks also hold sunfish in summer.

Sunfish in reservoirs, like those in natural lakes, will suspend in open water. Anglers find them feeding on plankton or insects over deep water.

In early fall, sunfish move back to their pre-spawn locations. They hang along breaklines adjacent to areas where they spawned in spring, but move shallower on warm days. But they do not go as shallow as they did at spawning time. Sunfish remain in these areas and continue to bite until the surface temperature drops to about 60°F. Then, they begin moving to deep wintering grounds.

In southern waters, few anglers pursue sunfish during the winter months. Fishermen catch some fish along sharp-breaking structure, usually at depths of 25 to 40 feet. The fish may move shallower after several warm, sunny days.

DAILY MOVEMENT. Weather and changing light levels affect daily movements of sunfish. Like almost all freshwater fish, they avoid bright sunlight. But they seem less sensitive to light than most other fish. They retreat to slightly deeper water on bright days, but do not move as deep as many other species. Most types of sunfish seek shade to escape the sun, but do not need dense cover.

Cold fronts affect sunfish much like other species. The fish move to deeper water and refuse to bite until a day or two after the front passes.

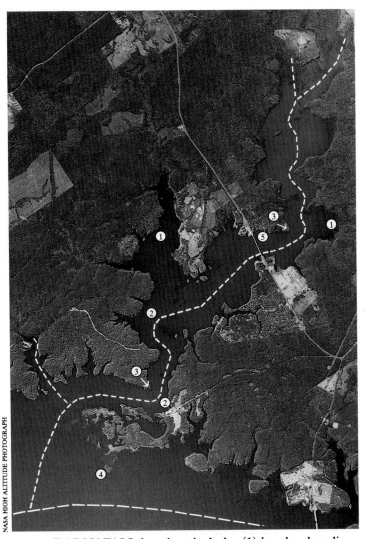

EARLY FALL locations include: (1) brushy shorelines, (2) outside bends of the creek channel, (3) shallow points near the creek channel, (4) shallow points in the main lake, (5) docks and marinas close to deep water.

LATE FALL-WINTER locations include: (1) creek channel-river channel intersection, (2) deep water in river channel, (3) deep main lake coves, (4) steep main lake points, (5) deep water at lower end of creek arm.

# How to Catch Sunfish

LURES include: (1) popper, (2) Timberwolf, (3) Western Bee, (4) Emmy Jig with mealworm, (5) rubber spider, (6) Creme Angle Worm, (7) Beetle Spin™, (8) Devil Spinner, (9) Panther Martin, (10) Black Fury® Combo, (11) Hal-Fly®, (12) Road Runner®, (13) Sassy® Shad, (14) Jiggly.

## Lures for Sunfish

Many sunfish anglers prefer artificial lures. Artificials eliminate the problems of buying and keeping live bait, especially when fishing in remote areas. And at certain times, lures are more productive.

Artificial lures work best in summer when the fish are most active. When you locate a concentration of active sunfish, artificials may outfish live bait because you do not waste time baiting the hook.

Many consider fly-fishing with surface lures to be the ultimate in panfish sport. Fly-fishing is most effective on warm summer evenings, at spawning time, or during an insect hatch. Surface-feeding sunfish will strike a popper, but may ignore live bait.

Sunfish prefer small lures. A big bluegill may strike a 6-inch plastic worm intended for bass, but an inch-long lure will catch sunfish more consistently. Always retrieve the lure slowly. Sunfish seldom strike fast-moving lures or those that produce too much noise or flash.

Anglers can make their own artificials or modify lures such as plastic worms and spinnerbaits to make them more effective.

## Tips for Sunfish Lures

SELECT a bug with ample clearance between the body and the hook point (top) rather than one with little clearance (bottom). If the hook point extends forward past the rear of the body, you will miss too many strikes.

TUNE a hair-bodied popper or diver if the lure will not pop. If it skims instead of popping or diving, bend the back of the hook down. This causes the face to catch more water when you pull.

## Natural Bait for Sunfish

Sunfish rely heavily on scent to find food, so it is not surprising that the vast majority of sunfish are caught on natural bait.

Natural bait works best early and late in the year when the water is too cold for sunfish to chase artificial lures. It is also the best choice for fishing deep or murky water. When a cold front slows fishing, sunfish may refuse artificials but continue to bite on natural bait.

Small baits like waxworms, red wigglers and mayfly nymphs usually work best in spring and fall. Larger baits like grasshoppers, crickets, catalpa worms, nightcrawlers and cockroaches may work better during summer when sunfish feed more actively.

Sunfish prefer a bait that squirms enticingly on the hook. When using worms, for example, let the ends dangle. To keep your bait alive as long as possible, use light-wire hooks because they do the least damage to the bait.

Some anglers chum with worms or bits of fish, clams or shrimp to draw sunfish into an area. Check local regulations before using this technique.

BAITS include: (1) cricket, (2) grasshopper, (3) piece of nightcrawler, (4) garden worm, (5) red wiggler, (6) small leech, (7) minnow, (8) grass shrimp, (9) clam meat, (10) waxworm, (11) mealworm. Hook sizes range from a #10 with a cricket to a #6 with a garden worm.

*Popular Natural Bait Rigs*

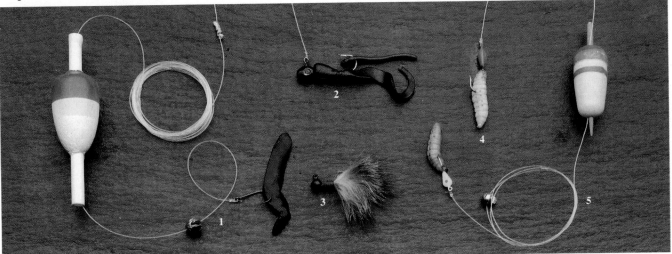

LURES AND RIGS: (1) slip-bobber rig with size 8 hook and small leech, (2) 1/32-ounce jig and piece of worm, (3) 1/64-ounce hair jig, (4) tullibee hook and waxworm. For ice fishing: (5) bobber rig with ice fly and waxworm.

# Turning the Worm on Sunfish

by Jake Barnes

*George LaFrance uses his homegrown crawlers to catch record numbers of "citation" sunfish*

Imagine a 60-year-old grandfather crawling on hands and knees across his backyard, punching holes in the ground with a long-shank screwdriver. Aerating the grass, you say? Or stabbing moles? Wrong. He's making nightcrawler condos.

George LaFrance resorted to this madness for good reason. He knew that nightcrawlers were the best bait for the plate-sized sunfish he loved to catch. But crawlers don't normally live in southern Virginia, so he hauled some in from the northern part of the state. At first, he tried putting the crawlers on top of the ground, but they wouldn't dig down. So he got a big screwdriver and started poking holes — nightcrawler condos, so to speak. Then he carefully inserted the worms one by one. He covered the holes with dirt; the new residents took over from there, boring tunnels of their own. Today, the LaFrance neighborhood crawls with his worms.

This scenario illustrates LaFrance's unyielding commitment to perfection when it comes to catching sunfish. He'll do whatever it takes to boost his odds of bagging jumbo bluegills and shellcrackers.

George now does most of his fishing on Western Branch, a 1600-acre reservoir in the tidewater plains of Virginia. The reservoir, one of seven supplying the Norfolk sprawl, can be reached only by a labyrinth of back roads. Its launching ramp, and its tidy new bait and tackle shop, do not draw itinerant fishermen, just the local hardcore.

Besides keeping the taps running in Norfolk, Western Branch grows lots of fish. Bass, catfish, bluegills, redears, white perch, yellow perch, pickerel, northern pike, gar, carp, even stripers swim in what Norfolk drinks.

LaFrance believes it's best to concentrate on one or two lakes rather than jumping around to dozens.

---

**George LaFrance**

**Home:** *Hampton, Virginia*

**Occupation:** *Retired, after 20 years in the Air Force and 18 years in the Postal Service*

*George LaFrance is a man blessed with an intuitive sense of how to catch fish — and also with the dedication, teetering on fanaticism, to stick with his intuition. When he was 3½ in Nashua, New Hampshire, he wandered down to the town pond alone and caught a stout pickerel with a bent pin and string. Since that tender age, he's been a diehard angler.*

*While in the Air Force, George caught Nile perch in the Philippines, trout in California, and bass in other parts of the U.S. On retiring from the military in the mid-1960s, he began to concentrate on sunfish — both bluegills and redears (also known as shellcrackers). His expertise in catching big sunfish throughout the year in deep water has made him the column of choice for tidewater Virginia sportswriters: when nothing new is breaking, do a George LaFrance piece.*

*Virginia issues citations of achievement for catching big fish. For sunfish, the minimum weight for recognition is 1 pound. George has more than 200 citations for sunfish, as well as citations for ten other species. His biggest sunfish is an eye-popping 2½-pound bluegill, from Folsom Lake in California.*

*Today LaFrance is less interested in winning awards than in simply having fun on the water. He puts in 300 days fishing a year, often in the company of one of his five grandchildren — each of whom, not surprisingly, has taken a citation fish while out with granddad.*

*Gathering worms at night; LaFrance often uses a flashlight covered with red cellophane to avoid spooking them*

He says he plans to study Western Branch "until I know every inch of it, until I know what the fish are doing on any day, in any weather."

Although George catches good-sized bass, catfish, and even stripers in Western Branch, he specializes in sunfish. It doesn't matter what kind. Whichever species is biting is George's fixation for the day.

He pursues sunfish with as much intensity and attention to detail as any muskie or trout addict. But he doesn't believe in buying every new lure and electronic device; instead, he holds to tackle, bait, and techniques that he's mastered over many years.

*LaFrance likes small, dull-colored boat*

A day on the water with George LaFrance starts at sunup, when he launches his modest boat on Western Branch Reservoir. The boat is a 14-foot Sears Gamefisher, made of fiberglass and painted dark green. He believes a bright-colored or shiny boat will spook fish in shallow water. He also believes that even the slightest noise will spook them. To deaden sound, George refinished the interior of his boat with a product called Liquid Carpet, a paint texturized with particles of rubber.

There's a souped-up 9.9-horse Evinrude on the stern, and an electric trolling motor with a foot control and a Maximizer on the bow. The boat is equipped with a flasher, but no graph or liquid crystal recorder. LaFrance has nothing against high-tech electronics, he just doesn't need them. A swivel seat amidships places George within a spin of a small cooler, where he keeps sodas and worms; a larger cooler, where he stores his catch; and a couple of storage compartments for terminal tackle, towels, and the other junk all fisherman acquire. The boat may not attract many admirers, but it's highly functional.

George goes after sunfish year around. He has studied the fish so carefully that he can tell you exactly where to find them every month of the year.

He finds bluegills and shellcrackers in pretty much the same places, although there are some differences in early season. Shellcrackers are the first to move into the spawning areas. In April and May he finds them on 2- to 4-foot shoreline flats. He pinpoints these flats by looking for areas where the land slopes gently away from the water. Bluegills move in to spawn a little later than shellcrackers, usually in May and June.

The larger females leave the nesting area first; the smaller males stay behind to guard the nests. After leaving the nesting area, the fish move to sunken islands that top off at 8 or 9 feet, or to creek channels between the spawning area and the main river channel. The fish remain in these areas, generally at depths of 8 to 12 feet, through June and July.

By August, most of the fish have moved to the main river channel where the water is deepest and coolest. This is LaFrance's favorite time to fish, because the big sunfish are concentrated. They seek out stair-step ledges along the channel edge, areas where a shallow ridge or sunken island meet the channel, and junctions where creek channels and old roadbeds meet the main channel. The most productive late-summer depth is around 15 feet.

One reason sunfish are more concentrated in late summer is that the deep-water structure is more pronounced than the shallow-water structure. "In the shallows the old channel edges get eroded by waves and currents," LaFrance says, "but in deep water they stay sharp. So in that deep water I like to fish right where the channel drops off. I'll try to pick up the fish on my flasher first. Once I lock on to the depth where they're holding, I'll stick there all day."

As the water starts to cool in September, the fish move somewhat shallower, 8 to 12 feet, but they stay on the same structure where they were in late summer. As the water continues to cool, they gradually slip into deeper water along the river channel. By midwinter, they're at depths of 20 to 25 feet. They stay deep until the water starts warming in spring, then they follow the creek channels to their spawning grounds.

George's tackle and rigging are simple. One rod is a floppy glass fly rod, rebuilt as a spinning rig with Fuji guides and a cork spinning grip; the other is a very soft, very old spinning rod. Unlike the stiff graphite rods popular today, these won't snap a lightly impaled worm off the hook on a cast. His well-used spinning reels are spooled with 8-pound yellow fluorescent mono. That's heavy line for sunfish, certainly, but remember that sunfish aren't the only inhabitants of Western Branch. George likes to know he has guts in his line should a bigger fish suck down his worm.

The water in Western Branch is cloudy enough that the fluorescent line doesn't alert the fish, yet it gives him an advantage in detecting the lightest bites. George does not use a bobber; he simply watches the highly visible line.

He rigs the business end in an unorthodox manner. The hook is a size 1 or 1/0 gold Aberdeen. He says this large hook doesn't discourage the heavyweight sunfish he's after, and it holds more securely than a tiny hook should he hang into a big catfish or striper.

LaFrance ties his rig a special way so the hook stands out at a right angle to the line. With the hook tied this way, George feels his hooking percentage is higher than if the hook were hanging straight down. To make the hook stand out, he ties the line to one side of the hook eye, then ties a 12- to 18-inch dropper to the opposite side. A single split-shot crimped to the dropper puts just enough pull on the hook to keep it at a right angle. The

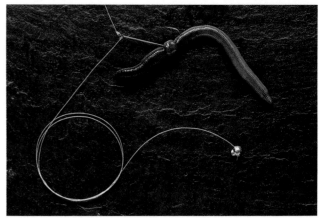

*The special right-angle rig LaFrance prefers*

split-shot rides along bottom with the bait above it. This way, the hook doesn't snag as often and the bait is more visible to the fish.

This is the rig George uses for practically all of his deep-water fishing. Only in water shallower than 6 feet does he omit the dropper and shot; there the hook and bait alone are heavy enough to get to the bottom.

*Where LaFrance Finds Sunfish in Shallow Reservoirs*

*In spring, sunfish spawn on (A) flats from 2 to 4 feet deep. After spawning, they move to depths of 8 to 12 feet in (B) old creek channels and around (C) submerged points and islands. From late summer through winter, look for them at 15 to 25 feet, where the old river channel meets a (D) point or (E) old creek channel.*

0-10 Ft.

11-20 Ft.

Over 20 Ft.

*Note: This map is intended to show the types of spots LaFrance recommends, not the actual spots he fishes.*

*Another citation redear, well over the 1-pound mark*

Nightcrawlers are his preferred bait for almost everything — even striped bass. For a day of fishing, he'll take along 200 of his homegrown worms. He generally uses a whole nightcrawler, inserting the hook in front of the collar and threading on an inch or so.

The rig, with or without the dropper, looks like something a child might devise. Most experts wouldn't even consider using heavy fluorescent line. They would argue that the hook is way too big for sunfish and far too obvious to deceive any fish at all. They would say that sunfish would nibble off the lightly hooked worm. But these objections wouldn't stop LaFrance — he knows the rig works.

When George approaches a piece of structure he wants to fish, he cuts the outboard, drops his electric and motors quietly into position. His usual plan is to start fishing shallow, then work progressively deeper until he hits big sunfish.

George rigs both rods alike. He drops one worm over the side, directly under the boat, then slides the rod handle under his thigh. He casts the other worm 30 feet out in a gentle arc so as not to flip it off the hook. He disengages the anti-reverse on the reel and ever so slowly retrieves the worm. By working the handle forward and then back, he can retrieve the worm in small increments and alternately place just a hint of slack in the line. When that slack twitches, a fish is on.

While gingerly working that rod, George continually jigs and fiddles with the other one clamped under his thigh. Concurrently, his eyes are locked on his flasher and he deftly controls the electric motor with his foot, holding the boat against a gentle breeze one moment, sliding closer to the structure the next, then moving sideways to another part of it.

At the slightest indication something might be wrong — weeds on his hook, or a messed-up worm — George reels in. If a small fish nibbles off some of the worm, he puts on a fresh one. He may pinch on an additional shot if the water is deep, or remove the shot and dropper if the water is shallow. He never stops thinking and adjusting his tactics.

LaFrance covers a given piece of water thoroughly in this manner. As he studies his flasher, he offers a blow-by-blow description of what's happening below: "Here come some weeds at 12 feet. Oh, look, now there's a fish. Perch probably, up that close. Now here's the channel. There're some bluegill, I bet, 18 feet." This monologue continues across every square foot of water. And most of the time, George's rods twitch out confirmation of his forecasts.

George may cover only 30 or 40 yards of channel edge in an hour. He moves his boat along very slowly, precisely following the contour while probing the channel with his worms. Sticking there is methodical, intense work. If someone were paid to fish this hard, from sunup till dusk, he'd call it grueling work.

"If a man loves what he's doing, though," says George, "it's art." The smile that never leaves his face from launch time until sunset widens. Out goes another worm. And in comes another 1-pound redear.

An artist is at work.

# Fishing for Yellow Perch

Perch are among the tastiest of freshwater fish. Closely related to walleyes and saugers, they live in many of the same lakes and rivers, although they rarely become abundant in extremely murky waters. The largest populations are in clear, northern lakes with moderate vegetation. Perch have been stocked in many southern waters.

Perch feed only during the day, because they cannot see well in dim light. In the evening, schools break up and the fish rest on bottom. The next morning, they regroup into large schools which feed in open water. In some lakes and reservoirs they forage along shore. They are active throughout the year, even when the water is near freezing. In the North, perch are a favorite of ice fishermen.

Perch normally have yellow to yellow-green sides, sometimes with a gray or brown tint, with about seven vertical bars. Spawning males have more intense colors with orange or bright red lower fins.

Spawning occurs in spring when the water reaches about 45°F. Perch lay their eggs in jelly-like bands that cling to rocks, plants and debris on the bottom. Staggering numbers of young are hatched, much to the benefit of predators such as largemouth bass, northern pike and walleyes. Because their reproductive potential is so great, perch can withstand heavy fishing pressure. Commercial fishermen on Lake Erie have taken as many as 30 million pounds in a single year. In many waters, perch become too abundant and, as a result, never reach a size large enough to interest anglers. A 7- to 8-inch perch is an acceptable size to most anglers, though sometimes perch grow much larger. The world record, 4 pounds, 3½ ounces, was caught near Bordentown, New Jersey in 1865.

Perch Range

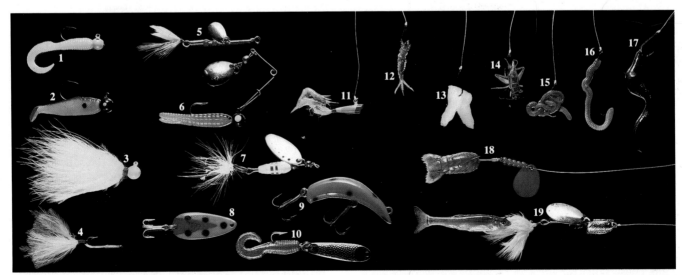

LURES AND BAITS for yellow perch include: (1) Twister® Teeny, (2) Sassy® Shad, (3) Maribou Jig, (4) no name spoon, (5) spinner/fly combo, (6) Beetle Spin™, (7) Toni™, (8) Dardevle®, (9) Lazy Ike, (10) Hopkins® ST, (11) Shad Dart with grass shrimp, (12) mayfly nymph, (13) perch meat, (14) cricket, (15) garden worm, (16) piece of nightcrawler, (17) leech, (18) snelled spinner with crayfish tail, (19) Paul Bunyan's® "66" with minnow.

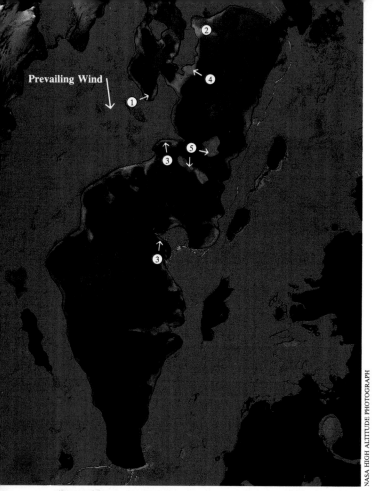

**SPAWNING AREAS** for yellow perch in natural lakes include: (1) isolated bays with scattered weeds, (2) main lake bays, (3) shallow water on protected side of points, (4) shoreline shoals, (5) tops of mid-lake reefs.

# Where to Find Yellow Perch

Finding small yellow perch can be as easy as dangling a worm off most any dock. But the angler looking for jumbo perch faces more of a challenge.

SPRING. Yellow perch begin moving out of deep wintering areas toward shallower water in early spring. In the southern part of their range and along the Atlantic Coast, spawning migrations begin as early as late February. Perch in northern lakes start their spawning runs in mid-April or early May.

Perch often migrate long distances, sometimes 20 miles or more, to reach their spawning grounds. In the Great Lakes, most perch spend their entire lives

**LATE SPRING-SUMMER** locations include: (1) deeper portions of spawning bays, (2) shoreline points, (3) drop-offs along mid-lake reefs, (4) edges of shoreline shoals with submerged weeds, (5) submerged points.

in large, warmwater bays. These fish edge out of deep water near rock reefs and islands onto reef edges. Others move into the mouths of tributaries or into man-made drainage ditches.

Perch are very selective as to where they spawn. They prefer sand, gravel or rock bottoms with scattered weeds or brush. In most lakes and reservoirs, they spawn in shallow, protected bays in water 5 to 12 feet deep. Generally, the larger the lake, the deeper they spawn. In the western basin of Lake Erie, perch spawn on off-shore reefs in 10 to 20 feet of water, and occasionally as deep as 30 feet.

Yellow perch in Chesapeake Bay and other East Coast estuaries winter in brackish water at the mouths of large tributaries. The fish move upstream after a series of balmy spring days or a warm rain. Many perch spawn just below small dams on the upper ends of the streams. Others deposit their eggs in quiet, brush-choked areas where the stream may be only 2 to 3 feet deep.

LATE SPRING AND SUMMER. After spawning, yellow perch in most natural lakes and reservoirs linger several weeks in their spawning bays. Look

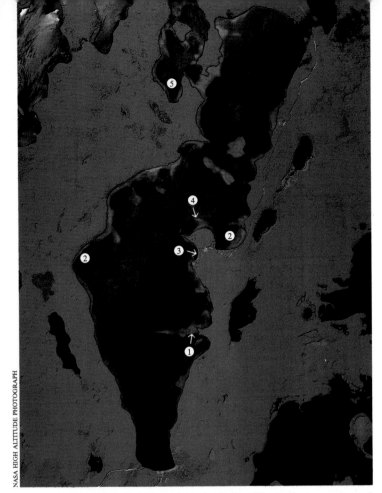

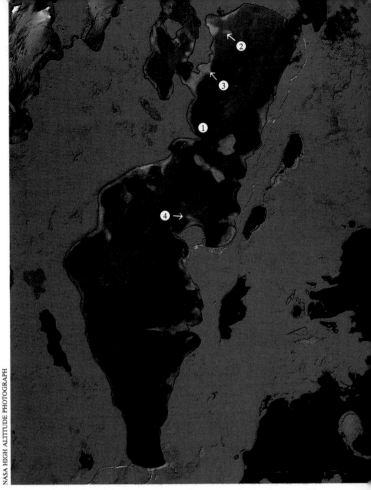

**EARLY FALL** locations include: (1) shallow portion of submerged point, (2) bays with sand or gravel bottoms, (3) rocky shorelines, (4) shallow flat with scattered weeds, (5) isolated bays.

**LATE FALL** locations for yellow perch include: (1) sharp dropping points along shore, (2) deep sunken islands, (3) deep edges of a shoreline shoal, (4) edge of a weedy flat in deep water.

for the fish in 15 to 25 feet of water. Some remain all summer unless the water becomes too warm, forcing them to find deeper, cooler water.

Jumbo perch prefer water temperatures between 65° and 70°F. Look for them in the thermocline, usually where it intersects with bottom. Some fish suspend in the thermocline over open water. Perch will also suspend in or above the thermocline to feed on plankton, baitfish or mayflies moving toward the surface to hatch.

In the Great Lakes, perch move toward open water in the bays, often gathering around rocky shoals and islands. The best reefs are isolated from other structure and have numerous projections or points. During the day, the fish feed along the points in 20 to 30 feet of water. Toward evening, they move onto the points in water as shallow as 6 feet. Great Lakes anglers also catch large yellow perch around breakwaters, pilings and docks. The best fishing spots are in 15 to 25 feet of water, with rock or sand bottoms and some vegetation.

Yellow perch in estuaries remain in the tributaries through summer. They school in deep holes at the

mouths of secondary streams, or around piers, bridges and old pilings.

**FALL AND WINTER.** In fall, perch in deep lakes and reservoirs move into the shallows around rocky shorelines and reefs. Great Lakes fishermen have recorded huge catches around concrete piers in only 6 to 8 feet of water. In East Coast estuaries, some fish move up secondary streams in fall. Others remain in their deep, summer locations. During winter, anglers catch few perch in waters that remain ice-free. But ice fishing is popular on many northern lakes.

**DAILY MOVEMENTS.** Schools of perch begin feeding in mid-morning, once the sun has moved high enough to brighten the depths. They may continue to feed off and on throughout the day. As twilight approaches, the schools move shallower and begin to break up. Schools re-form the following morning.

Cold fronts affect yellow perch less than they do most other panfish. Even during periods of extreme cold, anglers find and catch perch in the same areas they fished during mild weather.

# Icing Jumbo Perch

by Dick Sternberg

*Rod Sather divulges the jigging technique that has accounted for hundreds of 2-pound perch*

Rod Sather may be the only guide in the country who's disappointed when he lands a pound-and-a-half walleye. "Rather eat perch," he says. "Firmer meat and better tasting." His philosophy is easy to understand: the yellow perch he catches through the ice are often bigger than walleyes.

Before you can catch jumbo perch, you have to select a lake that's got them, preferably in good numbers. Sather does his guiding on Devils Lake in North Dakota, which he considers the top perch lake on the continent.

Devils Lake, like most good perch lakes, is big — 65,000 acres, to be exact. The maximum depth is 28 feet, so all the acreage is usable perch habitat. Interestingly, Devils Lake was almost dry during the drought of the 1930s, and there were no fish in the lake until the early 1960s.

Yellow perch and prime forage: freshwater shrimp

Rod explains that the lake water is highly alkaline: that is, the content of salts and other minerals is great. The unusually fertile water supports a tremendous crop of freshwater shrimp, which make ideal forage for the perch and account for their large size.

The largest perch ever caught from Devils Lake weighed 2 pounds 15½ ounces and was taken in 1982. This fish is also the official North Dakota record. However, Rod knows of several 3-pounders caught with test nets in Devils Lake, so he expects the record to topple soon.

Although Rod prefers Devils Lake, he's fished for perch in other alkaline lakes throughout the Dakotas. His top picks in North Dakota include Gackle Slough, Coal Mine Lake, and Lake

---

**Rod Sather**

**Home:** *Devils Lake, North Dakota*

**Occupation:** *Fishing and hunting guide; manager of Towers Bait And Tackle Shop near Devils Lake*

*If you walked into Ed's Bait Shop in Devils Lake, North Dakota, you'd be stunned by a wall display of thirteen mounted perch, each weighing 2 pounds or better. At first glance, they don't even look like perch. Their backs are more steeply humped than those of normal yellow perch, and their bodies look about twice as deep. But the most amazing thing about these fish is that all were caught by a single angler — a relentless perch-hound named Rod Sather.*

196

Sather is a modest man, not prone to bragging about his fishing accomplishments. It takes plenty of prodding to get him to reveal his catch statistics. On a typical day of ice fishing, Rod and his customers will catch a hundred perch, half of them running from 1 to 2½ pounds. Through an average winter, they'll catch more than a hundred fish weighing 2 pounds or heavier. Sather's biggest single perch went 2 pounds 9 ounces.

Rod also fishes for other species, often in tournaments. In fact, he's taken first-place honors in 25 different tournaments; in one recent competition, for northern pike, walleyes, and nongame species, his total catch weighed twice as much as the runner-up's.

*Sather likes to fish perch in morning and late afternoon*

Ashtabula. In South Dakota, he says, try Roy Lake, Lake Poinsett, and Lake Andes. He also recommends Mille Lacs Lake in Minnesota, although the perch there are not as big, topping off at about 1½ pounds.

Rod does most of his perch fishing in winter. The perch seem to bite best then, probably because food is scarcer than in summer and the water is much clearer, making the bait easier to see. And during the winter, female perch, which are considerably larger than males, dominate the catch. The females bite better in winter because their bodies need an ample supply of fat to nourish the developing eggs.

Early ice is best; in most years, the ice is thick enough to walk on by December 1. Rod does most of his early fishing on Creel Bay, because it's sheltered from the wind and freezes up earlier than the rest of the lake. Peak early-ice fishing continues until just before Christmas.

The perch continue to bite through the winter, but the action is not as consistent. There are good days and bad ones, depending on the weather and moon phase. Rod prefers a partly cloudy day a few days on either side of the full moon or new moon. The fishing usually slows right after a cold front, but after a few days of cold weather, the perch start to bite again.

### Prime Ice-Fishing Spots on Devils Lake

*Early-winter spots are usually in protected areas that freeze up first. Midwinter spots have extensive weedy flats extending from shore and dropping into deep water. Late-winter spots are near spawning areas and may be very shallow, sometimes only 3 feet deep. The best wintertime spots are generally next to moving water or springs.*

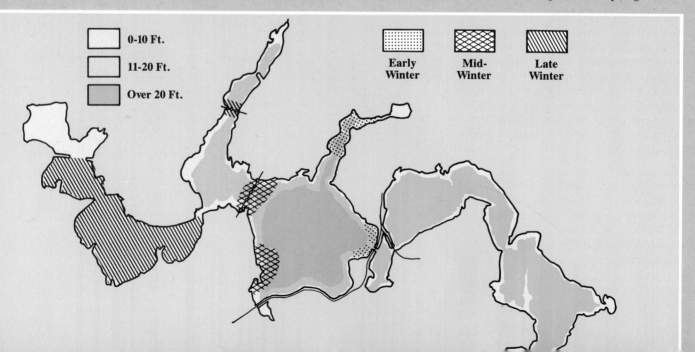

0-10 Ft.

11-20 Ft.

Over 20 Ft.

Early Winter

Mid-Winter

Late Winter

The action picks up in late winter, starting around March 1 and continuing until the season closes on March 20 or thereabouts. Even after March 20, perch fishing is still permitted on parts of Devils Lake, and the action is fast until ice-out around April 15. Late winter offers not only the biggest perch, but also the warmest weather.

Rod likes to fish in midweek, Tuesday through Thursday, when fishing pressure is lightest. He recommends staying away from crowds because the sound of power augers drives the perch away, especially in shallow water. If you locate a school of perch and have it to yourself, you can often enjoy good fishing for hours before the fish move.

You'll normally find Rod on the lake before sunrise. He believes the perch bite best from sunrise until noon, then again from 3 p.m. until dark. But when they're really biting, you can catch them all day long. Night fishing is usually poor.

His favorite technique for locating jumbo perch is to find a weedbed, then fish just out from the weedline. In Devils Lake, submerged weeds grow to a depth of 9 feet, so Rod normally starts fishing at about 10 feet.

Not all the perch are that shallow, however. Rod often finds deep schools and shallow ones at the same time. It's not unusual to find one active school at 10 feet, and another as deep as 28. On a trip the Hunting and Fishing Library staff made

with Rod, we caught most of our big perch on a 16-foot midlake flat with no vegetation and no structure. We found the fish by drilling holes over a large area and fishing no longer than a few minutes in each one.

In early winter, Rod uses a Si-Tex color flasher for locating perch. If the ice is free of slush and no more than 6 inches thick, he pours a little water on it, then sounds through the ice rather than drilling holes. The perch show up as red or orange blips just off bottom.

As a general rule, Rod fishes deeper on sunny days than on cloudy ones. After a storm front passes, he often finds the perch right in the weeds, as shallow as 5 feet.

Anyone can catch small perch, but it takes more skill to catch the big ones consistently. Rod's advice: "If you're catching little perch, move. You may catch a big one mixed in with the little guys, but the big ones are usually by themselves. The only way to find them is to keep looking."

Another tip: "If you want to catch bigger perch, use bigger bait. I like a ⅛-ounce Limpet spoon with the treble hook loaded with spikes or waxworms. I put three spikes [maggots or silver wigglers] or a single waxworm on each prong of the treble." Larger baits work best, probably because a big perch would rather eat a minnow than a freshwater shrimp or other small food item. If you use a small bait — a teardrop with a single

*Sather's Favorite Perch Baits and Lures*

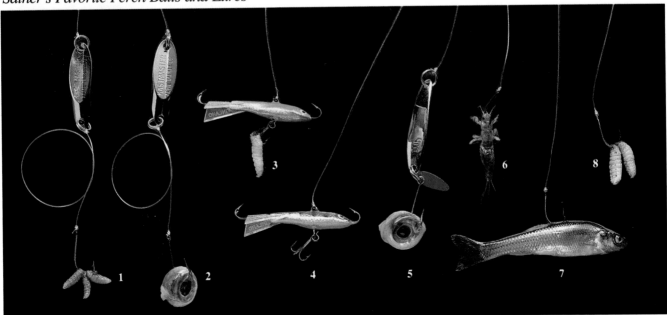

LURES AND BAITS for ice fishing include: (1) Kastmaster spoon baited with EuroLarvae, (2) Kastmaster spoon baited with perch eye, (3) Jigging Rapala® tipped with waxworm, (4) Jigging Rapala®, (5) Swedish Pimple® baited with perch eye, (6) mayfly nymph , (7) fathead minnow, (8) waxworms.

waxworm, for instance — you'll be pestered by little perch.

Besides the Limpet spoon, which is no longer being made, Rod uses a variety of baits and lures including:

• A ⅛-ounce blue-and-chrome Kastmaster spoon, with two or three spikes on a 4-inch dropper. EuroLarvae can be substituted for spikes. The small larvae evidently imitate freshwater shrimp.

• The same Kastmaster rig baited with a perch eye.

• A size 3 Jigging Rapala — in perch color for overcast days, chartreuse for bright days.

• A size 3 Jigging Rapala in orange and chartreuse, baited with a waxworm.

• A size 3 Swedish Pimple with a single hook instead of a treble, baited with a perch eye.

• A 2- to 2½-inch fathead minnow or a pair of 1½-inchers, hooked lightly just ahead of the dorsal fin with a size 8 hook and fished under a small slip-bobber.

When fishing is really tough, Rod uses an unusual bait: mayfly nymphs. The nymphs are difficult to get and must be imported from Wisconsin. They're soft-bodied and hard to keep on the hook, but when perch are fussy, the nymphs make a big difference. Another good bait for tough conditions is simply a waxworm or spike on a plain size 10 short-shank hook.

Rod's perch outfit consists of a 24-inch medium-action graphite rod; an ultralight open-face spinning reel; and limp 4-pound mono, either green or clear. Devils Lake has a good population of walleyes up

*Homemade sled carries all gear, has padded seat*

to 11 pounds, and they hang out in the same areas as the perch, so he uses a reel with a good drag. To reduce icing problems, he puts an oversized tip guide on his rod.

Other equipment includes an 8-inch Jiffy power auger; a 5-gallon pail with an elevated seat, which also serves for storing the perch; a small plastic tackle box for lures; and a homemade sled designed to carry his gear. In early winter, he carries an 8-inch Strikemaster hand auger: it's quieter than a power auger and doesn't seem to spook the perch. In late winter, he normally uses an 8-inch extension on his power auger, because the ice may be 40 inches thick.

Instead of using a bobber, Rod prefers to jig, lowering the bait to the bottom, then lifting it. With a bobber, you can't lower the bait far enough. A bobber isn't necessary to detect bites; a graphite rod transmits any light tap. If the perch are biting soft, Rod attaches a spring bobber to his rod tip. He may use a slip-bobber on a second line, however.

Rod's advice on jigging: "Jig down instead of up. Perch always are close to the bottom, and if you jerk the bait up too far, they won't chase it. I lift the bait slowly until it's a few inches off bottom, then I lower it to bottom while twitching the rod. Lots of times they grab the bait right on bottom. When you start lifting the rod, you'll feel weight. That means set the hook.

"I always tell my customers to sharpen their hooks. They'll tell me they're already sharp, but usually they aren't, even if the lure is brand-new. A sharp hook can make the difference between a pail of jumbos or just a few stragglers."

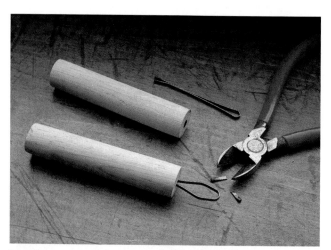

MAKE a perch-eye remover by drilling a small hole in a 1-inch dowel, then inserting a bobby pin with the ends snipped off. Spread the loop and sharpen the inside edges with a small file. Use the eyes to tip jigging lures.

*How Sather Jigs for Jumbo Perch*

LIFT the spoon slowly until it's about 10 inches off bottom. The spikes or waxworms will then be about 6 inches off bottom.

LOWER the spoon all the way to bottom, keeping the line taut and twitching the rod tip as the spoon is sinking.

SET THE HOOK if you feel a twitch, or if the line moves to the side. Sometimes perch will push the bait up, causing the line to slacken.

### How Sather Cleans and Cooks Perch

*In good perch country you measure your catch not in numbers of fish, but in numbers of 5-gallon pails. Many states, including North Dakota, set no limit on perch. That means you'll have a real cleaning chore when you get home.*

*If your perch are half-pounders or bigger, you'll probably want to fillet them. Rod makes short work of it by using an electric knife. The blades slice easily through the heavy rib bones, reducing cleaning time by as much as 50 percent. To save even more time, he cuts off the belly meat,* *rather than trimming around it. He loses a little meat this way, but the remaining fillets are of uniform thickness, so they cook evenly.*

*The real payoff in perch fishing comes at the dinner table. Perch have firm, flaky meat, with a hint of sweetness. Rod's recipe is simple: dip the fillets in a batter such as Shorelunch, then deep-fry them at about 375°F until they're golden brown. Once you try fillets prepared this way, you'll be sharpening your perch hooks too.*

# Panfish Tips

### Bobby Humphrey
## Split-Shot Jigs

Fishing with jigs in brush and timber is the number-one way to take crappies in many reservoirs and rivers. The drawback of the method is that usually it means lots of lost lures; if you're fishing with commercially made jigs, the snags can get costly. Some anglers mold their own jigs with hot lead, but Bobby Humphrey, a taxidermist from Strawberry Plains, Tennessee, has a solution that's even cheaper and easier. Humphrey modifies a stout-wire hook, then attaches a single split-shot for a head. Jigs made this way cost only a few cents; besides, they snag less to begin with, since the hook is shorter than on a typical jig. Another bonus: the stout wire won't straighten out if you hook a big fish like a bass, as the thinner and softer wire of ordinary jig hooks will. Humphrey finishes the jig with his own special tail with plenty of action to attract crappies.

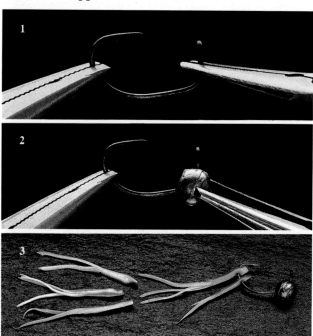

MAKE a split-shot jig by (1) bending the shank of an Eagle Claw 84 hook, size 4 or 6, to form a right angle about ⅛ inch from the eye. Before it's bent, the hook must be heated until red; but heating it too long will make it brittle. (2) Pinch a split-shot onto the bend just formed. The shot may then be painted, if desired. (3) Slice a 1½-inch squid tail into long strips, full length, then attach two or three strips onto the jig hook.

### Charlie Ingram
## Big Jigging Spoon for Crappies

Jigging spoons have more action than ordinary jigs, since their shape makes them flutter on the drop. In large sizes, they're popular vertical-jigging lures for bass schooling in deep timber during fall and winter. Charlie Ingram of Eufaula, Alabama, a guide on Lake Eufaula, has found that these same large spoons will take big crappies holding deep in heavy brush and treetops. His favorite is a ¾-ounce Hopkins with no dressing or bait on the treble. He

files the hook points to dull them slightly. The dull hooks are less likely to bite into woody cover and hang up, but are sharp enough to pierce the soft mouth of a crappie.

### Mike McKee
## Belly Strip for Big Perch

For yellow perch, the ideal natural bait is one that not only gets plenty of bites but also holds up well for fish after fish. After catching a perch, you need to get your bait back down to the school as quickly as possible, to keep them stirred up and feeding. Every time you stop to rebait, the fish start to lose interest. Mike McKee, a newspaper outdoor columnist from Michigan City, Indiana, fishes with a belly strip cut from a perch — a tough, appealing bait that will catch several fish before it's worn out. He rigs it on a size 6 or 8 hook. Two baits are fished at once, on a pair of droppers above a bell sinker. McKee works them just above the bottom, continually raising and lowering his rod tip a foot or two.

CUT a strip an inch long and ⅛ inch wide from the underside of a perch, just behind the anal fin. Leave a couple of rays from the tail fin attached to the strip. Hook the strip through its front end.

## How to Troll for Crappies With Multiple Lines

LURES include: (1) Mister Twister Teeny jig, (2) Napier Sand Hornet, (3) Napier Sand Hornet with spinner, (4) Bass Buster Super Beetle Twist.

TROLL slowly through a likely crappie area with several rods secured in rod holders. Set the front rods widest, the middle rods next widest, and the rear rods narrowest. Keep all lines at the same length, 25 to 30 feet behind the boat. This way, the lines won't tangle, even if you turn sharply.

## How to Catch Crappies Around Spawning Time

LOOK for crappies in old bulrush beds. The beds aren't as distinct as bluegill beds, but you'll see the fish between the broken-off shoots.

TIE a piece of cloth to an old bulrush shoot where you spot some crappies. They'll move away temporarily, but will return in a few minutes.

CAST a slip-bobber and jig over a bed. Twitch the bobber to give the jig action. Often, the bobber barely moves when a crappie inhales the jig.

## How to Catch Sunfish During a Mayfly Hatch

LOOK for mayflies clinging to leaves of willow trees or other plants along a lakeshore or streambank. Sunfish congregate below overhanging vegetation to grab insects that fall into the water. They also feed on mayfly nymphs that swim from the bottom toward the surface where they emerge as adult mayflies.

# How to Catch Suspended Sunfish

Large sunfish lack the strong schooling instinct of smaller ones. After spawning, big sunfish, especially bluegills and redears, retreat to deeper water. Many scatter along shoreline breaks, points and humps where they remain through summer, making it difficult for anglers to catch large numbers of fish.

Most fishermen assume that sunfish hug bottom most of the time. But large sunfish often suspend during the summer months. Expert anglers sometimes catch bluegills or redears 10 feet below the surface in water 20 to 30 feet deep.

Locating suspended sunfish can be one of the toughest challenges in panfish angling. Even if you find the fish, there is no guarantee you will catch them. Sunfish have no trouble finding food in summer, so they often ignore baits or strike halfheartedly.

Be persistent as you search. Cover a lot of water and use a depth finder to zero in on the fish. You may be able to concentrate sunfish, especially redears, with a chum bag. If the fish refuse live bait, try a spinner or other flashy lure.

## How to Cast for Suspended Sunfish

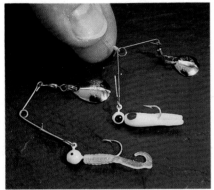

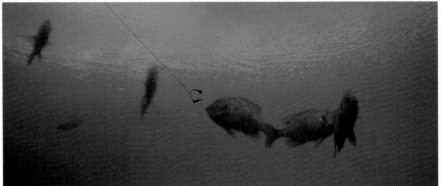

ATTACH a ¹⁄₁₆- or ¹⁄₃₂-ounce spinnerbait to 4- or 6-pound mono. Light line makes it easier to cast the tiny lure and allows it to sink deeper.

CAST the spinnerbait while drifting over open water. To locate fish, let it sink to a different depth before beginning each retrieve. Watch your depth finder closely for blips that may indicate the location of suspended sunfish. If you spot fish, work the area thoroughly before moving on.

## How to Drift for Suspended Sunfish

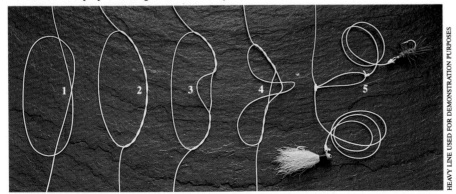

HEAVY LINE USED FOR DEMONSTRATION PURPOSES

TIE a blood loop by (1) making an overhand knot where you want to form the loop. (2) Pass the free end through the overhand knot five more times. (3) Form an opening halfway between the six wraps. (4) Push the loop through the opening, then pull on both ends of the line to snug up the knot. (5) Add a short mono dropper and a wet fly. Tie a ¹⁄₁₆-ounce jig to the main line.

LOWER the rig straight down while drifting over a potential sunfish area. Experiment with different lengths of line to find the fish. If you catch a sunfish, drift through the area again.

## No-Tangle Tandem Rig

Popper-and-nymph combos are great for bluegills in shallow water. The popper attracts the fish, but most of them, particularly the big ones, hit the nymph.

One common way of rigging flies in tandem is to cut your leader and join the pieces with a blood or barrel knot, leaving a tag end long enough for the dropper. But tying a dropper this way is time consuming, and the flies often tangle. Also, you need to tie up a new leader or cut the dropper off to go back to fishing one fly.

Here's a rig that's quick and easy to assemble, doesn't tangle, and is easy to take apart when you want to use a single fly:

ATTACH a small cork- or foam-bodied popper to a 6-foot leader. Tie 2 feet of 4-pound mono to the bend of the popper hook with a clinch knot, then attach a size 12 weighted nymph. The popper makes a good strike indicator, disappearing when a fish takes the nymph.

## A Little Leech Lasts Longer

Sunfish will gobble up a small jig tipped with a piece of garden worm or nightcrawler. Trouble is, after one or two bites, the worm is gone. Here's a bait that's just as appealing but lasts much longer. Tip a 1/32-ounce jig with a 1/2-inch piece of a leech, preferably from the narrow head end, where the flesh is toughest. The bait is small enough to catch nibblers, yet it will stay on the hook indefinitely.

## Modify Jigs for Papermouths

If you hook a crappie in the thin membrane around its mouth, the hook can tear out easily. Here's a way to increase your chances of hooking a crappie in the tough tissue in the roof of the mouth:

BEND the hook of a crappie jig about 10 degrees past its original position (dotted line). Now the hook is more likely to stick in the roof of the mouth than in the membrane.

## Brush Beater Crappie Jigs

Crappies often hang out in heavy brush and timber. No matter how carefully you work a jig through the branches, you snag up. Even if you don't lose the jig, you'll shake the branches as you try to rip free, usually spooking the fish.

One solution would be to put a mono-loop weedguard (p. 83) on your jig. Here's another way of rigging a snag-free crappie jig.

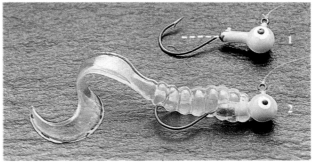

BEND the hook of a bare jig (1) downward about 20 degrees from the normal position (dotted line). (2) Thread on a plastic grub so the hook point is barely exposed.

## Pennants for Panfish

Catching spawning bluegills or yellow perch is easy because you can see them in the shallows. But once the fish move to deeper water, they can be hard to locate. Here's a way to bring the fish to you:

DROP a rope of colorful pennants (the kind car dealers use) in an area likely to hold bluegills or perch. A weight on one end of the pennants will keep them from drifting and a float on the other end will mark the spot. Leave the area for an hour or more. The bright flags attract these panfish and keep them in the area until you return. Fish around the flags with small jigs or live bait, either anchoring over the flags or casting from a short distance away.

## Scout Ice-Fishing Spots in Summer

Finding crappies under the ice is tough. You may have to drill dozens of holes before you get onto fish. And using a fish finder through the ice is far more time consuming than in open water.

When fishing in the spring and summer, find landmarks that will help you pinpoint your crappie spots once the ice forms. In early winter, the fish are found in the same shallow areas they occupy in the spring. By midwinter they move into the same deepwater spots they occupy in midsummer.

## Read Depth Through Bad Ice

In early winter, you can easily sound through the ice with a depth finder. But later in winter, snow, slush and air bubbles interfere with the signal, so you have to drill a new hole each time you want to take a reading. Here's how you can sound through the ice, even if the lake is covered by slush and snow:

SOUND through recently drilled holes, where the ice is smooth and clear. Pour a little water on the ice, set the transducer in the puddle and take a reading.

## See Light Bites in the Dark

In midwinter, panfish sometimes mouth the bait so lightly you don't feel a thing. Or they grab the bait and swim up with it. Here's a way to detect these soft bites and set the hook.

Fish from a darkhouse or cover the windows of your fish house so you can see down the hole. In clear water, you'll be able to watch the fish take the bait. In deeper or murkier water, you probably won't be able to see the fish, but if you're using a light-colored bait, it will disappear when a fish grabs it.

## Super-Tough Perch Bait ↑

The way yellow perch steal bait, you can spend more time baiting your hook than fishing. When you're jigging through the ice and fishing is hot, try this trick to make a bait that attracts perch with smell, taste and action and won't tear off the hook:

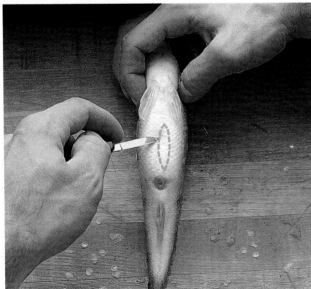

SCALE the belly of a small perch and cut out an inch-long strip (dotted lines). Split one end of the meat to form two tails. Hook the other end of the strip on the jig.

## Preserve Perch Eyes

Perch eyes make great bait for walleyes, saugers and even perch. So, when you clean a mess of perch, poke out the eyes with your thumb and save them. But don't put the eyes in a freezer or they'll get mushy. Instead, put them in a small jar and fill it with salt water. Keep the jar in the refrigerator until your next ice-fishing trip. Use an eye to tip a lure, or thread one on a plain hook and fish it on a 4-inch dropper beneath a small jigging spoon.

209

## Light up Ice-Fishing Holes

When ice fishing at night, it's tough to see a bobber. Most anglers set a lantern on the ice, but the bobber may be hard to see because of the shadow cast by the rim of the hole. And when a fish pulls the bobber under, you can't see it at all. Try this trick to help you see better. It works with a light source as small as a candle or as large as a lantern.

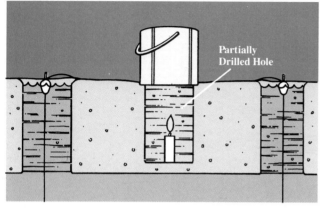

Partially Drilled Hole

BORE a hole in the ice between the holes you're fishing in, stopping just before the auger breaks through. Set a candle or lantern in the hole. Light will travel through the ice to nearby holes, illuminating the bobbers from the side and below so they're plainly visible (photo at right). Cover the hole on windy nights to keep the flame from blowing out, but be sure enough air gets in so the flame doesn't smother.

## Chum for Panfish

It's easier to bring panfish to you than for you to find them, especially when you're fishing through the ice. Borrow a tip from the saltwater angler's bag of tricks and try chumming. It works best for sunfish and perch, stirring up their competitive instincts so they feed more aggressively and keeping their interest so they stay around longer. Because fish must be able to see the chum from some distance away, chumming works best in clear water over a clean bottom, rather than in heavy cover. Here's how to do it:

DROP a few BB-sized chunks of frozen shrimp down the hole. Once the fish move in, chum sparingly but often to keep them around. As you change bait, use your old bait for chum. It's important to drop the chum in the same spot each time. When fishing in open water, drop the chum next to a marker or other stationary object.

210

TRY grass shrimp to catch bluegills and shellcrackers. You can find the small crustaceans by picking through clumps of water hyacinth.

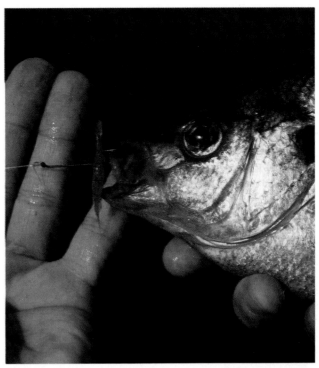

USE an extra-long-shank hook so you can unhook sunfish more easily. Even if the fish is hooked deep, you can still grab the end of the hook to push it free.

## Tips for Catching Crappies in Brush

DABBLE a small jig in the tops using a graphite extension pole. These ultrasensitive poles make it possible to feel the twigs so you can drop your jig into pockets in the brush. And you can easily feel even the lightest bite.

USE a 1/16- to 1/8-ounce brushguard jig, such as this Northland Weed-Less Sink'n jig head, when fishing in heavy brush. A brushguard will prevent most snags, but if you do hang up, free the jig as shown below.

UNSNAG jigs using a 1-ounce bell sinker with a snap attached to it (inset). Simply clip the sinker onto your line and drop it. If it doesn't free the jig immediately, jiggle the rod a little so the sinker bounces on the jig.

## Finesse Picky Perch

The motion and flash of a small jigging spoon will get a perch's attention. If the fish is aggressive, it will hit the spoon right away. A less active fish, however, will watch the spoon but won't bite.

When finicky fish are giving you fits, try this rig. It catches these inactive perch and the aggressive ones at the same time, whether you're fishing open water or through the ice.

MAKE a tandem rig by tying a barrel swivel to the line. Add 8 inches of 6-pound mono and tie a small jigging spoon on the end. Attach 6 inches of 4-pound mono to the swivel; add a small wet fly or nymph. Even perch with a full belly are curious; they'll move in to inspect the flashy spoon and may take a nip at the fly.

## Outwit Fussy Crappies

In spring, you'll find crappies preparing to spawn in shallow water near cover such as brush or bulrushes. But often they don't feed much and shy away from most lures and baits.

Coax them into hitting by casting a lively minnow without a sinker. With no weight to hold it back, the minnow moves naturally and appeals even to the fussiest crappies.

## Detect Light-Biters

At times, crappies swim upward as they suck in a small jig, so you can't feel the strike. If you're using a regular bobber, it moves too little to notice. Here's a way to catch these fish, no matter how delicately they take your lure:

USE a European-style slip bobber (inset) on a 2-pound-test mono to detect subtle takes. Tie on a 1/64- or 1/32-ounce jig. Add enough split-shot above the jig that only about 1/4-inch of the bobber sticks out of the water. Tiny European shot is best for the fine adjustment necessary. If a crappie swims upward as it sucks in the jig, taking some of the weight off the line, the super-sensitive bobber rises enough to clearly indicate a strike.

*How to Make and Use a "Crappie Stick"*

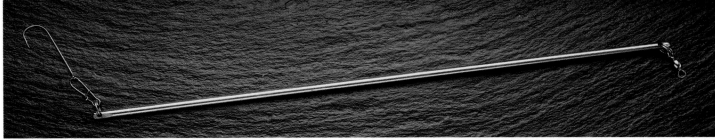

CUT a heavy metal rod into 12-inch lengths, drill holes in each end (you may have to flatten the ends first), add split rings, then attach a barrel swivel to one end and a snap with a size 1/0 Aberdeen hook to the other.

LOWER the rig vertically until you reach the desired depth. Make sure your boat is anchored securely so it doesn't swing. If you hook a limb, drop your rod tip; the weight of the crappie stick will usually free the hook.

HORSE the fish out of the cover quickly to prevent it from wrapping around a limb. The long metal rod reduces the chances that the fish will tangle in the branches, especially if you exert steady pressure.

*Other Crappie-fishing Tips*

USE a long-shank wire hook that will bend enough to pull free of snags. The larger the hook, the thicker the wire, and the less the hook will bend. Most anglers believe that a size 2 to1/0 hook is ideal.

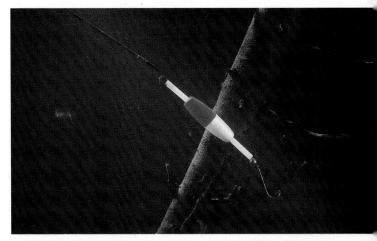

SUBSTITUTE a slip-bobber for a peg bobber if you're hanging up in shallow brush. When you get snagged, simply reel up slack and push your rod tip against the bobber, which then pushes on the split shot and hook to free the rig.

213

Catfish

# When, Where and How to Catch Catfish

Catfish bite best at night, but can be caught during the day, especially after a heavy rain when river levels are rising. Catfishing slacks off when the water temperature drops below 55°F, and below 40°F, they do not feed. In large northern rivers, catfish form huge schools in winter, lying dormant in deep water.

Catfish are primarily river fish. They also live in reservoirs and lakes connected to rivers, and have been stocked extensively in lakes and ponds throughout much of the United States.

Flathead and channel cats prefer similar habitats, but flatheads tend to be loners. Both like rivers with slow to moderate current, deep pools, downed timber and sunken logs for cover and bottoms of sand, gravel and rubble. Catfish live in deep pools during the day, then move into shallow feeding areas after dark. Blue cats prefer faster water, often living in swift chutes or pools with noticeable current.

Most anything goes when it comes to catfish baits, including soap, congealed chicken blood, animal entrails, rotten clams, dead birds, mice, frogs, worms, crayfish, grasshoppers, cheese, doughballs and stinkbaits. Live or dead fish, especially those with high oil content, such as gizzard shad and smelt, are also effective.

Whatever the bait, it should be fished on bottom. Catfish swim slowly, groping with their barbels to find food. Suspended baits are usually ignored.

Catfish anglers do not need sophisticated equipment, but it should be strong. For fishing around snags and rocks, 20- to 50-pound test line is best. Heavy tackle can turn a big catfish, preventing it from wrapping the line around a log and breaking free. In tailraces with strong current, up to a pound of weight may be needed to keep the bait on bottom and prevent it from drifting.

## Popular Catfish Baits and Rigs

BLUE AND CHANNEL CATS prefer cut fish, worms or baits that give off a strong smell, such as cheeses or stinkbaits. However, they occasionally take live minnows and even artificial lures such as spinners.

FLATHEAD CATFISH are caught almost exclusively on live fish, though a dead fish rigged so it flutters in the current can be effective. Baitfish weighing up to 2 pounds are used for big flatheads.

RIGS include: (1) slip-sinker rig, tied with a 1-ounce egg sinker and a size 1 hook baited with stink bait; (2) Wolf River rig, tied with a three-way swivel, 3-ounce pyramid sinker, and a 5/0 hook baited with a sucker.

*Typical Catfish Habitat*

STOCKED PONDS are common in the southern United States. Many are harvested commercially, though some are stocked for sport fishing.

DEEP POOLS below large dams are resting and feeding areas for larger catfish. Cats bite day or night in these turbulent waters.

LOG-STREWN CHANNELS, with deep holes and a combination of slow and fast currents, are prime catfish spots in many rivers.

SUBMERGED LOGS in deep holes along outside bends make ideal habitat for catfish, particularly flatheads.

Cats rest in deep water around the logs during the day, then move shallower at night to feed.

216

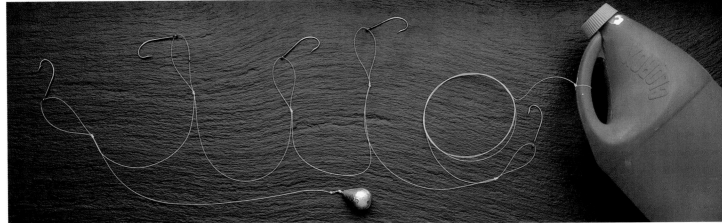

TIE 10 feet of 60-pound mono to the handle of a bleach bottle. Thread on 5 size 2/0 hooks, then add a 2- to 3-ounce weight to the other end of the line. Attach the hooks at 18-inch intervals, using the same knot as on a multiple-jig setup. Paint the jugs fluorescent orange so you can spot them from a distance.

BAIT each hook with a minnow, crayfish, shrimp or some cheesebait, starting with the bottom hook first. Check the wind direction before setting the jugs, then place them just upwind of the area you want to fish.

CONTINUE to toss out jugs as you motor along. Spread them in a line at a right angle to the wind so each one covers different water. Finding the jugs will be easier if you set them so they drift into shore, not into open water.

USE binoculars to find the jugs. On a windy day, they may drift a mile or two, but they will usually wind up in a fairly small area.

STORE your jug lines by first dropping the weight inside. Then gather all the hooks, stuff them into the jug and screw on the cap.

# Cats That Ain't Kittens

by Gerald Almy

*Using his cut-bait technique, Captain John Sellers has probably boated more giant catfish than anyone else in North America*

It's a warm Indian-summer day on 60,000-acre Lake Moultrie, the smaller of two sprawling impoundments that make up Santee-Cooper's 170,000 acres of fish-filled water. Thick mats of pewter-colored clouds block out the sun. A light wind blows the gray-green waters in a slapping drumbeat against the hull of John Sellers' boat.

Sellers grabs a fresh gizzard shad from the cooler, cuts off the head, slices the body into five ¾-inch steaks, then discards the tail. He impales the steaks and the head on 5/0 hooks. He strips line from his reels in carefully measured increments, then places the rods into sturdy, black iron holders, so the tips point parallel to the water and are just a few feet above it.

And now it's a waiting game — waiting and watching the rod tips, as we drift along rough bottom structure in 30 feet of water. The baits dangle just inches off the bottom. We pass over an old canal 40 feet down, dug by slaves to connect the Santee and Cooper rivers long before the famous lakes were formed half a century ago. Sitting back, we study the rods intently from the padded seats of the 22-foot Citation — once white, now with a tannish cast from the slime and grit of years of catfishing.

Though Santee-Cooper is the birthplace of freshwater striper fishing, and is renowned for cypress-loving largemouths up to 16 pounds and world-class crappies up to 5, the undisputed king of this huge pair of lakes is the catfish. And no wonder. What other fish can you go after in fresh water with a realistic chance of catching a 40-, 50-, even 60-pounder? Fish like that are a distinct possibility every day at Santee-Cooper. Cats now draw more interest than any other species on the lakes, thanks in large part to the tremendous catches made by "Big John" Sellers — a man who's 5½ feet of solid catfishing legend.

At the age of 22, Sellers became a full-time guide on Santee-Cooper. The lakes were young then, and channel cats, largemouth bass, and stripers were the main gamefish. When flatheads were added to the lake, and then blue catfish, John found himself catching bigger and bigger cats each season.

Although Sellers still guides for striped bass, the catfish is his first choice. Stripers run 5 to 15 pounds in the lakes; blue cats in the better spots average 10 to 25 pounds, with the chance of a 30- to 60-pounder ever present. The lake record is 86 pounds, and John has a hunch there are cats here that would top the century mark.

Sellers is a quiet, gentle man who in his own way — with action rather than talk — has promoted the

---

**John Sellers**

**Home:** *Cross, South Carolina*

**Occupation:** *Catfish and striped bass guide*

*Catching a 50-pound fish in fresh water is a pinnacle that few anglers ever reach. But for John Sellers, landing one that size or better is almost a weekly occurrence. He guides for giant blue, flathead, and channel catfish on the Santee-Cooper lakes in central South Carolina.*

*He's been a catfish fan since he first caught them as a youngster in the small tannin-stained creeks near his home. The Santee-Cooper lakes were formed in the early 1940s, and Sellers started guiding on these waters for catfish and stripers about ten years later. Since then, he has established a reputation as one of the finest catfishermen not only in the South, but in the entire country.*

*Sellers won two of the first major catfishing contests held on Santee-Cooper. In the first, he amassed a single-day winning catch of 263 pounds to win the total weight division, and his largest cat, a 54-pounder, took big-fish honors. During a single year, anglers guided by Sellers took 100 catfish weighing over 50 pounds. His top blue cat so far is a 64-pounder, and top flathead 49 pounds. On one incredible day, a single client from North Carolina caught five catfish weighing from 53 to 59 pounds.*

218

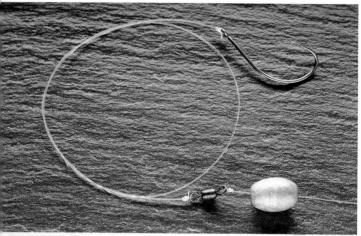

TIE size 4/0 to 6/0 hook to 18-inch, 50-pound mono leader; add barrel swivel to other end. Thread ½- to 2-ounce egg sinker onto 30-pound mono line; tie to swivel.

SLICE a large gizzard shad (shown), threadfin shad, mullet, or blueback herring into steaks ¾ inch wide. Only steaks and head are used as bait.

HOOK the head lightly through the snout. The steaks (not shown) are hooked in the belly, through one side and out the other.

sport and challenge of trophy catfishing. His catches speak louder than any sales pitch could. Calmly, without boasting, he has rewritten the record books on the number of 50-pound fish one guide has accounted for — he's also rewritten the how-to manuals on fooling giant cats. In this rural area where fishing and hunting are the main topics of conversation at roadside diners, Sellers has become something of a hero.

Once, in a single day, Sellers' clients came in with thirteen huge catfish. Their total weight? Four hundred and thirty-seven pounds.

The two anglers aboard today don't have their sights set quite so high. They do, however, hope they can latch onto at least a single trophy cat. Sharon Taylor has come 750 miles from New York to fish for her favorite quarry; I've traveled 500 miles from Virginia.

Hearteningly, the cats are there. Using his depth finder, Sellers locates appropriate structure — "anything rough or broken, or covered with stumps, or dropping off sharply" — then pinpoints fish holding near the lake floor. We can see them clearly on Sellers' Si-Tex LCR, hovering like huge logs just off the bottom.

Sellers begins a drift. "If the big cats are around," he says, "you can usually see them easily on the depth finder. The only exception is when it's real windy and rough. Then they're harder to see. They just kind of blend into the bottom."

He has dozens of favorite catfish locations on the lakes, discovered in endless hours of studying topographical maps, motoring around the lake with a depth finder, then test-fishing. Among these spots are hills, dropoffs, saddles, edges of creek channels, ditches, submerged islands, holes on an otherwise flat bottom, flooded bridges, roadbeds, sunken canals and building foundations. All are good structure and cover for blue cats. Occasionally he also fishes fields of dead standing timber, especially for flatheads.

The depth we're fishing now is 34 feet — a typical level in midday fishing for cats, according to John. "Early in the day and late in the evening the fish move shallower. I sometimes fish in as little as 8 or 10 feet of water in the morning or at dusk. The big ones often move in then to feed on flats, bars, points, and shallow humps. During the middle of the day like this, though, they hang deeper, 20 to 60 feet, around rough cover.

"Whatever depth you're fishing, it's important to keep your bait within inches of the bottom. I use anywhere from ½ to 2 ounces of lead, and let line out whenever necessary during the drift to make sure the bait stays close to the bottom. You'll get hung up some. That's just part of the game if you want to catch big cats."

A rod bounces with a sharp tapping in its holder. The two anglers jump to their feet, wondering if they should grab the rod and pay out line to the fish, or go ahead and strike.

"No need for that," Sellers says calmly. "I don't fish for little cats. I use big baits and big hooks so the small ones can't take them. We catch a few tykes, but most of the fish you see bobbing the rod lightly like that are just youngsters that can't get the big chunks of shad or mullet in their mouths.

"When a nice cat takes, you'll know it. They strike like a bolt of lightning. The rod jerks down hard and stays down. Sometimes the tip buries itself in the water. They hook themselves. I've never seen a fish in fresh water that strikes as violently as a big blue cat."

Sellers has actually had cats that were hooked in the shallows leap clear of the water like a largemouth or tarpon. Expect your heart to creep into your throat a bit when a 30-pound blue does that.

As we drift into the channel of the old canal, Sellers releases line from the reels so the baits stay on the bottom. Soon a tenacious 3-pounder scarfs down a chunk of cut mullet and holds on until it hooks itself. The fish is cranked in unceremoniously, and Sellers quickly twists the hook free and releases it unharmed — a potential trophy cat.

"I've tried fishing at night," he goes on, "but they don't seem to bite any better then. Big cats feed during the day as well as at night. You just have to know where they hang out, what they want to eat, and how to present it to them. Another thing — when you hook into a 50-pounder, he's a lot easier to deal with in daylight than at night. Big cats are going to feed an hour or two every day. The trick is to put a bait in front of them when that feed period occurs. It might be early in the day, late, or high noon."

Drifting is another of Sellers' secrets for catching giant cats. Most fishermen believe you have to anchor and wait for cats, letting a scent trail slither out in the current and waft its odor to the whiskered quarry. Keep the bait in place, goes the adage, so the slow, lazy fish can find and eat it. Sellers knows that big trophy cats are far more aggressive and faster than this. They can easily nab a bait that's drifting across the bottom, and do not hesitate to do so.

Only an hour into the afternoon, we've already swept across hundreds of yards of prime bottom

*Sellers uses 9-foot graphite rods, heavy level-wind reels*

## How to Drift-Fish with Cut Bait

PLACE rods in holders after lowering baits to a few inches from bottom. As you drift, watch rod tips for bites and check your sonar for changes in bottom depth.

ADJUST line length quickly when depth changes, to keep baits in fish zone and minimize snagging. Reel in periodically to check baits for debris or to add fresh bait.

contour, dragging six tempting baits that can attract cats with their scent as well as movement. "By drifting, I cover a lot more water and actually search for fish. Instead of waiting for the cats to come to me, I go to them."

There are times when Sellers will anchor: when the fish are less active in midwinter, when the wind is so strong that the boat rocks violently and it's hard to control the baits, or when the cats are in the shallows in March and April. "Big cats might be in as little as 3 to 5 feet of water in spring, because the shallow water warms more quickly than the depths. For drifting, there are too many stumps and snags to get hung up on, and you're likely to spook the fish if your boat goes over them in water that thin." Anchoring and casting up onto prime feeding areas such as bars, points, and humps is more effective.

Another myth John refutes is that big cats can only be caught on putrid blood or cheese concoctions, stink baits, or rotten fish. These baits are best for channel cats, but blues and flatheads prefer fresh fish. "You don't need a rotten, smelly offering to attract big cats," says Sellers. "They're used to feeding on other fish, usually live ones. They're a clean, strong sport fish. They're not garbage eaters."

Sellers uses fresh fish whenever possible; the rest of the time, he settles for the freshest frozen fish he can find. The best bait varies with the season. Whole threadfin shad are good during the winter months. Later, from mid-February into April, blueback herring are by far the top offering. These slender, oily, anadromous fish swarm up the Cooper River on their spawning run during this period. They get into the lakes via a lift at the dam at Moncks Corner. Sellers catches his herring below the dam with a cast net; sometimes he freezes an extra supply for later use.

By summer, cut gizzard shad becomes the prime offering. Sellers catches these baitfish at night in the canal between lakes Marion and Moultrie. He attracts them with lights and then hurls a cast net. Cut mullet, frozen or fresh, are equally effective. Cut sections of bluegills, or whole small ones, will work in a pinch.

Whichever bait he settles on, Sellers likes a sturdy, wide-gap hook such as the Eagle Claw Series 42. He uses a 50-pound mono leader, and a ½- to 2-ounce egg sinker. His 9-foot graphite rods are medium-heavy; the heavy-duty level-wind reels are spooled with 30-pound mono. It's sporting tackle, yet strong enough to handle fish in the 30- to 60-pound class, when used properly.

*Sellers struggles to hoist 53-pound blue cat*

At 3:30 p.m., that tackle gets a chance to show its stuff. A heavy fish nails a bait and Sharon Taylor grabs the rod. The big cat comes up grudgingly after ten minutes of stubborn fighting. Sellers gets ready with the long-handled net, but the cat wallows and thrashes just out of reach, astounding the anglers with its size. Then the monster dives deep again and slugs it out for another ten minutes.

"You rarely get them the first time they come up," says Sellers, reassuringly. "About twenty minutes — that's what it usually takes to get a big one in. He's giving up some bubbles from his air bladder now. That should mean he's about ready."

The long rod provides leverage to keep the cat away from the boat as it struggles to dive under the motor. Finally, 25 minutes after hookup, the grueling battle comes to an end. Taylor pumps the fish to the surface and the net enmeshes it. Hoisting hard, Sellers pulls in a 53-pounder. After photos, it's wrestled into the stash box in the front deck. Even when the fish is curled up, its tail sticks out — like the antlers of a trophy buck peeking out above a pickup truck's bed. And it is every bit as much a trophy.

The wind is rising now, kicking up out of the east at 10 to 15 knots. Sellers shakes his head disappointedly. "Strong wind is the worst thing in the world for this type of fishing. A light wind, almost calm, is best. When the wind kicks up, it stirs up the big cats and they move around a lot more, so they're harder to pinpoint. It also rocks the boat so much that the baits constantly bob up and down 2 or 3 feet. That makes it harder for the cats to connect when they strike." The best bet, according to Sellers, is to head for the lee side of the lake, where the water is calmer.

Unfortunately, the spots that have been producing best of late are on the windward side. So we stick it out, rocking and bouncing, hoping the baits are not moving too much to entice the cats. As it turns out, they aren't. The day wears on, and three more smallish fish come aboard. Many others rap the baits momentarily, then shake free.

Unless the weather gets extremely cold in your area, John feels you should be able to catch cats year around. And while natural bait is his overwhelming first choice, Sellers says that blues will occasionally strike artificials. He's caught them up

to 40 pounds while casting bucktail jigs for stripers. At times John has even encountered schools of big cats crashing bait on the surface like stripers or white bass will do. Tossing a shad-imitating lure or white jig into the melee can result in some jarring takes from 10- to 40-pounders.

The wind whips harder as the day grows long. Under the circumstances, Sellers feels fortunate we've landed a 53-pounder plus four smaller cats. But as the sun peeks through the clouds low in the sky and casts a warm orange glow on the lake, a rod throbs violently in its holder and line sizzles off the reel. After fifteen minutes of gut-busting battle, a 44-pounder comes thrashing wildly into Sellers' outstretched net.

Two catfish — together weighing an incredible 97 pounds. After quick photos, the second big cat is freed and lunges back into the murky lake to sulk over its rude encounter.

### Where Sellers Finds Catfish in Medium-Depth Reservoirs

*Good catfish spots include (A) creek-channel edges, (B) submerged hills and ridges, (C) flooded bridges, (D) old river channels, (E) flooded roadbeds, (F) flooded building foundations, (G) flooded standing timber, (H) sunken islands, (I) saddles between ridges, (J) depressions on a flat bottom, and (K) ditches and canals. These spots produce catfish year around. (NOTE: this is a hypothetical map intended to portray the types of spots Sellers fishes.)*

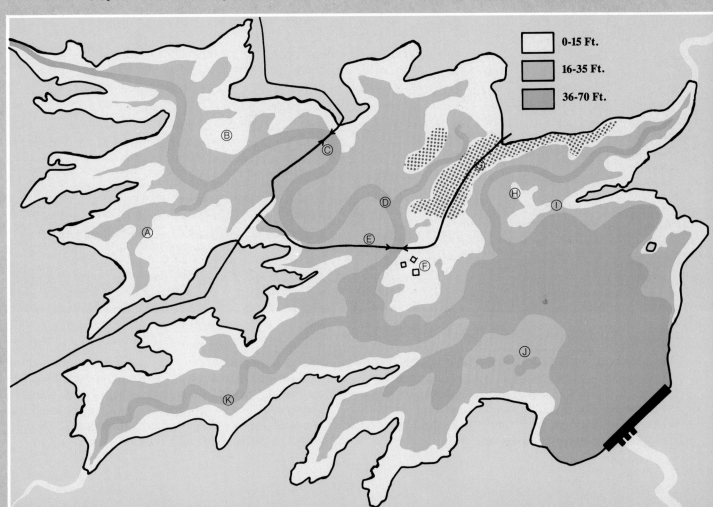

# Catfish Tips

## Keep Baitfish on a Short Leash

Flathead catfish anglers often weight a big, frisky sunfish, sucker or bullhead with a slip-sinker and put a sinker stop about 18 inches above the hook so the bait can move freely. But in the tangled timber big flatheads love, a baitfish on an 18-inch tether will hide in the wood or wrap your line around a snag.

Keep the baitfish close to the sinker by eliminating the sinker stop entirely or by placing a stop only a few inches up the line. Reel in the slack. If you want the baitfish to swim a little more, feed a few inches of line through the sinker. With the baitfish on such a short leash, a catfish can catch it easily.

## Line Release for Bank Fishing

When bottom fishing from shore with live bait, you should keep the line under a little tension so the wind or current doesn't carry it out. Yet line must pay out when a fish bites or it will drop the bait. To get just the right amount of tension, try this trick:

SLIP a loop of line under a matchstick held to the foregrip with a rubber band. The match will keep the line from drifting away, but will release the line when a fish hits. If the current or wind is strong, increase the friction on the loop by pulling the line in tighter to the rubber band. If there is little current, or if you feel that light-biting catfish are dropping the bait because they feel resistance, move the line farther from the rubber band. This way, the slightest tug will pull it free.

## Wild Baitfish Tame Cats

Veteran catfishermen know that baitfish caught from the river they're fishing are far superior to pond-reared baitfish purchased from the local bait shop.

Almost any kind of wild baitfish, including chubs, suckers and sunfish, will work.

The reason is simple: to baitfish that inhabit the river, catfish are natural enemies. When a hooked baitfish spots a cat, it struggles frantically to escape. The commotion arouses the cat's interest. A pond-reared baitfish, on the other hand, has never seen a catfish and has no reason to fear it.

## Keep Chicken Liver on the Hook

Chicken liver is a top channel cat bait, but liver won't stay on a hook if it gets warm and mushy. If you fish from the bank or a boat, keep the bait in a cooler. If you wade, pack the liver in a plastic bag and drop it in a canvas creel with an ice pack. Here are three other tricks that help keep the bait on the hook:

IMPALE the chicken liver on a number 8 or 10 treble hook, making sure each hook point pierces the bait. Whether the liver is firm or mushy, a treble hook holds it more securely than a single hook.

WRAP mushy liver in a patch of nylon mesh or stocking. The mesh lets odors escape yet keeps the bait from falling apart. Form a bag by gathering the edges of the fabric with the hook, twisting the hook to close the top and hooking the mesh again to keep the bag from opening up. Or tie the bag shut with thread before pushing a hook through it.

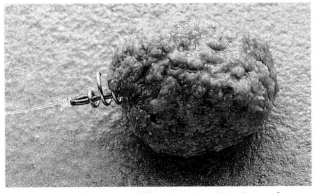

MIX chicken liver with Wheaties in a blender to form a thick paste. Mold the bait around a bait-holder treble hook to form a doughball.

## Longer-Lasting Scent

Catfish are drawn to some commercial and homemade scents, but many of these concoctions wash off after a few minutes in the water. Here's a way to make the scent last longer.

Cut a piece of sponge about 1-inch square and bury a bait hook in it. Soak the sponge in scent. Fish the sponge in one spot or drift it slowly along the bottom. Reapply scent every half hour or so.

The sponge stays on the hook well and releases the scent slowly. Because it has a soft texture like real food, a catfish will pick it up and swim off, giving you time to set the hook.

## Enhance Natural Odor

Flatheads, blues and big channel cats are lazy; they'll eat a good-sized baitfish but usually won't go much out of their way to do it. Here's how you can make any baitfish more appealing to big cats by slowing it down so they can catch it more easily, and at the same time increasing the amount of scent it gives off:

TRIM part of the tail and pectoral fins before rigging the bait with a slip-sinker. The smell of fluids that seep from the cuts will attract catfish. The bait will move frantically, but without normal fins won't be able to dodge a big cat.

226

## Jigs for Cats

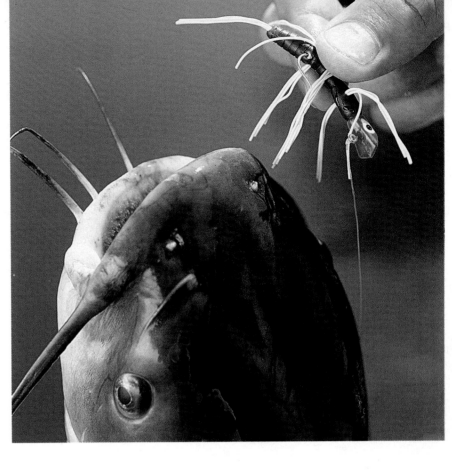

Few anglers think of jigs as catfish lures, but jig fishermen who target walleyes or bass in catfish waters catch plenty of cats by accident. It's not hard to understand why jigs catch so many catfish: They can easily be fished on the bottom, right where the catfish are.

Jigs tipped with live bait such as minnows, nightcrawlers or leeches work best, although it's not unusual to catch catfish on plain bucktail, twister-tail or rubber-legged jigs. Work the lure along the bottom in slow hops, just as you would for walleyes or bass.

## Keep Clam Meat on the Hook

Clams make good bait for catfish and many bottom-feeding saltwater fish, such as flounder and surfperch. The meat of a clam consists of the firm muscle mass, called the "foot," and some other tissue, which is softer. The foot is easy to keep on the hook; the other tissue is not. Most anglers use only the foot, but here's a way to make use of the soft meat as well:

WRAP the soft meat with about 8 inches of thread, leaving the hook point exposed. The thread will cut into the meat, making a knot unnecessary.

## Junkyard Slip-Sinkers

The debris-strewn bottoms of good catfish holes can gobble up a lot of sinkers. Here's how to cut your losses by making your own slip-sinkers out of otherwise worthless scrap:

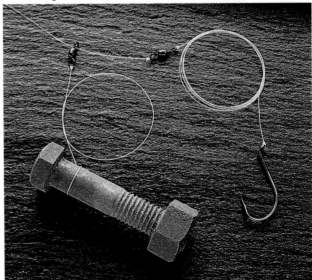

TIE a heavy washer, bolt, nut or other scrap to a 12-inch piece of mono. Attach a barrel swivel to the other end. Slip the line from your rod through the free end of the swivel, and tie it to a second swivel. Run a short leader and bait hook off the second swivel. The "junkyard dropper" should be lighter than the main line. That way, if the scrap hangs up, the dropper will break, sparing the rest of the rig.

## ← Toughen up Bait

Almost any kind of dead minnows will catch channel cats, but dead bait softens up with use and tears off the hook. Here's a way to keep it on the hook much longer.

Spread the minnows on a screen and let them dry in the sun for several hours. The screen lets both sides dry out and toughen up. Use the minnows as soon as they're dry, or freeze them in a plastic bag to use later.

## Cats Want Leeches — Dead or Alive

Most anglers think of leeches as good bait for walleyes, but leeches also work well for a lot of other species, including channel cats.

Walleyes seldom bite on dead leeches, but channels don't seem to care whether they're dead or alive. In fact, when cats are off the bite, the rank smell of the dead leeches often stirs their interest.

Save your dead leeches; you may want to use them in combination with live ones or with some other type of live bait. Dead leeches will keep for several days in cold water.

## Remove Catfish and Bullheads Fast

Catfish and bullheads often swallow the hook. Digging it out, even with a needlenose, is messy and time consuming. Here's a quick way to get a fish off your line and get back to fishing.

Tie up several bait hooks on 1-foot leaders, each with a loop at the other end. Tie a snap to your fishing line and clip it to a leader loop. These fish aren't leader shy and won't notice the snap. If one swallows the hook, unsnap the leader, clip on another, bait up and return to fishing. Recover the hooks when you clean the fish.

## Lift Baits Above Snags

Years after a reservoir fills, a tangle of roots, limbs and logs remains on the lake bed, making it difficult to reach bottom-hugging fish without snagging the debris on the bottom. Here's how some southern catfish anglers solve the problem. The technique will work in any snag-filled lake or slow-moving stream.

RAISE the bait off the bottom by pegging a 2- to 3-inch Styrofoam float about a foot up the leader (inset). The float lifts the hook and bait. The closer the float is to the hook, the higher the bait will ride.

## Feel Your Way Around Snags

Big flatheads lie in deep holes filled with sunken timber. It's tough to know where to cast. Get too close to the wood, and the sinker or hook will hang up. Stay too far away, and the big cats won't find the bait. To place the bait properly, you need to figure out the precise location of the logs and limbs. Here's how:

FAN-CAST with a 1-ounce bell sinker tied to the end of your line. Retrieve it along the bottom. The sinker seldom hangs up, and you can feel it crawl over logs, limbs, brush and rocks. Once you get a clear picture of the bottom, you can cast near snags but not into them.

## Steelheading for Catfish

Most catfishermen add a good-sized sinker to their line and let their bait rest motionless on the bottom of the river. In time, a catfish will usually find it. But enterprising anglers have discovered a quicker way to get a cat's attention.

Remove the front treble from a crankbait and substitute a leader and hook baited with a minnow, a gob of worms, chicken liver or cut bait. Except that the baits are different, this is the same rig steelheaders use to fish along the bottom of a swift run.

Anchor below a riffle, or wade out into it, and let the rig trail in the deeper run downstream. You can move the bait from side to side simply by repositioning your rod. Reel in or let out line to move the bait farther upstream or downstream.

Even if the catfish are not in position to smell the bait, they can home in on the vibrations of the crankbait using their lateral line sense. Once they get close, they smell the bait and grab it, though occasionally a cat will hit the plug.

# Chumming for Catfish

Chumming (below) can be the key to catching catfish at any time of the year. Mix the chum several days in advance to give the grain enough time to ferment.

In spring, spread the chum over an area about 50 feet in diameter, and anchor your boat alongside it. Then, cast the bait into the chum zone and fish it right on the bottom. In summer and fall, when the fish are deeper, chum a much smaller area and tie up to a tree or anchor right over it. Lower the bait straight down to the bottom, then reel it up a little.

Weather and time of day have little to do with cat-fishing success when you're chumming. The chum seems to activate fish that previously weren't feeding.

## Chum Recipe:

1  50-pound bag of wheat, mylo or cracked corn

3  cups sugar

Water

Fill three five-gallon buckets two-thirds full of wheat, mylo or cracked corn. Add one cup of sugar to each bucket. Add water until the level is a few inches above the grain. Cover the buckets and allow two days for the grain to absorb the water. Then, refill the buckets so the water level is again a few inches above the grain; reseal. Allow the grain to ferment five days at a temperature of 75°F; three days at 90.

## How to Chum Catfish

CHUM in early morning, using about a gallon of the mixture in each spot you intend to fish during the day. Give the chum an hour or so to work before you start fishing.

TIE OFF to a tree or anchor alongside the chumming area. Look for a distinctive tie-off tree or landmark. Then, you can easily find the same chumming area when you return.

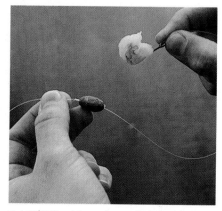

BAIT UP with a piece of shrimp, cut shad, hot dog or other preferred bait. Bury a heavy size 1/0 hook inside the bait so the point is not exposed. Otherwise, the fish might spit the bait.

PLACE your rods in rod holders. This enables you to fish with two lines at the same time, and makes it easier to see bites, which can be surprisingly subtle.

HORSE the fish out of the cover using a 6- to 7-foot, medium-heavy baitcasting outfit and 20-pound mono. If you let the fish run, it may swim around a branch.

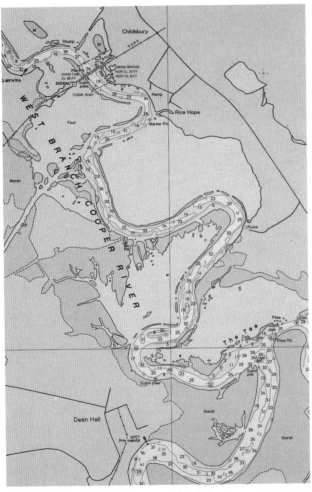

NAUTICAL CHARTS showing bottom contours can help you locate good catfish holes. The maps also show features such as navigation aids and bottom types. Maps like the one above are available from the National Ocean Service in Riverdale, Maryland.

FLATHEADS can be landed by grabbing the lower jaw and pressing down on the tongue area to partially immobilize the fish. A novice should not attempt to land flatheads this way without a leather glove.

*Drifting and Anchoring Tips*

SLOW your drift by lowering a sash weight off the bow of your boat. The weight also keeps the boat drifting lengthwise, parallel to shore.

ATTACH a jug to your anchor rope when fishing for big cats. This way, when a big one hits, you can untie the rope, toss it into the water (left), and follow the fish (right). After landing the cat, motor back to your jug and anchor up in the exact position where you caught the fish.

# White Bass & Stripers

# White Bass & Striper Basics

When a school of white bass churns the surface in pursuit of baitfish, there is no faster fishing. They instantly strike any lure cast into their midst. Fishing for striped bass can be just as exciting. Though schools are not as large, these trophy fish can put up a fight that rivals any other gamefish.

White bass, often called *silver bass,* have long been a favorite of freshwater fishermen. They are found in big rivers and connected lakes, and in large reservoirs. Striped bass, also called *rockfish* or *stripers,* were originally caught only in the ocean or in major coastal rivers during their spring spawning runs. However, when South Carolina's Santee and Cooper Rivers were dammed in 1941, striped bass were trapped above the dam. By 1950, stripers were thriving in Santee-Cooper Reservoir and fishermen were enjoying an exciting new sportfish. The success of stripers in Santee-Cooper Reservoir led to stocking programs in many other states and to development of the *whiterock,* a white bass-striper hybrid that has been introduced in many southern reservoirs.

Close cousins, white bass and stripers have similar lifestyles. Both species migrate up rivers and

streams in spring, spawning when the water temperature reaches about 58°F. Similarly, they both prefer large, open waters that have an abundance of gizzard or threadfin shad, their primary food.

White bass rarely exceed 3 pounds, while stripers often weigh more than 20 pounds. The record white bass, caught in Kerr Lake, North Carolina in 1986, weighed 5 pounds, 14 ounces. The largest striper taken from inland waters was caught in Lake Havasu, Arizona in 1977. It weighed 59 pounds, 12 ounces.

White & Striped Bass
Combined Range

WHITE BASS have a flatter body than stripers (top photo). Lines on white bass tend to be lighter and more broken than those on striped bass and usually fall short of the tail. On stripers, lines extend from the gills to the tail.

## When and Where to Catch White Bass and Stripers

White bass and stripers are constantly on the move. A school of hungry bass may appear out of nowhere, providing fantastic fishing for several minutes, and then disappear just as quickly.

Huge schools of white bass and stripers migrate upstream in spring, stopping in pools and eddies along the way. They move upriver until a dam, waterfall or other obstruction blocks their progress.

After spawning, both species retreat downstream where they scatter in the open water of lakes or reservoirs. They spend most of the summer in water from 20 to 40 feet deep. At daybreak and dusk, they move onto shallow sand flats to chase schools of shad or shiners.

In late summer and fall, white bass and stripers slash into schools of shad. Bass may suddenly begin feeding at any time of day. Gulls diving to catch injured shad reveal the location of feeding bass. During calm weather, fishermen look for swirls on the surface or shad leaping above water to escape.

In the North, late fall and winter fishing is slow because bass rarely feed in water cooler than 50°F. However, in the deep South, they continue to feed through the winter months.

CIRCLING GULLS pinpoint the location of white and striped bass feeding on schools of shad. Binoculars are helpful for spotting gulls. Watch for them wheeling and diving to grab shad that bass chase to the surface. Get to

TAILWATERS below dams offer excellent white bass and striper fishing in spring. Fish congregate in eddies or slack water near fast current, where they feed on shiners and other small baitfish.

WHITE BASS (above) and stripers roam open water in large schools. Unlike most freshwater fish, they feed in packs, surrounding shad in open water, or herding them along shorelines or into dead-end bays.

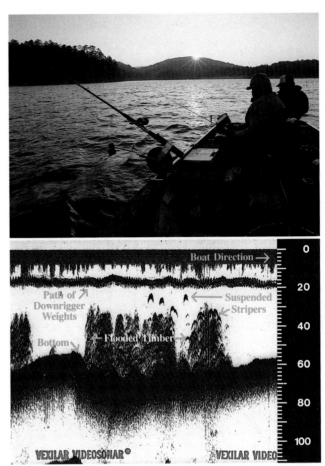

the spot quickly, because the action may be over within minutes if other boats spook the fish. Stop short of the school and drift within casting distance. If there is no wind, use an electric motor or oars.

FLOODED TIMBER provides cover for stripers in many reservoirs. This graph tape shows several stripers suspended just above the treetops. The downrigger weights can be seen tracking above the fish.

SHAD are super-abundant in many reservoirs. They form dense schools and feed on bits of algae and other tiny organisms near the surface. By late summer, shad are large enough to attract white bass and stripers.

WARMWATER DISCHARGES from power plants may attract millions of shad during winter. The shad, in turn, draw schools of white bass, providing fast fishing for anglers willing to brave the elements.

# Fishing for White Bass and Stripers

Methods for catching white and striped bass are quite similar, though the larger stripers demand tougher equipment and bigger lures. Recommended is 15- to 25-pound test line, a heavy-duty bait-casting or spinning reel and a stiff 6- to 7½-foot rod. For white bass, use an ultralight or light-action spinning rod with 4- to 8-pound test line.

Fishing tactics and locations change with the seasons. In spring, fishermen converge on rivers, usually below dams, where bass are spawning. When thousands of white bass jam their spawning grounds, they strike almost any bait or lure tossed their way, from minnows and jigs to strips of red yarn. Catching stripers is not as easy. Although many are caught on spoons, plugs or spinners, live or cut baits such as shad, herring, suckers and shiners usually work better at spawning time. Most anglers use slip-sinker rigs for bait-fishing, casting them into eddies and areas with slow current.

LURES for white bass include (1) Fat Rap, (2) Panther Martin spinner, (3) Pixee spoon, (4) Sassy Shad, (5) Mister Twister, (6) Super Sonic.

## Tips for Catching White Bass and Stripers

A POPPING PLUG (arrow) with hooks removed can be tied ahead of a small jig to add casting weight and attract bass. Anglers can cast into surface-feeding fish from farther away, with less chance of spooking them.

VERTICAL JIGGING is a technique for fishing white bass and stripers in deep water. Anglers troll until they locate a school, then stop and jig with spoons or lead-head jigs straight below the boat.

In summer, fishermen troll for deep-running schools of white bass and stripers, often locating them with depth finders. White bass are seldom deeper than 40 feet, though stripers may suspend as deep as 70 feet. To reach these fish, anglers use heavy slip-sinkers or lead-core lines, though downriggers are becoming popular for striper fishing in many reservoirs. Minnow-like plugs and spoons are favorite trolling lures for white and striped bass, but there are days when stripers want nothing but live or cut baits. To rig a shad or herring for drifting or trolling, slice off the head with a slanted, downward cut. Then rig the body with a harness consisting of two #1 or #2 hooks.

Beginning in late summer and through fall, anglers in lakes and reservoirs switch to a technique called *jump-fishing*. When a school of surface-feeding bass is located, fishermen race to the spot, casting into the school with surface plugs, spinners or jigs. The action lasts only a short time, then anglers must find another active school. Sometimes jump-fishing results in a limit catch in a matter of minutes. Some fishermen rig one rod with a surface plug and another with a jig or diving plug. If one fails to produce, they quickly switch to the other rig to avoid wasting time.

TWIN-JIG set-ups can improve the white bass angler's success. Where legal, fishermen tie a three-way swivel onto 8-pound test line. Then, they add different lengths of 10- to 12-pound test, each with a small jig.

LURES for striped bass include (1) bucktail jig with twister tail, (2) Spoonbill Rebel, (3) Hellbender, (4) Tinsel Tail jig, (5) T-Spoon, (6) King Spot.

Trout

# Trout-Fishing Basics

Trout are among the wariest of gamefish. Any quick movement or unusual sound, like the crunching of gravel or clattering of loose rocks when you wade, will send them darting for cover. But you can minimize spooking by following these guidelines:

- Keep a low profile (photo above); the lower you are, the less likely you will appear in the trout's window of vision. To fish a narrow stream, you may have to crawl to the bank and cast from a kneeling position.

- Wear drab clothing, something that blends in with the surroundings. A bright-colored shirt or cap can put the trout down in a hurry.

- In turbulent water, you can approach a trout more closely than in slow or slack water.

- Use objects such as boulders and trees to conceal your approach. If there is no place to hide, try to stay in the shadows.

- When you reach a likely spot, stand still for a few minutes before making a cast. When you first arrive, trout detect your presence and stop feeding. But after a few minutes, they may get used to you and start to feed again, even if you are plainly visible.

- Try to avoid casting over the trout's window of vision, especially with bright-colored fly line.

BOILS form when current deflects upward off an underwater obstruction, usually a boulder. When you see a boil, there is a good chance that trout are holding in the eddy just downstream of the obstruction. But the boil forms farther downstream, so you must cast well upstream of the boil to catch the trout.

# Reading the Water

An experienced stream fisherman can learn a great deal about a stream simply by walking its banks and "reading" the water. He observes current patterns, surface disturbances, coloration differences, changes in bottom type, and other clues that reveal trout and salmon hiding spots.

Current patterns pinpoint the location of rocks, logs or other underwater objects that shelter the fish from the moving water. Current pushing against a bank may indicate an undercut that offers cover. The seam between fast and slow current makes a good feeding station; trout hold in the slower water waiting for food to drift by in the faster water.

Novice stream fishermen pass up any water where the surface is broken and ripply, mistakenly assuming it is too fast and shallow for trout. But if you look carefully, this water may have slack-water pockets. A small pocket behind a rock might be home to a good-sized trout, even though the water is less than a foot deep.

Bottom makeup also dictates where trout will be found. A section of stream with a sandy bottom generally supports fewer trout than a section with a rocky or gravelly bottom. Important trout foods, especially larval aquatic insects, thrive among rocks and gravel, but may be completely absent in sand.

If possible, examine the stream from a high angle to get an idea of streambed contour and location of boulders, submerged logs, weed patches and other underwater objects. You can see most on a bright day when the sun is at its highest. Polarized sunglasses will remove the glare so you can see into the water.

Many trout streams have been damaged by erosion, beaver activity, channelization or logging. Natural-resources agencies and sportsmen's clubs sometimes reclaim these streams by installing devices to deepen the channel and provide good cover for trout.

Stream-improvement structures may be difficult to see because fisheries managers take great pains to make them look natural. The trick to fishing a reclaimed stream is simply learning to recognize the various structures and understanding how they work. Then you can use the fishing techniques that would work in similar natural cover. The most common stream-improvement devices are shown at right.

*Tips on Reading the Water*

UNDERCUT BANKS can be found by watching the current. If it is angling toward a bank, rather than flowing parallel to it, the bank is undercut.

DEEP HOLES appear as dark areas in the streambed. Trout move into holes to escape the current. The best holes have boulders or logs for cover.

WEED PATCHES may be difficult to see, especially in low light. But the weeds usually slow the current, creating slack spots on the surface.

CURRENT SEAMS are easy to spot because debris and foam usually collect in the slack water, near the edge of the fast water.

CHECK your favorite stream at low-water stage to find deep holes and objects like submerged logs that could hold trout when the water is higher.

*Common Stream-Improvement Devices*

CRIB SHELTERS, manmade undercut banks supported by pilings are built along outside bends. Water is deflected toward them by a rock or log structure on the opposite bank, scouring the bank under the crib. The left photo shows the shelter under construction, the right photo a year later.

HEWITT RAMPS, used mainly on high-gradient streams, function much like small dams. A deeper pool forms above; a scour hole below.

241

LIGHT RAIN or moderate wind disturbs the surface enough that trout cannot see you clearly. The fish feed heavily on terrestrial foods washed in by the rain or wind and are not nearly as spooky as they are when the surface is calm. But heavy rain pelting the surface or intense wind puts the trout down.

## Good Conditions for Trout Fishing

SLIGHTLY MURKY water allows trout to see the lure, but makes it difficult for them to see you. The clarity is best when the stream is rising or after it starts to fall.

OVERCAST skies eliminate harsh shadows that can spook trout. The fish do not hesitate to leave cover to search for food, sometimes moving into riffles in midday.

242

# How Weather Affects Trout

In stream fishing for trout and salmon, nothing is more important than weather. It affects the clarity, temperature and water level of the stream, which largely determine where the fish will be found and how well they will bite.

The most important factor is rain. Trout often start to feed when the sky darkens before a storm. A light to moderate rain slightly clouds the water, washes terrestrial foods into the stream, and increases the flow, causing more immature aquatic insects to drift downstream. These changes make for ideal feeding conditions and good fishing. A heavy rain, on the other hand, seems to turn the fish off. If the down-pour is prolonged, it muddies the water so much that the fish cannot see, and with the rising water, they abandon their normal locations.

Rain has even more effect on anadromous trout and salmon. Fish entering a stream to spawn tend to stage up at the stream mouth. A few will enter the stream at normal flow, but the majority wait for the increased flow resulting from a heavy rain. Fishing is poor as long as the stream stays muddy, but improves rapidly when the water starts to clear.

Air temperature also has a dramatic effect on feeding activity. Most trout and salmon species feed heaviest at water temperatures from 55° to 60° F. On a typical stream, warm, sunny weather early or late in the season will drive the water temperature to that range by midafternoon, triggering an insect hatch and starting a feeding spree. But in summer, the same type of weather warms the water too much by midafternoon, so fishing is poor. Trout bite better in the morning or evening, when the water is cooler.

Another important element is cloud cover. In sunny weather, trout are extra-wary, seeking the cover of boulders, logs or undercut banks. But in cloudy weather, they are more aggressive and more willing to leave cover to find food. Anadromous fish tend to migrate more under cloudy skies.

Windy weather also makes trout more aggressive. The wind blows insects into the stream and trout start feeding. But trout have difficulty spotting small insects when the surface is choppy, so dry-fly fishing is not as effective as it would be if the water were calm.

*Poor Conditions for Trout Fishing*

HIGH, MUDDY WATER makes it impossible for trout to see your bait. Fly fishing is usually a waste of time, but natural-bait fishermen still catch a few trout.

SUNNY, CALM weather makes trout extra-wary. They are quick to notice shadows from your body, your rod and even your fly line. They hold tight to cover until evening.

# Fly Fishing for Trout

Why fly-fish? After all, you can catch trout and salmon by spinning or baitcasting, both of which are easier to learn.

Fly fishing is by far the oldest of these methods, with a history stretching back at least six centuries. So the modern fly angler, equipped with a lightweight graphite rod rather than a buggy-whip wooden pole, has the satisfaction of carrying on a long and colorful tradition.

But nostalgia, no matter how strong, can't account for the survival of this old-time method into the space age, or for the manifold increase in its popularity in recent years. Despite its ancient origins, fly fishing remains a versatile and productive way to outwit wary salmonids.

Many of the most common foods of trout can be imitated only with flies; even the tiniest spinning and casting lures are much too bulky. Aquatic insects, such as mayflies and caddisflies, make up most of the diet of stream trout. Imitations of these delicate creatures are much too light to be cast with ordinary spinning or baitcasting techniques.

In fact, any trout food can be imitated successfully with flies. With a 6- or 7-weight fly line and a rod to match, you can fish anything from the tiniest midge imitations, not much bigger than a gnat, on up to streamers that simulate minnows several inches long.

th
O
w
m

In
yo
in
ha

Al
ni
na
to
be
sli
pa
br
ba
fo

Fo
kno

*Tyi*

DUI
the l
(2) l
and

*Tyin*

DOU
the h
ing li

The most frantic angling for stream trout comes during cloudlike insect hatches. Yet it can also be the most frustrating. The fish may be rising all around you, but if you're limited to casting hardware, you're almost certainly out of luck. When rising to a hatch, trout generally refuse all imitations of other types of food.

Some of the biggest trout feed almost entirely on baitfish. In lakes, spoons and minnow plugs usually work better for these fish than streamer flies, which don't have much action in the still water. But in streams the current gives streamers an erratic, undulating movement more lifelike than the steady wobbling of hardware. And generally you can mimic the size, shape, and color of particular baitfish more closely with flies than with plugs or spoons.

Many famous trout streams have flies-only regulations. Although spinning and baitcasting equipment is sometimes allowed, such tackle makes it difficult to present a fly realistically enough for the educated trout found in these waters. For casting flies softly and maneuvering them like living creatures through a maze of currents, fly-fishing tackle nearly always works best.

Some anglers hesitate to try fly fishing because matching the hatch seems too complicated. But you don't have to know the insects by their species names, or carry scores of different fly patterns. In nearly all cases, an approximate imitation will do the job. Actually, a hatch is not so much a problem as an opportunity. Seeing exactly what the fish are feeding on is a big advantage; in most other kinds of fishing, all you can do is guess.

It's true that learning to fly-fish takes time and effort. To become really skilled may require several seasons of experience on the water. But it's also true that you can start enjoying this traditional way of angling, and start catching fish, after only a couple of brief practice sessions.

As in any other kind of fishing, the learning is part of the fun. Actually, it's a process that never ends, even if you fish a lifetime. The tips on the following pages will get you started right.

Ri

Wh
mai
perl
fail:
mac
mig

Mar
even
cally
tack
the
strea

*Tyin*

PERFI
ing lin
(3) Wra
the top

*Tying*

BLOOD
With on
section.

## Casting a Fly

Fly casting differs from other methods of casting in several important respects:

- Because a fly weighs so little, you cast the weight of the fly line itself, which is thicker and heavier than other kinds of line.

- Each casting stroke, forward or back, consists of two movements blended together. Using your forearm, you *load* the rod, raising the tip to start the line moving and to put a deep bend in the rod. You finish the stroke with a *wrist snap*, which forms a loop in the line and speeds it on its way.

- The keys to smooth fly casting are the proper timing and gradual acceleration of each stroke, not a sudden application of force as in spinning.

Gradual acceleration insures that the line will flow out straight on the cast. If you apply too much power

### How to Make the Basic Overhead Cast

1. EXTEND about 30 feet of line. Set your feet comfortably apart, the foot on your rod side slightly back. Place your thumb on top of the grip, wrist cocked down. Point the rod low, and pull in any slack with your other hand.

2. BEGIN the backward stroke, raising your forearm smoothly but keeping your wrist cocked. The rod tip should move straight back, not swing outward in a semi-circle. As the rod nears vertical, stop your arm abruptly.

3. SNAP your wrist rearward and upward (arrow), forming the loop. The unrolling line should have no waves, and the loop should be narrow. Pause until the line is nearly unrolled (dotted line), then begin the forward stroke.

too soon, the rod tip will bounce at the end of the stroke, throwing waves of slack into the line. On the following stroke, this slack will make it impossible to load the rod.

The loop formed in your line as it travels forward or rearward should be narrow, no more than 2 feet in width. A narrow loop has little air resistance, so your line travels fast without sagging to the water and with less chance of blowing off target. To form narrow loops, your wrist should break only slightly on each snap. A longer wrist movement will drop the rod tip too far, widening the loop.

Before attempting to fish, spend some time practicing on water or an open lawn. Any balanced trout outfit will do, but a 6-weight rod with a weight-forward floating line is ideal. Tie on a leader 7½ feet long and a piece of bright yarn to simulate the fly.

Start by learning the basic overhead cast. Once you have it mastered, practice false casting, shooting line and roll casting. Then you'll be ready to catch trout. The double haul is an advanced technique for distance casting, which you can learn later on. Usually, the most effective range for trout is just 25 to 40 feet.

4. PUSH your arm smoothly toward the target, accelerating gradually. Stop the arm suddenly when your rod reaches the 45-degree position. Your wrist is still bent at the same angle it took at the end of the rearward snap.

5. SNAP your wrist forward (arrow), forming a narrow loop. As before, the snap is very short but powerful. For a soft presentation, the cast should be aimed 2 or 3 feet above the spot where you want the fly to settle.

6. LOWER the rod gradually to a horizontal position as your line unrolls forward. The line will drop softly to the water. The leader should straighten completely, and the fly alight directly on the target.

## False Casting

The false cast is a necessary supplement to the basic overhead cast. Instead of letting your line and fly settle to the water on the forward cast, you keep them in the air and make another backcast.

False casting serves several purposes:

- You can cancel an off-target cast; just pull into a back-cast and correct your aim on the next cast forward.

- You can change directions from one cast to the next. It's difficult to pick your line off the water, make a single backcast, and aim the forward cast at a target off to your side. Instead, you false-cast once in an intermediate direction and then hit the target on the next cast.

- In fishing with dry flies, a succession of false casts helps air-dry the hackle so the fly floats high and keeps its natural appearance.

- For additional distance, shoot line on a false cast. Generally, the more line you strip in on the retrieve, the more false casts it will take to cast the same distance again.

## Shooting Line

Usually you will want to cast more line than you pick up from the water. If your previous cast was 40 feet long and you retrieved 15 feet while fishing the fly, you need to *shoot* line if you want to reach out more than the 25 feet you pick up. To do so, you simply release line while the loop is in the air; the unrolling line pulls more out behind it.

Before starting a cast, make sure you have enough running line stripped off the reel. Let it lie on the water, or hold it in loose coils with your line hand. You can shoot line on a forward cast (shown below) or on a backcast.

SHOOT line by forming a large *O* with your thumb and forefinger immediately after the wrist snap on the cast. Allow loose line to flow, or shoot, through it.

BRAKE the cast as it nears the target by closing your fingers on the line. For maximum distance, you can release the line completely while shooting.

## How to Roll-Cast

When obstructions prevent a normal backcast, use the roll cast. With this technique, you cannot reach out as far as with a normal cast; the maximum distance is about 40 feet. Roll casting must be practiced on water, not land. A double-taper line works best; with a weight-forward, the running line is too light to pick up the belly.

EASE your rod tip rearward and tilt it away from you, so the line hangs outside the rod and slightly behind it. Then wait till the line stops moving.

MOVE your arm forward and downward smoothly, then make a short wrist snap. The line will roll toward the target in a wide loop and straighten.

# The Double Haul

Long casts are often necessary in salmon and steelhead fishing, and occasionally in other types of trout fishing. The double haul increases line speed on the backcast and again on the forward cast, so you can make long casts and punch into the wind. This technique can increase your casting distance by 50 percent.

GRASP the line several inches ahead of the grip. Start with your rod tip low. The entire belly of the line should be extended on the water.

RAISE your line hand as you make the backcast, keeping it alongside the rod. Stop the rod suddenly as it reaches the vertical.

PULL your line hand down sharply at the instant your rod hand makes the rearward wrist snap. The pull, or haul, is only a few inches long.

BRING your line hand up near the rod as the line unrolls to the rear. If desired, you can shoot line on the backcast by forming an *O* with your fingers.

PULL down again as you make the forward stroke. This pull is longer; it begins when the rod first moves forward and ends with the wrist snap.

RELEASE the line, and hold the rod nearly level as you shoot. With a weight-forward line, it's possible to cast more than 100 feet.

*Common Mistakes in Fly Casting*

STARTING the backcast with the rod pointed high allows slack line to sag from the rod tip. With this slack, you cannot fully load the rod.

TURNING the arm or wrist so the reel aims outward waves the rod in a semicircle, widening line loops. The rod must go straight back and forward.

BREAKING the wrist too far rearward on the backcast widens the loop and throws the line too low behind you. Keep the wrist snap very short.

# Fishing Trout with Dry Flies

Nothing is more suspenseful than watching a big trout or salmon rise slowly to a floating fly, perhaps to reject it at the last moment or perhaps to engulf it and give you a battle demanding all your finesse.

Despite the intimidating technical discussions in books and magazines, dry-fly angling is generally the easiest way to fool a trout with a fly. It offers these advantages:

- You can read surface currents easily.

- If the trout are rising, you can see where they are and often what they're feeding on as well.

**MAYFLIES**

Royal Wulff     Rusty Spinner     March Brown

Blue Wing Olive

Hexagenia     Green Drake Wulff     Pale Evening Dun

**STONEFLIES**

Bullet Salmon Fly

Improved Sofa Pillow

**CADDISFLIES**

Coachman Trude

Goddard Caddis

Henryville Caddis

Elk Hair Caddis

- You know exactly where your fly is and whether it's working as it should.

- You can detect strikes by sight.

Dry flies are designed to imitate the adult stages of various aquatic insects. The classic dry, with a stiff tail and hackle and a pair of upright wings, is a good approximation of a mayfly. Stonefly imitations are similar but larger, with a single hair wing angled backward. Caddis patterns are small, like mayfly imitations, but have wings lying tentlike along the body; they are sometimes tied without hackle. Midge flies, almost microscopic, have hackle but no wings.

When selecting a dry fly on the stream, most anglers attempt to match the hatch. Recognize, however, that trout often feed selectively; and the particular insect you notice first, the biggest or most abundant species, may not be the one they want. Examine the rises and the naturals adrift on the stream to determine what the fish actually are taking. If you don't have a fly that duplicates it in size, shape, and color, settle for matching the size. An artificial slightly smaller than the real thing usually works better than one that's bigger.

Traditionally, dry-fly anglers have fished in an upstream direction. The fly drifts toward you, so you strip in line and can easily pick up the short length remaining on the water when you're ready for the next cast. Cast diagonally upstream, rather than straight up, so your leader and line won't drift over the fish and spook it. To reach difficult lies, you may want to cast across stream or downstream.

Regardless of the direction you cast, always drop your fly well upstream of the fish and let it drift into position. Remember, the rises of a fish are misleading; they do not indicate the spot where the trout actually lies.

On the drift, you must avoid drag. If the current pulls your line so the fly is dragged across the surface of the water, the trout will refuse the fly and may even stop rising. Keep some slack in your leader at all times, and also keep some slack in your line if needed. Use special slack-line casts. Once the line is on the water, you can mend the line to maintain slack. When you fish in a downstream direction, simply pay out your line as fast as the current takes it.

At times, the drag-free drift may be less productive than skating a dry fly across the surface. You do this by making a short cast downstream, then holding your rod tip high and shaking it gently from side to side while stripping in line. The fly will skip erratically on the water like a caddisfly attempting flight. The action is very different from the steady slide across the surface resulting from drag.

Dry flies often catch trout and salmon when they aren't rising, and even when no insects are hatching at all. Under these conditions you drift your fly naturally to the spots where fish are most likely to lie, or skate it over them. An effective tactic is to make several casts to a single spot, creating the illusion of a hatch.

Dry flies are used in sizes 8 to 28 for most trout, and sizes 2 to 8 for steelhead and Atlantic salmon.

*Rigging Up for Dry-Fly Fishing*

APPLY paste floatant to the hackle and tail of a dry fly to reduce water absorption. Rub the paste on sparingly with your fingertips.

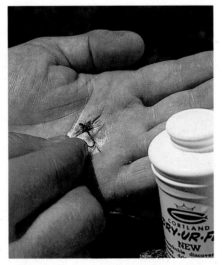

REMOVE water or fish slime with a desiccant powder. Rub the fly gently in powder, then blow the powder away and reapply floatant.

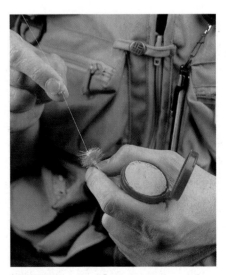

SPREAD a leader-sink compound on your tippet. A sunken tippet is less visible to trout in flat water and casts less shadow than a floating one.

## Fishing Trout with Wet Flies

The standard wet fly has almost become a museum piece. A century ago, it was the only artificial fly in use in America; today the angler who wants a sunken fly is far more likely to tie on a streamer or nymph, which more closely resemble important trout foods such as baitfish and larval insects. Yet there are excellent reasons for using the wet fly even now, none of them sentimental.

Traditional wet-fly techniques are the simplest and most effortless in fly-fishing. There's less casting than with dry flies, so you cover the water more quickly. Also, wets are effective in fast, broken cur-

rents that would quickly drown any dry. Wet flies are generally much smaller and less air-resistant than streamers, so they're easier to cast. And your presentation and retrieve need not be as precise as in fishing with nymphs.

Wet flies have soft, absorbent hackle for quick sinking and lifelike action. The standard wet has a feather wing; dull-tinted patterns of this type are thought to represent drowned adult insects. Feather-wing wets with gaudy colors and metallic tinsels may suggest tiny baitfish, but serve mainly as attractors useful for brook trout and Atlantic salmon. Some wet patterns, called *hackle flies*, lack wings; these may resemble insect larvae or leeches.

The most popular wet flies today are specialized types. Large patterns with wings of hair or marabou, often in bright attractor colors, are commonly used for steelhead and salmon. And fat-bodied hackle flies called wooly worms, which have hackle along their entire length, are favorites for trout of all kinds on big western rivers.

Wet flies are often drifted at random, covering lots of potential holding water rather than particular lies. The wet-fly drift technique, with a floating or sink-tip line, works especially well in long runs and riffles that lack large boulders or other obvious cover. In such places, trout take shelter near small obstructions

or in depressions in the bottom that may be invisible from the surface.

You can also fish specific targets. Cast across stream and let your fly drift into the calm pockets around logs, rocks and other objects. When it reaches a pocket, feed line into the current; the fly stays where it is, but the belly expands downstream. Otherwise the fly would be swept away immediately.

An old reliable method, all but forgotten by modern anglers, is to fish with two flies at once. The second fly is tied to a dropper 3 or 4 inches long. To make the dropper, leave one of the strands untrimmed when you tie your tippet to the leader with a blood knot. Cast across stream and drift the flies to a likely spot. Then raise your rod tip and jiggle it, so the dropper fly skips on the surface while the tippet fly works underwater.

In fall and winter steelheading, it's usually necessary to fish wet flies very deep. Use the wet-fly drift with a fast-sinking shooting head or a lead-core head. Many wet flies designed for steelhead have weighted bodies or bead heads; they will bounce along bottom without snagging if the rocks are rounded.

Wet flies are used in sizes 10 to 18 for most trout, and sizes 2 to 8 for steelhead and salmon.

FEATHER WINGS
Professor • Light Cahill • Leadwing Coachman
HAIR WINGS
Green Butt Skunk
Skykomish Sunrise • Fall Favorite
HACKLE FLIES
Bread Crust • Green Soft-Hackle • Silver Soft-Hackle
PALMER HACKLE FLIES
Olive Wooly Worm • True Wooly Worm
SALMON FLIES
Silver Doctor • Jock Scott

*How to Fish with the Wet-Fly Drift*

CAST across stream, then let the fly swing in the current. Follow the drifting line with your rod, keeping the tip up to absorb the shock of strikes. Mend the line as it swings. Slight drag won't turn the trout off, but a wet fly dragged rapidly won't get many strikes.

RETRIEVE the fly in twitches after it swings below you. Trout usually strike at the end of the drift, as the line is straightening below you. After retrieving, take one or two steps downstream and make another cast, shooting the line you retrieved. Repeat, continuing downstream.

255

## Fishing Trout with Nymphs

Day in and day out, the odds favor the fly fisherman who uses a nymph. No matter how low or high the stream may be, no matter how cold or warm, the naturals that nymphs imitate are always present and available to the trout.

Nymphs are intended to copy the immature forms of aquatic insects, including mayflies, stoneflies, caddisflies, dragonflies, damselflies and midges. Some nymphs are close imitations of particular species, as exact as fly tiers can make them. Others are impressionistic, meant to suggest a variety of naturals in form, size and coloration. Many nymphs of both these types have bodies that are thick at the

front and thinner at the rear, simulating the wing pads and abdomen of the real thing. Usually, there's a soft, sparse hackle to serve as legs.

A nymph pattern may be tied in weighted and unweighted versions. Weighted nymphs have lead or copper wire wound onto the hook shank under the body material. They are used for fishing near bottom, especially in fast currents. Unweighted nymphs work well for fishing shallow; and because they have livelier action, many experts prefer them for fishing deep in slow water as well. To carry them deep, split-shot or lead wrap is attached to the leader. A few nymphs are designed to float, imitating the immature insect at the moment it arrives on the surface to transform into an adult.

No one becomes a complete nymph fisherman overnight. Techniques for fishing nymphs are far more numerous and varied than those for any other type of fly. Some are simple, but others are the most challenging of all ways of catching trout.

Depending on species and stage of life, the naturals may crawl across the bottom, burrow in it, swim or simply tumble along with the current. Thus the nymph fisherman can work his fly realistically by drifting

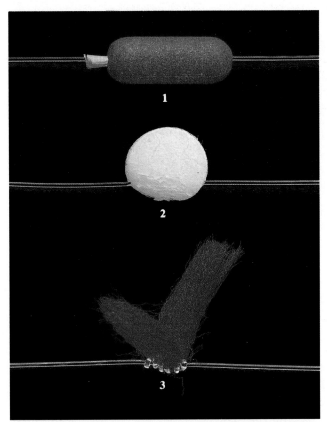

POPULAR STRIKE INDICATORS include (1) styrofoam float pegged in place with a toothpick; (2) Stay-On, which pinches onto your leader and sticks in place; and (3) colored yarn tied into a blood knot in your leader.

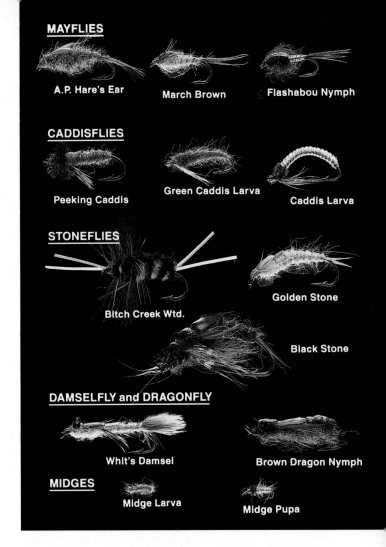

**MAYFLIES**

A.P. Hare's Ear

March Brown

Flashabou Nymph

**CADDISFLIES**

Peeking Caddis

Green Caddis Larva

Caddis Larva

**STONEFLIES**

Bitch Creek Wtd.

Golden Stone

Black Stone

**DAMSELFLY and DRAGONFLY**

Whit's Damsel

Brown Dragon Nymph

**MIDGES**

Midge Larva

Midge Pupa

it freely with the current, or by twitching or stripping it along at various depths.

Detecting strikes in nymph fishing can be difficult. When you use a natural drift, it's generally impossible to feel the hit. The best solution is to use a floating line with a bright-colored tip, a leader with a fluorescent butt, or some kind of strike indicator (see photo) attached to the leader. If you see any twitch or hesitation, set the hook.

For greatest sensitivity, strike indicators should be positioned as close to the fly as possible. To fish shallow, place the indicator just above the tippet knot; to fish deep, move it back toward the leader butt.

Keep your casts short so you can see the twitch more clearly. If you use a sink-tip line, keep an eye on the point where the lighter-colored floating portion disappears below the surface.

One of the easiest nymph techniques, and one of the most effective, is the wet-fly drift (p. 255). It's a good way to fish runs and riffles that lack obvious cover to cast to. By planning a drift carefully, you can also use this technique to swing your fly close to boulders or logs, or to nymphing trout you can actually see.

Sometimes these nymphing fish are visible only as flashes near the streambed as they turn and dart in the current to feed. At other times, their tails make swirls on the surface when they tip nose-down to take nymphs on the bottom, or their backs may break water when they feed on naturals that are only a few inches deep. Anglers often mistake these swirls for rises to adult insects, and make futile attempts to catch the trout with dry flies.

When drifting a nymph to a feeding fish, try to sink it exactly to the fish's eye level. To increase the depth of a drift, angle your cast farther upstream so the fly will have more time to sink before reaching the trout. Use a weighted nymph if necessary, or add a suitable amount of weight to your leader.

In the still water of pools, try making a long cast, letting the nymph sink near the bottom, then retrieving it in short twitches. In very cold water, especially in the early season, a nymph allowed to lie motionless on the bottom and twitched only occasionally may be more effective than anything else except live bait. Stay alert for strikes; a trout may pick up the loitering nymph and drop it instantly.

Nymphs used for trout range from size 1/0 to 18.

## How to Fish a Nymph Upstream

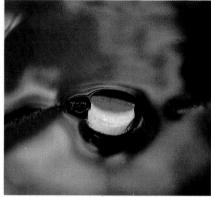

MAKE a short cast upstream, so your nymph will drift to a visible fish or probable lie. If possible, cast at an angle rather than straight upstream, so your line won't drift over the fish and spook it.

STRIP line in as the current carries the nymph toward you. Let the fly drift naturally; to prevent drag, your line should have slight curves of slack. Twitch the fly when it reaches the fish or the lie.

WATCH your strike indicator closely. If it flicks or pauses at any time during the drift, set the hook instantly. Too long a delay, or too much slack in the drifting line, will cause you to miss the strike.

## How to Fish a Nymph in the Surface Film

DEAD-DRIFT a nymph in smooth water. It should drift an inch or less beneath the surface, where trout feed on naturals about to emerge. To keep your fly from sinking too far, rub paste floatant on your leader, except for the last few inches of tippet. Because the leader floats, you may have to give a tug to sink the nymph. To detect strikes, watch the point where your tippet goes underwater; if more of it goes under, set the hook.

## How to Fish a Current Edge with a Downstream Mend

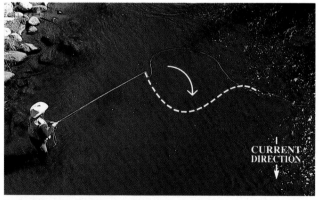

ANGLE your cast upstream into the edge of a fast current. Trout will hold in the slower water near shore, watching for nymphs to wash down in the fast current and darting out to grab them.

MEND your line by flipping a curve of slack downstream. Because the tip of the line is in the faster water, a belly forms upstream, the reverse of the usual situation. Without a mend, the fly would drift slower than the current.

## How to Imitate an Emerging Caddisfly

MIMIC a caddis pupa rising rapidly to the surface by first (1) aiming a short cast, 25 to 30 feet, at an angle upstream; lower your rod near the water as the fly alights and the drift begins. Then (2) raise the rod tip gradually as the nymph drifts toward and alongside you. The line is lifted off the water, so no mending or retrieving is needed. As the nymph washes past you downstream, (3) lower the tip slowly. This technique gives you a drag-free drift. When the nymph is directly below you, (4) lift the tip again. The fly will dart toward the surface.

## Tips for Fishing with Nymphs

APPLY floatant paste to the first 5 feet of a floating line for maximum buoyancy. To detect strikes, the line tip must stay on the surface.

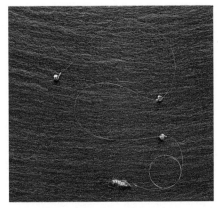

SPREAD tiny split-shot along your leader for smooth casts, rather than using one large shot. On a knotted leader, put shot just above the knots.

TIE an overhand knot around a removable split-shot before squeezing it shut. The knot keeps it from coming off during casting.

259

# Spinning & Baitcasting Techniques for Trout

For the average fisherman, spinning and baitcasting are much easier than fly fishing. And in many situations, they catch more and bigger trout. Because trout eat more baitfish and fewer insects as they grow larger, good-sized baits and lures have more appeal than small flies.

The monofilament line used with spinning and baitcasting gear offers several advantages to stream fishermen. The small-diameter line cuts the current much better than fly line, so drag is not as much of a problem, and you can fish deep more easily. Mono is also less wind-resistant, which makes casting in a headwind or crosswind considerably easier. And fly line is highly visible; if you cast over a trout, or allow your line to drift ahead of the fly, the fish may spook. With mono, your presentation need not be as precise.

When heavy rains cloud a stream, fly fishing may be tough, but spinfishermen and baitcasters continue catching trout. The fish can detect the scent of natural bait or the sound and vibration of plugs and spinners.

On a narrow, brushy stream, fly casting is almost impossible because streamside obstacles foul your backcast. But with a short, ultralight spinning outfit, you can flip small lures beneath overhanging branches and fish pockets that otherwise would be difficult to reach. Spinning gear is also an advantage on wide streams because you can make long casts and cover a lot of water in a hurry.

Baitcasting gear is the best choice for exceptionally large trout and salmon. The level-wind reel eliminates the line-twist problems that plague spinfishermen when big fish strip line from their reels.

## Casting for Trout with Hardware

The term "hardware" means all hard-bodied lures like spoons, spinners and plugs. Hardware attracts trout by flash and vibration. By casting with hardware, you can cover a lot of water in a hurry. The technique works best from late spring through early fall, when higher water temperatures make trout more aggressive.

Compared to most other trout-fishing techniques, hardware fishing is easy. Simply cast across stream, then regulate the speed of your retrieve so the lure ticks bottom. When trout are actively feeding, ticking bottom may not be necessary; the fish will swim upward to grab the lure.

Exactly how you angle your cast depends on the lure, the water depth and the current speed. The more you angle it upstream, the deeper the lure will run. If the lure is bouncing bottom too much, angle the cast farther downstream. This way, water resistance from the current will keep the lure off bottom.

Standard spinners and thin spoons are popular in small streams, where distance casting is not important. Sonic spinners, which have a shaft that passes through the blade, are extremely popular in the West. The blade starts turning at a very low retrieve speed.

Weight-forward spinners and medium to thick spoons are a better choice in bigger rivers or in those with deep water or fast current. These heavier lures can be cast much farther, and they run deeper.

Floating minnow plugs work well in small streams, but sinking minnow plugs and diving crankbaits are more effective in deeper current.

With spinners, spoons and sinking minnow plugs, the slower you retrieve, the deeper the lures will run. Floating minnow plugs and crankbaits run deepest with a medium to medium-fast retrieve.

For casting spinners, small spoons and minnow plugs, use a 5- to 6-foot light spinning outfit with 2- to 6-pound mono; for larger spoons and diving plugs, a 5½- to 7-foot, medium-power spinning outfit with 6- to 8-pound mono. Steelhead and salmon fishermen often use 8- to 9-foot, medium- to heavy-power spinning rods with 8- to 17-pound mono.

To avoid line twist, attach spinners and spoons with a small ball-bearing snap-swivel. Or, splice in a swivel about 6 inches ahead of the lure. Attach minnow plugs with a small snap or a Duncan loop knot; crankbaits, with a snap or a double clinch knot (p. 247).

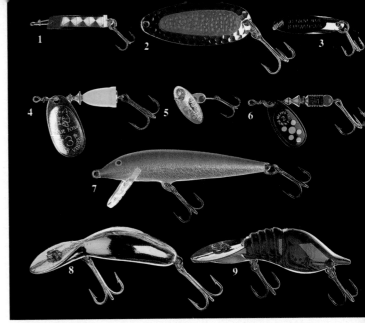

HARDWARE includes spoons like (1) Super Duper®, (2) Pixee™, (3) Kastmaster®; spinners like (4) Super Vibrax®, (5) Panther Martin®, (6) Black Fury®; plugs like (7) Countdown Rapala®, (8) Tadpolly®, (9) Crawdad®.

*Tips for Casting Hardware*

HANG your lure in the current to fish hard-to-reach pockets such as holes beneath log jams, brush piles, overhanging limbs or undercut banks. From an upstream position, cast just short of the pocket, let out a little line, then allow the current to work your lure.

CRANK a floating minnow plug through a riffle in early morning or late evening to catch feeding trout. From a downstream position, cast to the head of the riffle, then reel rapidly through the riffle and downstream run. After a few casts, move to the next riffle.

WORK the cover farthest downstream and closest to you first. Then, a hooked fish will not spook others in unfished water when the current sweeps it downstream, or in unfished water close to you when you reel it in. Make your casts in the order shown in the photo.

STANDARD BUBBLE RIGS work best for casting across stream or downstream; if fished upstream, the bubble would drift ahead of the fly. Tie the rig by threading a plastic bubble on your line, then attaching a dry fly, wet fly, streamer or nymph. Twist the ends of the bubble so it locks in place a foot up the line. With a dry fly, you can put a little water in the bubble for casting weight; use a drag-free drift. With a sinking fly, you can fill the bubble with water or add split-shot for more depth; dead-drift the fly or twitch it for extra action.

## Spinfishing for Trout with Flies

Even if you don't own a fly rod, you can fly-fish with spinning gear. In fact, spinning with flies works better in some situations. In deep water, for instance, you can attach split-shot to mono line and reach bottom more easily than with fly line. And in high winds, mono is easier to control.

In streams with flies-only regulations, spinning gear is usually legal, as long as the lure is a fly. But to cast a fly, you must attach some extra weight.

With a sinking fly, simply add a split-shot or two about a foot up the line. Leader wrap, lead sleeves or a good-sized strike indicator will also add weight. Strike indicators help detect light pickups as well.

Dry flies and sinking flies can be rigged with a weighted float or a plastic bubble, which can be partially filled with water for extra casting weight. If you use a clear float or bubble, trout will pay little attention to it. But a float or bubble splashing down close to a fish, or drifting over it ahead of the fly, may cause it to spook.

A long, soft rod is best for casting flies and manipulating them in the water. A stiff rod doesn't flex enough to cast a light weight, and could snap a light leader when you set the hook. A 6½- to 7½-foot, slow-action spinning rod or an 8½- to 9½-foot, 4- to 6-weight fly rod with a spinning reel is a good choice. Spool your reel with 2- to 8-pound, limp mono.

Many spinfishermen use line that is too heavy, and add too much weight, inhibiting the movement of the fly. Always use the lightest line practical for the conditions, and the lightest weight that will allow you to cast and reach the desired depth. Too much weight causes snagging problems; and even with minimal weight, strikes are more difficult to detect than with fly-fishing gear.

## Natural Bait for Trout

Fly-fishing purists frown on the idea of using spoons, spinners and other hardware to catch trout, and the idea of using natural bait is even farther down their list of tolerable tactics. But there's no denying that natural bait catches lots of trout; in fact, there are times when it badly outfishes flies and hardware.

Trout and salmon rely on their sense of smell to a greater extent than most other gamefish. They can detect dissolved substances in minute concentrations, as evidenced by the ability of sea-run salmon and steelhead to return to their home stream on the basis of its unique odor. So it's not surprising that they use their remarkable sense of smell to help them find food.

Natural bait appeals to this highly developed sense. Smell is especially important during periods of high, muddy water. Under these conditions, trout cannot see flies or hardware, but they can easily detect the odor of natural bait.

In early spring, when the water is still cold and few insects are hatching, natural bait usually out-produces flies by a wide margin. Natural bait is also a good choice in streams that do not have many insects. And big trout or those in heavily fished streams can be super-wary, closely inspecting any potential food item. They're likely to recognize any imitation as a fake.

Bait fishermen often make the mistake of using heavy line and a big hook, then adding a heavy sinker and a golfball-sized bobber. This type of rig is fine for northern pike, but will seldom catch a trout. For most stream trout, bait-fishing specialists use light spinning tackle with 2- to 4-pound mono, size 6 to 12 hooks, and a split-shot for weight. Of course large trout and salmon require heavier tackle, but seldom will you need line heavier than 8-pound test or a hook larger than size 2.

The major drawback of natural bait is the problem of deep hooking. Even a small trout often takes the bait so deeply it's impossible to remove the hook without causing serious injury. If you plan on releasing your trout, don't use live bait. If you must release a deeply hooked trout, cut the line rather than trying to remove the hook.

Another disadvantage of many natural baits is the difficulty of keeping them alive and carrying them, especially if you're wading. And in some states, certain natural baits, like minnows, are illegal for trout.

The variety of trout and salmon baits is nearly endless. Garden worms, nightcrawlers and salmon eggs are the most common baits, along with minnows and cut fish. Leeches, adult and larval insects, and crayfish are not as popular, but are no less effective. Fishermen have also discovered that certain "grocery baits," like marshmallows and corn, work extremely well, especially for stocked trout.

Although most trout will take any of these baits, some have a distinct preference. Also, a given bait may be more productive at certain times of year or under certain water conditions. Following are details on the most common live baits used for trout:

GARDEN WORMS. Any trout will take a worm. The bait is effective anytime, but works best in early spring when streams are high and discolored. For convenience, carry your worms in a box that attaches to your belt.

Push a size 6 to 10 hook through the middle of the worm, letting the ends dangle; or hook the worm two or three times, letting the tail dangle (photo, opposite page).

NIGHTCRAWLERS. You can use nightcrawlers and garden worms interchangeably; for small trout, half a crawler is better than a whole one. Crawlers must be kept cooler than garden worms.

Push a size 6 or 8 hook through the broken end of a half crawler (top), or through the middle of a whole crawler (bottom). Or, hook the crawler two or three times, like a garden worm.

MINNOWS. Trout fishermen commonly use fathead minnows and shiners because of their availability, but almost any kind of minnow in the 1½- to 3-inch range will work. Minnows catch trout year around, but are most effective in spring and early summer, when young baitfish are most numerous. Live minnows are best in slow-moving water; in current, dead ones work nearly as well.

Trout, particularly browns, eat more fish as they grow older, so minnows are a good choice for the big ones.

Sculpins, often called bullheads by mistake, are the prime bait for trophy browns in numerous western streams. But other baitfish are illegal in most western

states, and many other states ban any type of baitfish. These regulations are intended to prevent introduction of non-native fish species, and to reduce the trout harvest. Always check your local fishing regulations before using any kind of baitfish.

To carry minnows when you're wading, put them in a small bucket with a perforated lid, then tie the bucket to your waders. Fatheads are the easiest to keep alive.

Most minnows are hooked through the lips with a size 4 or 6 short-shank hook. You can also hook a sculpin by pushing a size 4 or 6 double-needle hook through the vent and out the mouth (photo above), then attaching a special clip to the front of the hook.

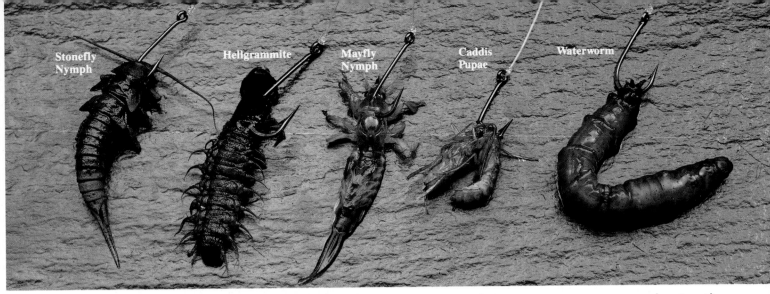

Stonefly Nymph | Hellgrammite | Mayfly Nymph | Caddis Pupae | Waterworm

**AQUATIC INSECTS.** Immature aquatic insects work better than adults, mainly because they're easier to keep on the hook. Stonefly nymphs and hellgrammites (dobsonfly larvae) top the list, but mayfly nymphs, caddis larvae, waterworms (cranefly larvae) and other immature forms also catch trout.

Any of these baits will take trout year around, but stonefly nymphs are best in midsummer; hellgrammites, in spring and early summer. You can find stonefly nymphs clinging to the undersides of rocks and logs in cold streams; hellgrammites are found in warmer water, and can be caught by turning over rocks in a riffle while someone holds a small-mesh seine just downstream. Mayfly nymphs can be found by sifting through mud on the stream bottom; waterworms, by digging through sticks and debris on the bottom or in a beaver dam; caddisworms, by checking the undersides of rocks.

Adult aquatic insects are not as common in a trout's diet as larval forms. But some adults, such as stoneflies, make good trout bait. Watch for them as you walk along the stream, and don't hesitate to give them a try.

Stonefly nymphs should be hooked through the collar with a size 8 or 10 light-wire hook; hellgrammites, under the collar with a size 4 to 8 hook; mayfly nymphs, through the hard plate just behind the head with a size 10 or 12 light-wire hook; caddis pupae (shown in photo) or larvae, by pushing a size 12 to 16 light-wire hook through the head or threading it through the body (use several larvae or pupae, or a larva inside its case); waterworms, through the tough skin just ahead of the tail lobes using a size 8 or 10 light-wire hook. Adult mayflies and stoneflies (not shown) stay on best when hooked through the head with a size 10 or 12 light-wire hook.

Grasshopper

Cricket

Waxworms

**TERRESTRIAL INSECTS.** In late summer, trout often lie near the bank, waiting for grasshoppers to get blown into the water. Where hoppers are plentiful, you can easily catch them by hand or with a small insect net. They can be fished alive or dead, floating or submerged. Crickets are not used as widely, but are equally effective.

Fishermen have discovered that waxworms (bee moth larvae), maggots (fly larvae) and other larval baits used for ice fishing are excellent for trout. They work particularly well in winter, when most other baits are hard to find. Their small size is an advantage when the water is cold and trout feeding slows.

Hoppers and crickets are hooked with a size 6 to 10 light-wire hook, either under the collar (left photo, top), or through the body so the point protrudes from the underside of the abdomen (left photo, middle). Waxworms and maggots are hooked through the head with a size 10 or 12 light-wire hook (left photo, bottom); some anglers hook on two or three.

Crayfish Taii

Scuds

Crayfish

Mud Shrimp

CRUSTACEANS. Crayfish from 1½ to 3 inches long make good summertime bait for big trout, especially browns. For smaller trout, use only the tail. Crayfish work best in streams with high crayfish populations.

You can often catch crayfish by quickly grabbing them after turning over rocks in the streambed. Or, use the seining technique. You should try to select crayfish in the softshell stage. Live crayfish can be hooked through the tail, from the bottom up, with a size 2 to 4 hook. Crayfish tails can also be hooked in this way.

Mud shrimp and ghost shrimp are actually soft-bodied crabs. They are popular for steelhead and salmon in Pacific coastal streams, particularly in spring and summer. They average about 5 inches in length, so they are not likely to catch small trout.

Rig the shrimp on a 1/0 plastic-worm hook with an egg loop. Push the hook through the top of the tail and out the bottom, bring the point through the body from the bottom up, then cinch the egg loop over the tail. Tie a small piece of yarn to the egg loop for attraction and to open the loop when rebaiting.

You can buy mud shrimp at bait shops or catch them on tidal flats with a clam tube, a device used to suck them out of their burrows. Keep them alive in a container with an inch of water or a layer of moist weeds, sawdust or paper towels.

Scuds, small crustaceans found among submerged weeds, are commonly eaten by trout but seldom used for bait, because they are difficult to keep on the hook. The best way is to thread them on a size 12 or 14 light-wire hook, two or three at a time.

EGGS. All species of trout and salmon feed on each other's eggs. Salmon eggs are most popular for bait because of their large size and commercial availability, but trout eggs also work well.

A single egg will catch anything from an 8-inch brook trout to a 50-pound chinook. But for salmon and large trout, most anglers prefer egg clusters, either plain or tied in a mesh spawn bag. Eggs are effective year around, but they work best during and after a spawning run, when the fish are eating eggs.

Fresh salmon eggs deteriorate quickly, but you can preserve them by rolling them in powdered borax or soaking them in a boric-acid solution.

To hook a single egg (1) pierce one edge with a size 10 to 14 salmon-egg hook, (2) slide the egg up the shank, (3) turn it 180 degrees, then (4) push it down so the point is buried.

Attach a spawn chunk by tying an egg loop on a size 4 to 8 hook with a turned-up eye, putting a chunk of spawn into the loop, then tightening.

**SPAWN BAG.** (1) Wrap eggs in a 2- to 3-inch square of nylon mesh or a piece of nylon stocking. Gather the corners of the mesh; the bag should be ⅜ to ⅝ inch in diameter. (2) Wrap five loops of thread around the mesh, and secure the bag with a series of half-hitches. Put the finished bags in a jar of borax, then shake the jar. Refrigerate for up to two weeks, or freeze. (3) To hook a spawn bag, push a size 4 to 8 short-shank hook through the bag so only the eye and point are exposed (inset).

**YARN FLY.** Salmon and steelhead anglers often drift-fish with a spawn bag and yarn fly. To make a yarn fly, (1) pass the line through a turned-up-eye hook, then tie a *snell*. (2) Make a loop in the line you passed through, and hold it against the hook shank. (3) Wrap the free end through the loop about five times, and (4) snug up by pulling on the free end and standing line. (5) Place a short piece of yarn under the line between the snell and the eye, then (6) pull the line to secure the yarn. Hook the spawn bag.

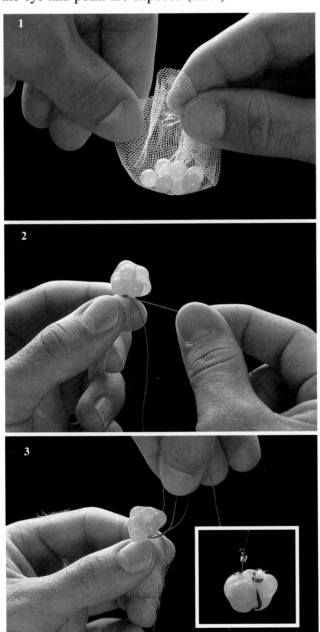

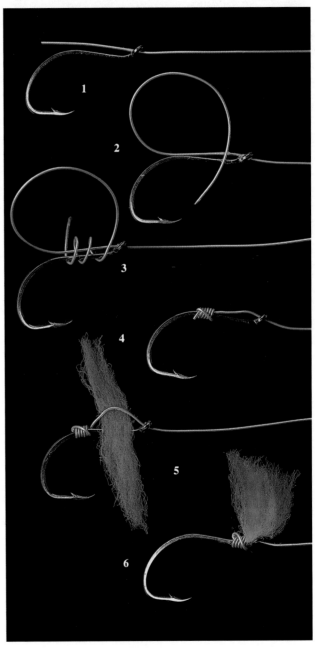

**GROCERY BAITS.** Though unappealing to many fishermen, grocery baits such as whole-kernel corn, small marshmallows, and soft cheese like Velveeta® catch lots of trout. Single corn kernels and small marshmallows are simply pushed onto a size 8 or 10 hook. Soft cheese can be molded around the hook. Grocery baits may suggest the pellets that stocked trout have been fed in hatcheries. They work best for trout that have been recently stocked; they are not as effective on wild trout.

269

# Fishing for Trophy Trout

An average stream fisherman seldom catches a big trout. It's not that the big ones aren't there; anglers occasionally see them following lures or hear them taking insects on the surface. As proof that big trout exist, fisheries workers regularly take them with shockers during stream surveys, even on streams that are fished heavily.

The trophy fisherman catches considerably fewer trout, but the challenge of outwitting a big one makes up for the lack of quantity. To improve his chances of taking a trophy, he fishes in different places and uses different techniques than other anglers.

Look for big trout in the deepest pools or undercuts, or at least in areas where they can easily reach the deep-water retreat. Just how deep is relative; in a small creek, a 4-foot pool is deep enough to hold a big one. In a large river, an 8-foot pool may not be deep enough.

Big trout prey on smaller ones, so when a likely-looking pool fails to produce even a small trout, this may be a clue that the pool is home to an exceptionally large trout. It pays to try such a pool from time to time rather than giving up on it.

Of course, some streams are more likely to produce big trout than others. Tailwater streams, coastal streams, and streams connected to large lakes generally yield the biggest trout. Some of the very best streams in these categories are identified in the following chapter.

A trophy trout is more likely to be near bottom than a small one, so sinking flies or deep-running lures are usually more effective than dry flies or shallow-runners.

Because fish make up a greater percentage of a trout's diet as it grows older, fish-imitating lures like minnow plugs, spinners and streamers take larger trout than small, insect-imitating flies. Some trophy hunters use 5-inch minnow plugs, or streamers that measure up to 4 inches.

Trout that have lived in a stream for many years and seen almost every possible lure are difficult to fool with even the most realistic artificial. But these old-timers can often be duped with live bait, preferably

HARD-TO-REACH pockets, like a deep hole beneath roots or branches, often hold big trout. Most anglers shy away from such spots because of snags.

DOWNSTREAM reaches that would seem too warm and muddy for trout usually have high baitfish populations that attract trophy browns.

REMOTE stream stretches or those where brushy banks restrict access usually hold bigger trout than easily accessible stretches.

a natural food captured in the stream. Western anglers, for instance, know that big browns have a weakness for sculpins, small fish that spend most of their time hiding under rocks. Other good baits for big trout include salmon eggs, chub tails, crayfish, waterworms, hellgrammites and nightcrawlers.

Big dry flies can be deadly during a hatch of large insects. In the northern Rockies, trophy-class trout that normally ignore insects go on a feeding rampage when large stoneflies, known as salmon flies, are hatching. On many eastern streams, big trout gorge themselves during the green drake mayfly hatch.

A hefty trout does not like to exert itself too much. Rather than racing smaller trout to catch fast-moving foods, it lies in wait for the chance to grab unsuspecting prey. Regardless of the type of bait or lure, a slow presentation generally works best.

Any type of trout fishing requires an inconspicuous approach to avoid putting the fish down. But when you're after trophies, stealth is even more important. The reason these trout have grown so large is that they have learned to sense predators, including fishermen. If they detect any unusual movement or vibration, they immediately head for cover and refuse to bite. Some trophy specialists go to extremes to avoid detection; they cast from behind bushes, or stay upstream of the pool and let the current carry their bait to the fish. For trophy browns, serious anglers do almost all their fishing at night.

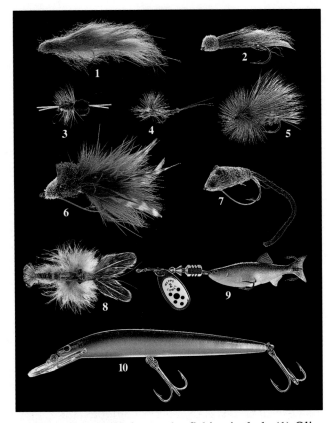

POPULAR LURES for trophy fishing include (1) Olive Wool-Head Sculpin, (2) Muddler Minnow, (3) weighted Bitch Creek Nymph, (4) Extended Green Drake, (5) Elk Hair Salmon, (6) Dahlberg Diver, (7) Mouserat, (8) Dave's Crayfish, (9) Comet, (10) Diving Bang-O-Lure.

# Movin' On for Tailwater Trophies

by Dick Sternberg

*On a typical day, Carl Jones drifts 20 miles to catch world-class trout in tailwater streams*

It didn't take Carl Jones long to convince me he was a pro. On the first cast of our three-day trip on Arkansas' famed White River, I hooked and landed a gorgeous 5-pound brown trout.

We had just motored away from the dock at White Hole Acres, Carl's base of operations. "Water's comin' already," Carl noted in his typical Ozark drawl. "We'll hafta fish fast and fish hard." I tied on a number 9 CountDown Rapala and cast toward the bank across from the dock. I made about six cranks, then *wham!*

And I'd always thought that fishing for big browns was tough.

Of course, the White River is famous for its trophy trout, so a fish like my 5-pounder doesn't raise an eyebrow. Since 1952, when the Bull Shoals Dam was completed, the White has produced a North American record brown trout no fewer than five times, the largest a 33-pound 8-ouncer in 1977.

Before the dam was built, the river held only warm-water fish. Cold water drawn from the depths of the reservoir now feeds the river and enables it to support trout.

"Guess I know the river well as anyone," Carl surmises. "Been fishin' it since I was a kid. My dad used to guide here starting back in the fifties, just after they built the dam. We guided together for eleven years, and he was real good competition. We'd find a bunch of good fish, then he'd fish for 'em one day and I'd fish for 'em the next. He taught me more about fishing than anybody."

One thing that separates Carl from most other guides on the river is his versatility. His strategy depends mainly on how much water is being discharged from the dam. When the lake is too high, or more power generation is needed, more water is discharged. "You got to fish different at different water tages," Carl explains. "The water level can

---

**Carl Jones**

**Home:** *Yellville, Arkansas*

**Occupation:** *Trout guide at White Hole Acres Resort near Flippin, Arkansas. Also guides deer and turkey hunters in the fall.*

*In 23 years of guiding on the White River, Carl Jones has tallied 25 brown trout weighing over 20 pounds for his customers and himself. The heaviest fish of all, caught in 1976, weighed 30 pounds 2 ounces. And on September 19, 1987, he boated a 20-pound 12-ounce brown, a pending world record for 2-pound-test line.*

*"I'd been trying to break the 2-pound line record for seven years," Carl says. "Then one day when the water was low, I floated over a deep hole and spotted fifteen big browns. Threw out a blown-up crawler and it no more than hit the water when the big one grabbed it. I fought that fish for an hour and 45 minutes."*

*Carl can entertain you with fish tales all day as you float down the White. He'll tell you about 15-pound rainbows, 25-pound browns, and 10-pound cutthroats that live in different holes along the river. And he should know . . . he's caught and released a good share of them. "I ask my customers to throw back any big fish they don't want to mount. Most of them cooperate real good. They understand that fishing won't hold up if you keep those big ones. There's plenty of small rainbows for people who want a meal."*

*Early-morning low water on the White River, before release starts from dam*

change as much as 18 feet overnight. Where you caught fish one day can be dry land the next.

"Love to fish low water," he says. "Seventeen of my 25 biggest browns were caught when the river was down. Water's usually lowest in summer, but it can be low anytime the weather's been dry.

"Best time for big trout is June and July," he continues. "When the gates are shut, the downstream water warms up and the trout are forced to move toward the dam where the water is cooler. They're concentrated in a smaller area, so they're a lot easier to get at.

"When you're fishing low water, trout seem to bite best right in the middle of the day. You'd think it'd be just the opposite. But when the water's higher, time of day doesn't seem to make much difference.

"Nice thing about low water is you can see where they're at. They get schooled up in certain holes, and if you know where they are, you can catch a bunch. I like a calm, clear day because you can see 'em a lot better. If it's windy, you can't spot 'em."

When Carl is scouting for trout, he stands on the rear seat of his boat and steers the outboard with his foot. "Yeah, I've gone in a few times, but it's the best way to see the trout," he maintains. "You've got to look way ahead of the boat — they won't sit still and let you drift over them. They're real spooky because the water's so clear.

"Once you find some, the best way is to anchor above a hole and throw bait at 'em. If there's a lot of trout in the hole, I'll wait 'em out. Sometime during the day, one of 'em's gonna feed. If there's only a fish or two, then I'll move to another hole where I've seen some.

"I use the same rig for most any kind of bait. It's just a dropper rig with a number 7 to 10 bell sinker — depending on depth and current speed — and a hook. "If I'm after big fish, I'll put two big crawlers on the hook. Another good big-fish bait is sewed-on sculpins. You can pick 'em up on certain flats after the water has been high for a few days and then drops fast. You've got to fish 'em dead. First thing a live one'll do is swim under a rock and hang you up. Softshell craws work good, too."

For live-bait fishing, Carl prefers a light spinning outfit. He normally uses 6-pound monofilament, but goes as light as 2-pound when the fish are extra-spooky. "Don't use anything lighter than 6-pound for sculpin fishing," he advises. "A big brown'll mouth a sculpin and then chew on it; and when he turns, his teeth'll fray the line."

Using two anchors, Carl positions his boat broadside to the current just upstream from a hole where he has seen trout. Anchoring broadside makes it easier for two or three people to fish the hole, but is not recommended in fast current. As a safety precaution, Carl ties both anchor lines to the boat with slip knots. This way, he can untie them quickly should the current pick up and threaten to overturn the boat.

Navigating the White River in low water can be treacherous. Carl, and practically everyone else who fishes the river regularly, uses a special boat originally designed by Carl's father. It looks like a long, skinny jonboat, with a length of 20 feet but a beam of only 4 feet. Both ends are swept up so the bow won't take on water; the stern can be maneuvered easily with a paddle. The fiberglass hull draws only a few inches of water, for skimming over gravel bars, and its thin shape makes it easy to steer

## How to Make a Dropper Rig for Live Bait

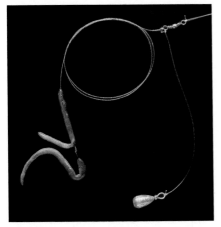

TIE rig as shown with 6-pound mono and size 4 long-shank hook. Thread one crawler up line; another over hook.

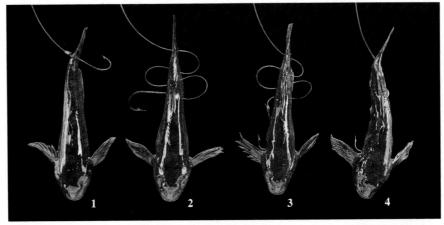

HOOK a sculpin on same type of rig by (1) inserting a size 4 long-shank hook through base of tail, then (2) back through body three times. (3) Push hook through side so point protrudes behind pectoral fin. (4) Snug up line.

## How Jones Fishes at Low Water

USE a narrow, shallow-draft jonboat for navigating in low water. A boat of this design will steer easily through narrow chutes, and will float over shallow bars.

LOOK for trout while motoring downstream. Jones wears polarized sunglasses and stands on the boat seat so he can see into the water. Avoid motoring over the fish.

ANCHOR just upstream of a pool where trout were spotted. Jones uses two anchors to keep the boat broadside to the current so two anglers can fish the hole effectively.

PULL hooked fish away from the hole quickly so you don't spook the others. The bell-sinker rig with two crawlers or a sculpin works best for trout during low water.

*Sternberg's first-cast brown*

through narrow chutes. The boat is powered by a 15-horsepower outboard.

Rising water is another story, a race against time. When Carl tells you "water's comin' already," he means the dam gates are open and the water is rising fast. When he says "we'll hafta fish fast and fish hard," he means the river will soon be too high to fish effectively, so you'll have to motor downstream quickly to stay ahead of the swelling water, stopping to fish some likely spots along the way.

Carl calls this technique "fishing the bulge," the bulge being the advancing surge of high water. "The bulge seems to turn the fish on," he explains. "If you can get on at just the right time and ride it, you'll catch more trout than you would at low water."

When you stop to fish a spot, the bulge catches up with you in a hurry. You can tell when it arrives by watching the clarity. When the White is low it's very clear, but when it starts rising it gets murkier and you'll see bits of weeds and algae floating downstream. "When you start to see a lot of trash, you've got to run down and get away from it," Carl says. "Otherwise the trout can't see your bait too good, and it'll pick up lots of weeds.

"When I'm fishing the bulge, I like to throw a CountDown Rapala, either size 7 or 9. Rapalas are big-fish baits, and a lot of guys don't have the patience to throw them all day. But if you're after big trout, they work a lot better than live bait. Early in the season, silver works best because the trout are eating shad. By June, they start eating creek minnows which are gold-colored, so I switch to a gold CountDown. The big browns can be real particular — color makes a big difference."

For casting Rapalas, Carl uses a 5½-foot medium-action baitcasting outfit spooled with 8-pound-test

*How Jones Fishes the Bulge*

BEGIN fishing just downstream of the bulge. The location of the bulge may not be immediately apparent, but if the bulge passes you, the water will carry bits of weed that catch on the hooks of your lure.

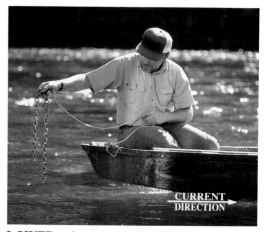

LOWER a drag chain off the bow as you start drifting. The chain will keep the bow pointed upstream.

276

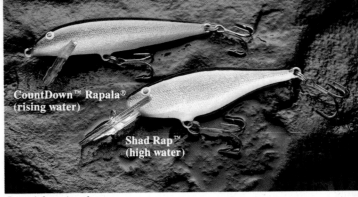

*Jones' favorite plugs*

mono. In this type of fishing, he says any line lighter than 8-pound will snap too easily when you set the hook.

"Cast just downstream of the boat, let the plug sink a few seconds, then twitch it hard a few times before you start to reel," Carl suggests. "Browns usually hit just when you start reeling. But don't twitch when you're fishing rainbows.

"I throw out a drag chain to slow my drift. This gives you more time to work your spot, plus it keeps the bow pointing upstream so the boat stays at the same angle. When I'm running over deep water, I just leave the chain out. The rope's short enough so the chain doesn't get in the motor. In shallow water, I pull it in just to be safe. The chain works real good. In fact, a lot of fly fishermen want to see it banned. They say a chain rips up too many weeds on the bottom, but they rip up just as many when they're wading.

"When I'm fishing the bulge, I always look for break-offs. You know — spots where a rock pile or a bar drops into deeper water. The drop may be only 8 inches, but that's enough to hold trout. They rest in the deeper water because there's less current. Usually, they're not far from the deep pools where you find 'em when the water's low."

High water — after the bulge has rolled on past — presents yet another set of challenges. "Most important thing to remember when the water's high is to cast close to the bank," Carl advises. "Not as much current in there, so it's the best place for trout to rest. The higher the water, the closer you need to cast.

"I use pretty much the same technique I do for fishing the bulge, but instead of throwing a Count-Down I may throw a Shad Rap. The big bill makes it run deeper, and it starts diving as soon as you reel it away from the bank, so the big trout can see it. If the water's not too high I'll go with a number 7 Shad Rap, but when it's really high, I switch to a number 8.

"When all the gates are open, the current rolls along at 5 or 6 miles an hour. Before you know it, you're 20 miles downstream, and it'll take you the rest of the day to motor back up. If you plan on floating with the current, get a buddy to meet you at a downstream landing with a trailer. That way you can fish a lot longer.

"If the water's already high when I start fishing, I usually float a ways, then run back up and float again. Never try to anchor in high water. Current's fast enough to suck your bow under. Hardly a year goes by when I don't pull somebody out of the river after they anchored their boat and it turned over in the current.

"Personally, I'd much rather fish when the water's low. The fast current makes it tough to get your lure deep enough, 'specially when the trout are tucked up tight to the bank."

It's probably a good thing the water gets high once in a while. The White River trout can enjoy life a lot more when Carl's working on his garden.

ANGLE your cast just downstream of the boat, using a CountDown Rapala. When casting downstream, the plug has a chance to sink before the line tightens up.

TWITCH the rod hard several times as the plug is sinking. The twitching action seems to attract big browns, which often strike when you start to retrieve.

# Trout & Salmon Tips

## Wormin' for Salmon

During their life at sea, chinooks, cohos and other Pacific salmon eat small eels of various kinds. Once the salmon enter rivers to spawn, they no longer feed, but they still strike lures resembling eels. As a result, they can be caught on the curly-tailed worms normally used for bass.

Hook a 3- to 5-inch worm on a stout-hooked jig heavy enough to run just off the bottom. Bright or fluorescent colors are usually best, but black and purple work well on bright days.

Anchor your boat above a holding area, then angle your cast down and across the river. Let the current swing the worm in front of the salmon. Or troll the worm through deep water on bends or by creek mouths. Salmon usually hit these lures hard; set the hook as soon as you feel the strike.

## Offbeat Colors for Steelhead

When drift-fishing for steelhead or salmon, many fishermen use bright or fluorescent yarn. Fish probably mistake these flies for spawn. But don't limit yourself to old standards, such as orange, pink and chartreuse. Here are some other colors and color combinations that often work when the usual colors don't:

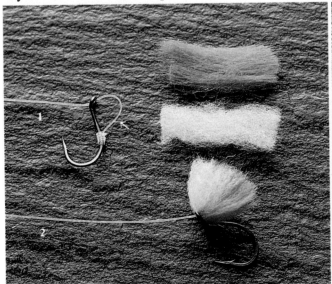

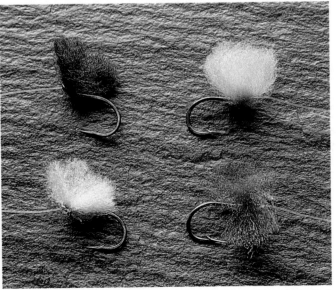

INSERT (1) two pieces of contrasting yarn into the loop (arrow) of a snelled egg hook. (2) Pull the line to cinch up the yarn, then trim so the yarn is ¼ to ¾ inch long. The two-toned pattern will sometimes catch fish when neither color alone draws a strike.

MAKE a fly from black, tan or brown yarn. These flies don't resemble spawn at all, but rather natural foods, such as stonefly and mayfly nymphs. Also effective at times is blue yarn, though it resembles nothing steelhead or salmon would normally eat.

## Keep Reels Dry When Wading

Wading anglers who fish with a fly rod or long spinning rod are familiar with the problem: to unwrap line from the rod tip or restring the tip section of the rod, you must dunk the reel in the water to reach the last few guides. But then sand gets in your reel. Immersion also causes the drags of some reels to slip.

You can avoid these problems by pulling the rod apart at the ferrule. Now you can untangle the line from the end of the rod or string up the tip section without putting the reel in the water.

## Better Fly Floatant

Silicon gel fly pastes are handy but are difficult to apply to flies evenly and thoroughly. If you don't apply enough, the fly won't float long. If you dab on too much, the hackles, wings and tail mat down. What you need is a dressing that cleans and treats every part of the fly, evaporates quickly, and floats a fly a long time. Here's how to make a dressing that does just that:

MIX one part silicon gel fly floatant with three parts lighter fluid. Store the mixture in a small jar or squeeze bottle, after first adding a little to the bottle to make sure the plastic doesn't dissolve. Squeeze a drop or two directly onto the fly or apply it with your fingers or a toothpick. The lighter fluid will evaporate in seconds, leaving a thin coat of the gel on the hackles and body of the fly.

## Ice Jigs Score in Streams

If you're fishing worms for stream trout, you'll generally need a bit of weight to aid casting and get the worm down to the fish. Pinching a split-shot or two several inches above the bait does the trick, but the shot and hook will revolve around one another on the cast, making accurate placement difficult. Here's a way to make your bait easier to cast and also more appealing to the fish:

HOOK the worm on a gold, silver or fluorescent panfish ice fly. For best casting, use 2- or 4-pound mono on an ultra-light spinning rig. The ice fly and worm will cast as a unit, improving your accuracy.

## Ski Wax Tames Dubbing

Spinning short animal hair onto a thread, a process called "dubbing," is the first step in forming the bodies of many dry flies, wet flies and nymphs. However, the process can be tricky and messy, especially for a beginning flytier, because short hair doesn't adhere very well to the thread. Instead, it sticks to the tier's fingers or falls into his lap.

Here's a way to make the hair stick so it's easier to spin onto the thread:

1. APPLY a light coating of soft (warm-weather) cross-country ski wax to several inches of thread.

2. DAB on the hair. Pinch the thread below the hair; roll the thread between your thumb and forefinger to form yarn.

## Watching Hard-to-See Flies

It's important to watch the drift of a dry fly so you can detect strikes and set the hook. But there are times glare or darkness makes it hard to see dry flies, especially those that imitate small naturals, such as midges. The next time poor lighting makes dry-fly fishing difficult, try this trick:

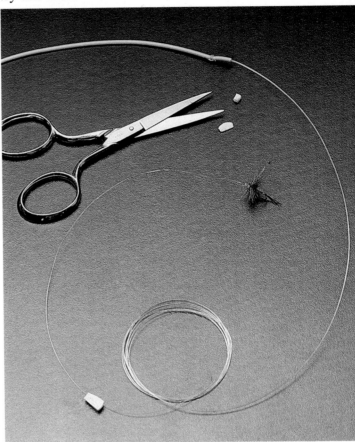

WRAP half of an adhesive foam strike indicator (the kind used by nymph fishermen) around the tippet, about 10 inches above the fly. Trim it to the size of a BB so it doesn't hinder casting or spook fish. This small piece of white foam will be much easier to follow in poor light than a tiny, dark fly. When a fish takes the fly, the foam disappears.

## Stopping a Strong Run

When hooked, a big salmon or steelhead makes a swift, powerful run, sometimes stripping off a hundred yards of line or more. If you're fishing in a boat, you may have no choice but to turn around and chase the fish. When wading in a stream, you may have to follow the fish downstream. If you can't, it will break off in seconds. Here's a trick that will stop a streaking fish nine times out of ten.

Give the fish complete slack. They run because they feel resistance; when there is no resistance, they usually stop. In a stream, they often swim back upriver. Once you gain back some line, you can put the pressure on again.

# Index